Our Fragmented World

An Introduction to Political Geography

W. Gordon East

Professor Emeritus of Geography
in the University of London

J. R. V. Prescott

Reader in Geography in the
University of Melbourne

First published 1975 *by*
THE MACMILLAN PRESS LTD
London and Basingstoke
Associated companies in New York Dublin
Melbourne Johannesburg and Madras

SBN 333 15109 7 (hard cover)
333 15169 0 (paper cover)

Photoset, printed and bound
in Great Britain by
REDWOOD BURN LIMITED
Trowbridge & Esher

The authors dedicate this book to
Dorothea East and Ada S. Prescott

Contents

List of Maps

Note on References

References in the text within square brackets relate to books and articles listed, alphabetically by author's name, in the relevant chapter-section of the References, beginning at page 255.

Preface

We live in a world which has always been differentiated regionally and locally, being made up of parts, distinguishable at different scales, each with its own character and potentialities yet, with all others, part of a single whole. It remains one of the main tasks of geography to study the diversifications and divisions of the earth's surface that derive from natural and human causes. On the one hand, it is to the forces of Nature that one turns to explain the broad patterns of our terrestrial world – the distribution of land and sea, the areal extent of climates of sharply different types, and the variety of regions of mountain, plateau and lowland, all of which present the stage and set limits to human effort. On the other, it is in man and his works that one finds the cause of areal differences in the degrees of settlement and population density, as in the levels of material culture, economic achievement, living standards and political organisation. In this book we have dared to look at the world as a whole, but from only one particular standpoint, that of political geography. This investigates the two-way relationship between geography and politics as exhibited in states, which are the most significant and exactly defined of all the many regions, actual and perceptual, studied by geographers.

In contrast to the earth's surface in its physical aspect, which has been fashioned during geological time and changes its main features only slowly, the world political scene is the product of man's short history and undergoes continual and rapid change. Political geography, which must take note of the findings of many social sciences whose interests it shares – notably history, political science, economics, and international law and relations – rests its claims to be heard on the political appropriation and division of the surface of the earth that its discipline exists to study. We live in a world of states, complex human organisations, none of which is exactly like another, yet all of which, associated together, present an ever-changing world map and ever-changing internal and external relationships. By an approach from the stage to the drama thereon enacted and by applying his own method, the political geographer seeks to cast one ray of light on the complex conditions and problems of life lived necessarily within a world of states on a finite and differentiated stage.

As political geographers, we have long shared academic and professional interests when engaged in teaching university students, in research and in writing which, if we pool our efforts, we have done in four continents. *Our Fragmented World* is offered as our joint work, shared equally, for we have collaborated closely, industriously, happily – and antipodally: certainly it gained much therefrom. Without any intention or attempt to write a compendium, we have, as the contents list shows, sketched the field of interest, indicated the range of concepts and methods, and also highlighted, by analyses of selected 'cases' drawn from various parts of the world, many topics of current, continual, and in some instances, contentious interest. It is our hope that our book will serve the needs, and arouse the interest of students within the English-speaking world who are seeking an introduction to political geography, and also that it may encourage some of our readers to enquire into specific problems that they choose – or may be required – to study.

'This world', said Horace Walpole, 'is a comedy to those that think, a tragedy to those that feel.' Slick, epigrammatic and arguable – yes, but it suggests rightly that the restraints, difficulties and problems of life, with one aspect of which political geography is concerned, are too serious not to be taken seriously. We believe that political geography as it refines its methods and concepts and deepens its scholarship can make a useful contribution to the understanding of many of the major issues that divide the world.

July 1974

W.G.E.
J.R.V.P.

Acknowledgements

We wish to thank Mr H. J. Collier of the University of Melbourne, who drew the maps, and Mrs Rita Davis and Mrs Mabel Sealy (respectively at Melbourne and Ashtead, Surrey) who typed the manuscript.

1 The World Political Map

Society is indeed a contract. Subordinate contracts, for objects of mere occasional interest, may be dissolved at pleasure; but the state ought not to be considered as nothing better than a partnership agreement in a trade of pepper and coffee, calico or tobacco . . . to be dissolved by the fancy of the parties. It is to be looked upon with reverence.

(Edmund Burke, *Reflections on the French Revolution*, 1790)

A local state is not a god. It has been treated as a god. People have sacrificed their lives for it. But a local state is really just a public utility, like the gasworks, the electricity grid or the telephone system.

(Arnold Toynbee, *The Times*, 11 July 1972)

We live in a divided world, and not the least evident and formidable of the divisions with which we are familiar are the many states which make up the jigsaw pattern of the world map. Professor Toynbee rightly reminds us that states exist to serve communities of individuals and that they have been accorded excessive importance. Doubtless if states were subordinated to a world authority, much of the violence, danger and fear implicit in everyday life would disappear. World government, however, is at present very much a hope, difficult of achievement; in a world of remarkably rapid change, men's minds are, in contrast, slow to throw off old attachments, attitudes and beliefs. The real world of today is organised into over 150 states and, although they carry out service functions as do public utilities, they behave very much like Greek gods, so much so that, given the great powers which they wield, they need to be taken very seriously.

1

1 The Nature of States

States, each with its own identity and characteristics, are concepts of
international law, which has grown up to define and in some measure
to control their relationships. The nature, purpose and functions of
the state could be discussed at great length, for it is a many-sided
entity, the study of which is shared by political scientists, historians,
geographers, sociologists, philosophers, international lawyers and
others. Here it is important to note that understanding of the state
falls within the orbit of geography since one of its requirements is
'territory', that is, a part of the earth's surface, which this discipline
exists to study. Successive chapters of this book discuss, with attention turned to specific illustrative cases, those features of states that
geography specially illuminates, and it is enough here to indicate certain basic facts and concepts necessary to comprehend the political
divisions of the world which confront us.

For some thinkers, notably the German philosopher Hegel, the
state is a mystic concept which most citizens would fail to grasp. For
the purposes of political geography a state can be described very
simply as a group of people organised politically within a specific territory. Territory, to which subject we return in chapter 3, consists of a
more or less well-defined area of land, together with the air space
above it, and usually also a zone of sea. Without territory states
cannot exist, although we may recall that a 'government in exile',
when a state's territory has been militarily occupied by an enemy,
can survive, sustained by the active purpose of recovering its control. The groups of people for whom a state exists and from whom
their rulers, legislators, officials, armed forces and labour forces are
drawn, present remarkable variety – in numerical strength, language, nationality and cultural level – and to this topic the next
chapter is devoted.

States have become so normal a division of the world and come to
engage such strong loyalties as possibly to obscure their origins, purposes and functions. Discussion of these will serve to explain the
third essential requirement of states, namely political organisation.

Thomas Hobbes [1651, pp. 84–100] conceived of states or, as he
called them, 'commonwealths', as arising in two different ways. In
one case, 'sovereignty' – the supreme power exercised by the state –
was freely handed over by the majority of citizens, either to one man
or to an assembly, thus creating a 'commonwealth by institution'. In
the other, a 'commonwealth by acquisition' resulted from the win-

ning by force of sovereignty which, through fear of death or enslavement, a people agreed to accept. Hobbes's view provides a
theoretical rather than a historical view of the origin of states,
although it underlines the distinction between those states that arise
in response to the desires and efforts of particular groups of people
and those that are created by outside powers with little or no regard
to the popular will. However, the historical record indicates that
states are only very rarely instituted by an act that expresses the collective will of a people, whether this is exercised freely or under constraint. Certainly states are man-made organisations, not organisms
in the strict sense, even though they appear to be born, to grow and
even to die. It is unlikely that any state was created as a result of a
solemn decision of a nation or people to hand over to chosen rulers
the full political powers of sovereignty that it already held. One can
recall that in 1815 Malta, already an organised state, chose to be
ruled by the British Crown. Also, after the thirteen American colonies of Great Britain successfully revolted, they solemnly established a
federal union, but this was made up of thirteen separate states, each
of which retained very considerable powers.* In general, states have
emerged in specific areas after long periods of active life, which
involved struggles both within their own areas and against enemies
outside them in their efforts to establish their own political identity
and stable institutions of government. Other states, in contrast, had a
more arbitrary and datable birth as the result of the successful policies of strong, external powers. Rousseau's revolutionary teaching in
his *Du contrat social* of 1762 [Tozer 1920] underlines the idea that
states exist, or should exist, for the benefit of their citizens, although
it would be naive to believe that this was, or is, everywhere achieved.
It should be emphasised that 'the State is never given; it is always
forged' [Febvre 1925]. Military force and some degree of coercion
normally enter into the making of states. Indeed, already in the late
sixteenth century the political philosopher Jean Bodin asserted that
force and not a contract is the origin of commonwealths [Tozer
1920]. Even so, the purpose of the state is essentially a civilised one.
Its creation marks a mature stage of social organisation and, in the
main, brings relative peace and order to peoples otherwise divided
and conflicting. States exist to establish and uphold laws, to advance

* Clearly, as is discussed later (pp. 118–20), the United States and its member states
share sovereign power. As D. W. Brogan wrote, '. . . neither the United States nor any
state is sovereign . . . the United States and the states are equal. The United States is
not sovereign but is superior'. (*The Times*, 26 June 1961)

in peace the well-being of their citizens, and to provide them with security and defence against external dangers. In this attempt they seek to control and administer the territories to which they have legal title, for which purposes institutions of government are set up and armed forces organised. Here we are concerned with 'political organisation', the third of the requirements of every state.

'Political organisation' relates to the institutions and means by which state populations are governed. 'Politics' are concerned with the activities of states both within their territories and in their relations with other states. On the one hand, local government is necessary at different levels and, on the other, a state pursues its policy with outside states or groups of states, usually by means of discussions and negotiations or by coercive action involving, at worst, actual warfare. Note that, although the State is commonly personified and acquires attributes, it is only in the legal sense a person and acts always through individual representatives or groups of these. 'Politics' derive from the existence, sharing and use of the powers that states possess and need to carry out their functions and purposes. In modern times the powers of the State have usually been conceived to be 'sovereign' or absolute, implying that such states exercise powers subject to no restriction. In fact, even legal theorists concede that state sovereignty is often in some measure curtailed, if only because in formal engagements with other states or groups of states, they have bound themselves to behave in certain ways – as did the United Kingdom when it joined the European Economic Community in 1973 [Oppenheim 1955, pp. 120–3].

The ways in which state powers are shared show marked variety. At one extreme stands the democratic state, where adult citizens of both sexes, on occasions at least, exert their collective power to choose their government and, by the free expression of public opinion, by the activities of political parties, by pressure groups and other means, seek to modify its policy. At the other extreme, the totality of citizens are allowed little scope to express views on policy, which remains in the hands of a small number of decision-makers who have won control of government and, at best, seek to realise what they think is in the best interests of all citizens. Between these extreme types are found numerous variant systems. A fully democratic state, where every citizen in turn plays an active part in the business of government, might appear to have been achieved in ancient Athens, but citizen rights there were restricted to free men, being denied to slaves. If only because of the size of populations of modern states, even the most democratic systems can work only through elected representatives, so that the powers that be – 'them above' as T. S. Eliot called them – act as agents of the people who, even so, enjoy some freedom to follow their own lives. In short, although states have many purposes in common, notably the maintenance of law and order and of peaceful conditions for economic and social life, they diverge in respect of the sharing of political power as well as in their ideological beliefs and avowed ends.

To the varied categories of states, as distinguished on different bases and in the structural arrangements adopted for their internal administration, we shall turn in later chapters. Here it is enough to note that central governments, concerned with the most important functions, such as law-making, administration and courts of law, defence and security, currency and commerce, are supplemented by regional and local bodies, which in widely varying degrees share political power with the central government. We should note here also that the apparatus of government does not always and everywhere succeed in ensuring the administration of all the peoples of a state over all its territory, since this last, although usually well-enough defined, cannot always be effectively controlled.

2 The Variety of States

States of several kinds, some of them rudimentary in structure, have always been recognisably present, if only in certain areas, as responses to social needs, for, as Aristotle put it, man is a 'social animal'. Among precursors to the absolutist or sovereign state of modern times most noteworthy are city-states, feudal states and empires. The city-state, as well-exemplified in classical Greece, was a relatively simple organisation – small in area and population (free and unfree), yet exhibiting several forms which reflected the way political power was held and exercised, as by a monarchy, an aristocracy or a democracy. These were the only forms, Thomas Hobbes [1651, pp. 89–90] insisted, although the same forms 'misliked' are called (he wrote) tyranny, oligarchy and anarchy respectively. Classical Greece, even in its heyday, was never a political unit but its component states, within their limited territories, often girt around by mountains and woodlands, functioned effectively, although they would appear today to have been little more than municipalities. The city-state long persisted, notably in Germany and Italy, until the latter part of the nineteenth century, and this form was adopted under treaty settlements after the First World War, when the Free States of Danzig and Trieste were set up as temporary solutions to particularly difficult territorial wrangles. Since 1965, when it withdrew from the Federation of Malaysia, Singapore, with an area of only 581 square kilometres (226 square miles) and a population – mainly Chinese – of over two millions, presents the best modern example of an independent city-state – and one that flourishes.

The feudal state, widely represented in Europe during the Middle Ages, was built on a system of contractual relationships related to land-holding and involved a hierarchical political and social structure. Such states were characterised by their continual changes of area, the sharing of governmental powers between emperors, kings, barons and bishops, the looseness of central control, and the vague limits of their territories which were by no means necessarily continuous. The feudal state, like the city-state, was doomed to disappear with the emergence by stages of the absolutist state, which concentrated in royal hands political power formerly shared with the nobility and Church. The absolutist state, which in England was formed by its Tudor monarchy, was the outcome of a revolutionary process which involved the drastic curtailment of baronial and ecclesiastical power. It was brought about by kings seeking to win supreme power for themselves by an alliance with men of business and by selecting their own ministers and officials. A sharp contrast is presented in the late sixteenth century between the relatively strong and stable centralised government achieved under Elizabeth I and the weak government of Scotland which still presented the features of a feudal state. Despite her legal and accepted title to the throne, Mary, Queen of Scots, was unable to control the inter-feuding Scottish magnates who were virtually autonomous in their own lands and resisted the enlargement of regal power [Fraser 1970].

Lastly, among forms of state of especial interest as background to the present state system, are those imperial structures that existed at all periods of history, and contrived, with more or less success, to hold together complex groupings of peoples occupying extensive territories.

3 Empires

These large and composite states even now have not wholly disappeared despite the strong and successful reactions against them, especially during the last fifty years. Empires grew by the sword but also by marriage and inheritance, and by discovery and colonisation of new lands. Their survival depended on skilled leadership and, in varying degrees, on the coercive powers of armed forces. Usually, too, they depended on the services of an effective bureaucracy and police system and, in some cases, on the co-operation with governments given by the Church. No less necessary for the functioning of empires were capital cities, as the seats of political power, and effective and safeguarded routes by land or by water or both. To the ancient Greeks the Persian Empire, based on Arabia, appeared both an alien political structure and a dreaded enemy. It was, however, a Hellene, Alexander the Great (died 323 BC) who, in striking down this empire, created for a brief time an even larger dominion stretching from Macedonia, Thessaly and Egypt through South West Asia into Afghanistan and what are now Pakistan and Soviet Central Asia. The imperial form of state was not restricted solely to the older continents of Asia and Europe, for Spaniards in their conquest of South America encountered the remarkably centralised and civilised Incan Empire. Doubtless among the most famous and long-lasting empires, alongside many that had their base in China, was that of the Romans, which grew from Latium in central Italy to encompass territories in southern, western and central Europe, northern Africa and South West Asia. This empire was remarkable not only for its endurance but also for the broadly civilised government which it provided. Over fourteen centuries elapsed from the accession of the first emperor Augustus in 30 BC to the final disappearance of the last remnant of this empire, when in 1453 AD the Ottoman Turks captured the imperial capital of Constantinople, now Istanbul.

This is not the place to attempt a balanced assessment of the pros and cons of past imperialism, for it is more important here to enquire how the geographical pattern of empires has changed and why in the twentieth century so many empires have fallen and with what effects on the political map of the world today. This type of state has generated, not without good reasons, strong and often violent censure and has been decried in terms often emotional rather than academic. It is clear that bloodshed, oppression, persecution, greed and stupidity have figured in the history of empires, as in that of other kinds of states, and also that those who held the reins of power dominated over those unable effectively to resist.

Before the Renaissance in all previous civilizations the individuality of the human being was only dimly realized and counted
for little or nothing in the ethics and organization of society; men,
women, and children were not individuals, were in no sense 'I's',
they were anonymous, impersonal members of classes and castes.
[Woolf 1969]

Yet imperialism in the Old World brought leadership, stability and
the chances of improved social and economic life in replacement of
conditions unlikely to have proved superior. In the New World, too,
one form of imperialism, characterised by the formation of colonies
settled from an overseas base, brought civilised rule and explains the
origins of several of the nations of today. And it is of interest to recall
and reflect upon the view of an eminent historian, Lord Acton, who
had been a citizen of the Austro-Hungarian Empire. He wrote:
'Those states are substantially the most perfect which include distinct
nationalities without oppressing them [Acton 1862].

4 Past Political Maps of the World

A cursory glance at the pages of an historical atlas of the world indicates that, except in relatively recent centuries, only parts of the
earth's surface were politically organised and that these were, for the
most part, empires holding together many different peoples speaking
many different tongues. Great stretches of the world, many wholly or
virtually unknown to the old-established, civilised societies of
Europe and Asia, remained at best tribally organised, often little occupied and settled. Whatever their shortcomings, the empires of the
past managed to contain diverse peoples under a relatively well-
ordered system of government and territorially they waxed and
waned, thus representing on the map ever-changing patterns. As new
and hitherto unexplored lands were brought into contact with those
maritime nations of Europe who first reached them, imperialism
tended increasingly to hold sway. Thus, alike in the Americas, Africa
and Australasia, political dependence on outside powers, all at first
European, became and long remained characteristic. The 'mother of
continents', Asia, no less in the course of time became a congeries of
dependencies [East, Spate and Fisher 1971]. The vigour and enterprise of certain Europeans in extending political control over peoples
overseas – alike in old populous and new unsettled lands – as well as
in providing their own peoples as colonists and administrators, have

been remarkable features of the last few centuries. As a result, independent states in both Africa and Asia became exceptional, so vigorously had European powers (and the United States, too) espoused their colonising and mercantile missions.

In Africa territories were carved out by European powers mostly after 1870, although parts had been acquired earlier, as Algeria by France, the Cape Province by the Netherlands, passing to Britain in 1815, and Angola and Mozambique by Portugal, which had pioneered the Cape route to India. Only two fully independent states – Ethiopia and Liberia – adorned the map of Africa in 1914. Asia, no less a dependent continent, was shared by Russians, who held Siberia and parts of the Far East and central Asia, by British (in India, Burma, Ceylon, Malaya, Singapore and Hong Kong), by French (in Indo-China), by Dutch in what is now Indonesia, by Portuguese who retained holdings in Timor (East Indies), Goa (in India) and Macau on China's coast, and lastly by Americans in the Philippines. Already too, early in the twentieth century, Japan gained control of Korea and Taiwan (Formosa). It is worth noting that it is this overseas or 'salt water' imperialism that has most engaged the interest of those who, in relatively recent times, have sought the overthrow of imperialism, and certainly by their scale and success the empires of Britain, France, the Netherlands, Portugal, Spain, Italy and Belgium presented spectacular targets for criticism and attack. But it should be remembered that for both the United States and Russia territorial expansion took place landwards, and with it went the subjection of those – admittedly small in numbers – who were native to the acquired lands; this is no less a form of imperialism. Nor was the territorial expansion of the United States and Russia wholly continental, for the one moved beyond its own shores to acquire Hawaii, Puerto Rico and the Philippines, and the other held for a time Alaska and other Pacific coastal holdings of North America.

5 Political Maps of Europe

Europe, which gave rise to so many empires stretching far beyond its shores, also nourished many within its bounds. And for several centuries, until fairly recent times, Europe was the political nerve centre of the world because its numerous and skilled population commanded so much financial, commercial, political, military and diplomatic power. What happened in Europe during the last century or so had widespread effects overseas, so that it is helpful to the understanding of the present political fragmentation of the world to ponder a little on certain events and movements in Europe itself. The political map of Europe in 1815 affords a useful vantage point at a time when this continent included several multi-national empires, notably those of Britain, Austria, Russia and Turkey, within which peoples were held in political subjection.

The way in which the political map of Europe was redrawn, by decisions reached at international conferences held in 1814–15 after the Napoleonic Wars, illustrates how little national sentiments had then to be considered by statesmen. The extensive territories of the Austrian Empire, as also those of the much larger Russian and Turkish Empires, were left intact. Indeed, the Russian Empire was actually enlarged in Europe by the incorporation of the Grand Duchy of Warsaw – all that remained of the old Polish Kingdom – with the Tsar as Grand Duke. The British Empire no less firmly survived and was substantially enlarged by the accession of colonies formerly held by France and Holland. France, stripped of its conquests, was only marginally reduced in territory and the Low Countries, made up of Walloons, Flemings and Dutch, as also of Roman Catholics and Protestants, was set up as a new kingdom, intended to act as a buffer state between France and Prussia and to help in the defence of Britain from continental attack. Both Germany and Italy appeared in 1815 as congeries of states. In Germany the kingdom of Prussia, the strongest single state within the newly formed German Confederation, made important territorial gains, notably in the Rhineland, which paid tribute to its military power and effective statesmanship. Prussia, however, existed alongside sizable kingdoms such as Bavaria, Württemberg, Saxony and Hanover, grand duchies, duchies and principalities as well as city-states like Hamburg and Bremen. And Italy, which like Germany awaited political unification until 1871, was split into a wide variety of states, largest of which were the kingdoms of Lombardy and Venice, and of the two Sicilies (Sardinia and Naples) and the Papal States. Two of the richest lands of Italy – Lombardy and Venice – remained in 1815 outlying parts of the Austrian Empire.

In retrospect it is clear that the statesmen who remade the map of Europe in 1815 thought primarily about the re-allocation of territories in favour of the victors, who had shared the burdens of the prolonged war against the French, and (more remarkably) paid little or

no regard to the views of the populations who were politically transferred with them. Moreover, even though it offended liberal thinkers
in Britain and elsewhere, there was a general understanding among
statesmen, then as later during the nineteenth century, that the multi-
national empires would and should persist. Doubtless the desire to
preserve the peace after a long period of war helps to explain this
policy, but basically the idea that nations should seek to obtain
separate statehood was thought to be revolutionary, since it involved
disturbance of the status quo and rebellion against legitimate rulers
such as the Russian tsar, the Austrian emperor and the Turkish
sultan. As a result, with some success but above all through control
of the armed forces, police and bureaucratic systems, the empires in
Europe managed to contain their many nationalities, even though in
the course of the nineteenth century national leaders tried to arouse
national feeling and to direct it towards political ends. Concessions
and compromises had to be made: thus Rumania, for example, won
its independence of the Turkish Empire in 1878; Austria made concessions (in 1867) to the Hungarians in the interests of imperial unity,
and lost to the new kingdom of Italy its provinces of Lombardy and
Venice; while the Turkish Empire, although clearly weak, lasted on,
thanks only to the efforts of the Great Powers, fearful of who might
inherit its many territories if it collapsed.

But the forces of nationalism ultimately emerged to sponsor revolutionary claims to national self-determination. In the history of this
powerful movement we should recall how the revolutionary wars of
France, with their call to liberty, equality and fraternity, had tried to
arouse the peoples of Europe, reached by its armies, against their
rulers. The French revolution of 1789 owed much to the thinking of
the Swiss philosopher Rousseau, who held it as an evident truth that
nations, not kings, personified states and were themselves the hol-
ders of complete sovereignty. The French armies as they conquered
carried with them this revolutionary message, which appeared to justify action not only against existing rulers but also against the French
when later, under the Emperor Napoleon, they tried to establish
imperial dominance. Many peoples experienced anew the realisation
of their national identities, so much so that this spirit, geared to war,
contributed measurably to the defeat of Napoleon. It should also be
remembered that the New World, even before the storming of the
Bastille in 1789, had shown that revolution could successfully challenge imperial strength, for by 1783 the thirteen colonies of Britain –

from Maine southwards to Georgia – had set up their own federal system under a written republican constitution. So also in Central and South America, notably under the military leadership of Simon Bolívar during the first few decades of the nineteenth century, the colonists of the Spanish Empire revolted and set up their own independent republics.

During the nineteenth century, indeed until after the First World War, governments succeeded in repressing many national movements. The attempts of the Poles, for example, to free themselves from the Russian Empire in 1830, and again in 1848, failed; so also a revolutionary movement in Hungary, led by Kossuth in 1848 and aimed at restoring Hungarian independence of the Austrian Empire, was suppressed by Russian military intervention. The creation in 1871 of the German Empire under Prussian leadership and its policy of co-operation, based on common interest, with the neighbouring empires of Austria–Hungary and Russia, served further to make impossible successful national movements. The United Kingdom, too, managed to retain Ireland by admitting Irish members in 1801 to the Parliament at Westminster. Outside Europe empires, based on the seaways and commerce, not only flourished but even grew in extent.

6 The Collapse of Empires

The First World War, since it required at its end a world-wide review of territorial problems by the Great Powers, provided the climate and the opportunity for the assertion and consideration of national claims. As a result, political maps were redrawn – but not everywhere. In Europe the continental empires collapsed, their ends caused or confirmed by military defeat. By partitioning Ireland and by conceding the Irish Free State, now known as Ireland, Eire or the Republic of Ireland, the United Kingdom made adjustments in Europe but retained its dominions and colonies overseas. Other victors in the First World War – France, the United States, Belgium and the Netherlands – retained their overseas empires. The Russian Empire, although effaced by the Bolshevik revolution of 1917, survived under new management as the Soviet Union, but within boundaries markedly redrawn in Europe since political independence was won by Finland, Estonia, Latvia, Lithuania and Poland. The German Empire, as such, disappeared to become the German Republic, little reduced in area. However, both the Austro-Hungarian and Turkish Empires in their passing gave rise to a number of new states, some broadly national in character like Austria and Hungary, others markedly multi-national like Czechoslovakia and Yugoslavia, or even (as in Arab lands) scarcely national at all.

It was the Second World War, however, which produced, by relaxing imperial bonds both during its course and more especially after its end, a remarkable spawning of independent states by a process commonly referred to as 'decolonisation'. But we should note here that only a few of these, such as Egypt, the Philippines and Mongolia, could be broadly regarded as nation states, the others being either multi-national in character, like India, Malaysia and Pakistan, or even still at a tribal level of social organisation as is true of many African states.

7 The Political Map of Today

In 1914 the world map represented fifty-four independent states and during the inter-war period 1919–39 this number increased by one-third. In the decades which followed the end of the Second World War, the inter-war total almost doubled – to over 140 in 1974 when decolonisation was nearly complete. One effect of these changes can be measured by the striking contraction of the area of colonialism from rather more than 51.8 million square kilometres (twenty million square miles) in 1900 to less than 23.3 million (nine million square miles) at the end of 1971. These figures are equivalent respectively to forty per cent and barely eighteen per cent of the inhabited earth taken as 129.5 million square kilometres (fifty million square miles). The success of decolonisation is more vividly grasped when it is noted that already by 1961 less than two per cent of mankind remained colonial, and this percentage has further shrunk [Wainhouse, 1964, p. 14].

The dependent peoples who moved to independent statehood had been held under widely differing degrees of political dependence as they had been exposed to widely differing imperial systems. British colonies, in particular, achieved by stages a measure of self-government which at most allowed for autonomy, that is, control of their domestic government subject to imperial powers in certain spheres, notably defence, foreign affairs and commerce. Some dependent territories were held as 'protectorates': such were Morocco and Tunisia held by France, where again the imperial power had in theory only certain specific powers. A special category of dependency was created after the Second World War when the United

Nations set up Trust Territories. Here it was required of the trustee power to report to the U.N. on the progress made towards the self-government and independence of the subject people. As to the variety of principles which imperial powers applied, it is enough to note here that some sought assimilation between their colonials and their own nationals, as did France and Portugal, while others, notably Britain, seldom made any effort to achieve this. But essentially and inevitably an imperial power exported to the dependencies its own language, ideas and culture generally, some of which have had permanent effects.

The rapid dwindling of empire and the spawning of new states were especially marked after 1960. Since the end of that year France, which had held vast territories in Africa, notable more for their sheer extent rather than for their densities of population, has decolonised over 7.8 million square kilometres (3,000,000 square miles). For the United Kingdom the corresponding figure exceeds 3.9 million square kilometres (1.5 million square miles). Similarly, the Netherlands, Belgium and Italy all witnessed the emergence of new states from their former colonial possessions. Virtually all of the great colonial powers of the past retain only vestiges of their former holdings. Thus in 1972 Britain had some fifteen colonies, but their total area (if that in Antarctica is excepted) fell short of 103,600 square kilometres (40,000 square miles). The old empire of Portugal, which accounted for 2,072,000 square kilometres (800,000 square miles), largely in Africa, appeared in 1974 to be decolonising. But note that the above figures relate to colonies as conventionally conceived and imperialism beyond doubt assumes many different forms. Dependent areas of large scale still exist and have become the responsibility of states which were once themselves colonies. Canada has responsibility for its North-west and Yukon Territories (over 3.9 million square kilometres or 1.5 million square miles in area), Australia for its Northern Territory (over 1.3 million square kilometres or 0.5 million square miles), as it had for Papua–New Guinea (453,250 square kilometres or 175,000 square miles), until it became independent in 1974. Similarly, the former German colony of Southwest Africa, although never legally ceded to the South African Republic, is effectively under its rule. And a substantial degree of political dependency akin to that of the old imperialism can be discerned within the Soviet realm, made up of the Soviet Union and its satellites in Europe and Asia.

8 Decolonisation

Changes in world attitudes towards colonialism were crystallised in the policies and decisions of, first, the League of Nations and then, the United Nations [Wainhouse, 1964, p. 3]. The former body, created at the end of the First World War, laid it down that the well-being and development of the dependent peoples of the defeated powers (Germany and Turkey) was 'a sacred trust of civilisation' and, to give effect to this belief, instituted so-called 'mandated territories'. These were graded into three types in recognition of the differing needs of the peoples concerned and formally allocated to one or other of the victorious powers, who were answerable to the League for their administration. In 1945, at the end of the Second World War, the United Nations Charter went further by assigning powers to its General Assembly and Trusteeship Council designed to ensure that all non-self-governing territories of victors and vanquished alike should be guided speedily towards independent statehood.

The time was then ripe for the process of decolonisation which took place rapidly and dramatically. It appears to have been effected much more peaceably than might have been expected, although much blood was shed in certain cases, as for example, in Algeria, Indo-China, India and the Belgian Congo. The once strong imperial powers were exhausted by a war which, starting like the First World War as a European civil war [Acheson 1970], had spread to Africa, Asia and to the approaches of the mainland of the Americas.

These powers, too, had failed in their first duty as imperialists by not successfully defending from enemy attack many of their colonies, especially in Asia, which were thus able to hope for escape from the control of an outside metropolitan power at the end of the Second World War. Further, marked changes of attitudes towards colonialism, even by imperial powers themselves, had taken place. While on the one hand, colonies brought certain advantages to their overseas masters, notably those of 'captive' markets for their manufactures and opportunities for capital investment, on the other they involved increasing costs both for defence and for the provision of improved standards of health, education and living. Curiously, though for different reasons, the two strongest powers to emerge from the Second World War – the United States and the Soviet Union – were agreed in promoting decolonisation. Not surprisingly the former, which as a group of colonies had won its independent statehood by revolutionary action, favoured in its external policy the disbandment of empires which were thought wrong in principle, outmoded and obstacles to free competition among nations. The Soviet Union's policy rested upon Marxist thinking that empires were capitalistic structures that deprived workers of their fair rewards; it included also the hope that free nations, making their own way, might provide profitable fields for Soviet propaganda, infiltration and trade.

The peoples caught up in this movement of decolonisation were moved in varying degrees by nationalist feeling and expressed liberalist attitudes which urged them to shake off old political bonds and to try to control their own destinies. How far such feelings and attitudes were widely spread and how far they were only grasped by leaders educated, trained and ready to act, could doubtless be discussed at length. It should be noted that some imperialists had advanced far along the road towards an ultimate transfer of sovereignty merely by having introduced their own political institutions, ideas, language, literature and democratic ways; as also by the education in their home universities of abler colonial citizens, who were destined to become anti-imperial leaders and even rebels against them. Yet it must be admitted that some of the nationalism widely expressed and claimed scarcely existed. Nationalism surely is based on the existence and recognition of national identity yet, widely in Africa above all, societies were still illiterate and organised tribally. This is not to say that there were not good and valid reasons for overthrowing imperial yokes. It has meant, however, that many new states have faced problems of great difficulty in their attempts to integrate peoples in no sense so cohesive and single-minded (if only about themselves) as nations tend to be.

9 Nations and Nationalism

The emergence of so many new states over the last fifty years owes much to the powerful and explosive force of 'nationalism'. This emotive force springs from consciousness of national identity and the will of a nation to seek political independence. Nations as such have long existed and been recognised by their distinctive traits, usually of language, customs and history; but only by stages did they assume the role of political protagonists.

It is not easy to define briefly the concept 'nation', but it is clear that many nations originated in Europe and were known as such, where peoples, localised and relatively secluded in and around 'core areas', developed a common language, common defensive attitudes, a common history, and thus a sense of togetherness and, eventually, an awareness of their distinctive identities. 'Core areas' were those well-suited geographically to become food bases (in earlier times especially, when agriculture was the chief element in the economy), to support somewhat denser populations, to become foci of routes, and to provide sites for capital cities from which political power could be directed. While nations are normally distinguished by their own national language, this alone is not a sure guide to the identity of all nations, some of which share, for example, English or German, yet, like Australians, New Zealanders, Swiss and Austrians, nevertheless clearly form separate national groups.

It should be emphasised that the concept 'nation' includes the presence of a spirit, a consciousness or, as Renan put it, a soul: nationals develop a sense of togetherness, and value – indeed tend to overvalue – their own specific virtues and qualities. Also, in the making and survival of nations, external pressures from similar (or multi-nationally organised) groups certainly played an important part. In the recollection of most nations, as for example in those of the English, Scots, Poles, and Vietnamese, are the battles fought, lost and won throughout their histories against their enemies, and those battles and the history associated with them helped to bind together and mould the national group. And let us note lastly that the growth of a nation marks a mature stage in social and political development, for it is clearly a larger and more complex community than one which is either tribal or provincial.

10 State Patterns by Continents

The pattern of states shown on a world map appears neither simple nor rational. Everywhere states are of unequal size and framed within irregular limits. Even during the short span of the last few hundred years these patterns have changed continually and very markedly in quite recent years. Clearly the political map represents a stage in history and the outcome of social and political processes which have been long operative, especially in the Old World of Asia and Europe. Among these processes the occupation and settlement of land areas and wars leading to either territorial expansion or contraction are outstanding. Statesmen of the leading powers at periodical conferences have given recognition to new states as they have sanctioned boundary changes, but the map remains bizarre. Note how sharply the patterns of states differ between the continents. Table I enumerates the independent states, dividing the Americas into three units, and ignoring Antarctica, the parts of which have been partitioned on the map into dependencies of the United Kingdom, Australia, Argentina, Norway, Denmark, the United States and the Soviet Union.

TABLE I
THE NUMBER OF INDEPENDENT STATES BY CONTINENTS IN 1974

Europe	34
North America	2
South America	11
Central America	13
Asia	32
Africa	42
Australasia	5
Total	139

SOURCE: *The Statesman's Year-Book 1973–4*, Macmillan, London.

This apparently simple enumeration raises some points for arbitrary decision. The figure for Europe includes the Soviet Union, Turkey and Cyprus, although their territories are either largely or wholly Asiatic, and also three microstates; however, it excludes the Holy See, Andorra and Gibraltar – the last two of which are dependent states – and also the City of Berlin, which has a legally anomalous status. The figure for Central America includes Mexico and island states both within and at the approaches to the Caribbean Sea. Asia's total allows two states for China, Korea and Vietnam, and Africa's includes the Indian Ocean state of Mauritius but excludes Rhodesia. Lastly, in Australasia the tiny independent states of Western Samoa and Fiji are grouped with Australia, New Zealand and Papua New Guinea.

It is evident from this table that Europe, with seven per cent of the world's inhabited area and twenty-five per cent of its independent states, presents an exceptional pattern. In contrast, in relation to their areas, North America and Australasia show remarkably little political subdivision. Asia has fewer states than its sheer area might suggest and Central America's share of states is high for its small area. Africa has above average proportion of the world state total –

about thirty per cent. South America conforms best to the average number of states proportionate to land area.

By way of commentary on these inequalities, note that the large number of states in Europe is related to the development there in the course of a long history of many distinct nationalities and their eventual desire to secure separate statehood. Note also that physical geography insinuates another explanatory factor. When so much of the land is hot desert, as in Africa and Australia, or tropical forest as in Africa and South America, penetration and settlement are mini-mised: the cores of settlement, with which the origin and growth of states are associated in Europe, were thus lacking in such lands, which also were opened up relatively late. The fragmented insular world of the Caribbean clearly has a bearing on the number of states which emerged in Central America. Another point to be borne in mind, to which we return later (chapter 5), is that Australia, Canada and the United States are federated states made up of six, ten and fifty units respectively, each of them states. So also, the vast Soviet Union incorporates fifteen state units.

Conclusion

The bizarre pattern of states, which the political map represents, gives no hint of the political efforts of many different kinds which have combined to produce it. It is enough here to indicate the princi-pal ways international boundaries have changed and provide, for a time at least, stability to the present map. First, we should note that in the past conquest was the major means by which states were forged and their territories expanded – or contracted. If open warfare may be ceasing to be an accepted method of state-making, we can be in no doubt that many present-day states occupy territories which have been wholly or in part acquired by the sword. Algeria's detachment from France is a relatively recent instance. Both the United States and the Soviet Union extend to Pacific shores, thanks to efforts, in part at least, military, exerted in earlier times. The United Kingdom, although ultimately united by dynastic and diplomatic means, finds an earlier stage of its state-building in wars successfully waged by England against both Welsh and Scots. Certainly, and in contrast, the beginnings of statehood may be seen in claims made by right of discovery and this would help to explain the origin of Australia and New Zealand as states. Some changes in the political map result from the break-up of old, composite imperial states with new state units emerging. The passing of the Austro-Hungarian Empire – a territorial continuum – and of the British and French Empires, which were widely extended and mostly in Asia and Africa, gave rise to many new independent states. Further, the processes of partition and secession, which can be distinguished [Prescott 1970], have also contributed to the patterns of the political map.

The partitioning of states, a not uncommon historical phenomenon, has been called 'this century's awkward form of compromise'. It is usually the result of decisions taken jointly by major powers and involves 'overtones of outrage or abuse' [Pounds 1964]. Partition accounts, for example, for the division into two states of Germany, Korea and Vietnam, all three of which were historically single political units. Acts of secession explain the separate statehood of Ireland (the Irish Republic) and Bangladesh: the former seceded from the United Kingdom, the latter from Pakistan, of which it was the detached and more populous eastern part. Yet another way in which the political map changes relates to states with dependent or independent status which are joined to other, usually neighbouring states. Thus Eritrea, which became an Italian protectorate in 1889 and was later federated within Ethiopia, is now absorbed by the unitary state of Ethiopia. And, as we have already noted, the Baltic states of Lithuania, Latvia and Estonia, formerly independent, are now incorporated as units within the Soviet Union.

The above discussion does not review all the many causes of changes in the pattern of states. In earlier dynastic times territory was often acquired, as by the Hapsburgs, by inheritance and by marriage. So, too, there are remarkable cases of territory acquired by purchase. Two notable purchases were made by the United States: in 1887 it bought Alaska from Russia and even earlier – in 1802 – it purchased Louisiana from the Emperor Napoleon, succeeding in a transaction which has been called the greatest real estate deal in history. Lastly, let us note that frequent adjustments in boundaries, recorded in formal agreements, produce minor and less dramatic changes in the political map (see chapter 4).

2 The Inhabitants of States

The strongest States are those in which the political idea completely fills the body of the State in all its parts. Those sections of the State in which the idea does not gain acceptance fall away.

(Friedrich Ratzel, *Politische Geographie*, 1923 edn)

Although mankind is conceived by biologists to belong to a single species (*Homo sapiens*) and was once called, by the sociologist Graham Wallas, 'The Great Society', it has come to be divided between states which, in respect of both their internal and external affairs, largely go their own way. And just as the territorial niches which these states occupy vary greatly from one to the other (see chapter 3), so also do their inhabitants. States are often lightly referred to as 'nations', thus carrying the implication that the inhabitants of each state form only one national group and, as such, are easily distinguished and characterised. In fact, it is the norm rather than the exception that they reveal differences of nationality as well as many other differences, some of which, like the literacy and natural growth of the population, can be quantified, while others, like political unity and strength, are qualitative and less easily measured. It would be easy to make a long list of the differences of many kinds among the inhabitants of states. Some of these are indicated by vital statistics, which tell of rates of natural increase, total numbers, proportions by age groups and numerical trends. Other differences relate to alleged 'racial' and ethnic characteristics and to levels of material culture within the wide range from so-called 'simple' (or primitive) societies to those which have reached high technological levels. But among these many criteria of differentiation, particular importance attaches in political geography to language and nationality. This is because these two cultural factors may markedly affect the cohesion and strength of a state. They are, in fact, elements of the 'state-idea', to which Friedrich Ratzel, the father of political geography, referred (see above), and we shall find that an analysis of the population of a state which seeks to establish its state-idea can throw a clear light on its cohesion, functioning and viability.

1 Racial and Ethnic Differences

The problems of 'race', which are primarily a matter for biologists, are still an unsolved puzzle; ethnic differences, some of which may appear visibly simple, can also be difficult to establish and understand. On the one hand, we learn that races today are mixed and impure; on the other, we can speak confidently of races that are 'White' (or Caucasian), 'Black' (or Negroid), and 'Yellow' (or Mongoloid), although these colour labels apply very loosely. In other words, it is relatively straightforward and convenient, if not all that meaningful, to allocate the present peoples of the world to specific ethnic categories on the basis of visible and measurable criteria, such as skin colour, head shape, stature, hair texture or the shape of eyes and noses. Such classifications can be quantitative, thus depending in part for their limited validity on the statistical techniques employed, but whatever interest these may arouse, we are left in much doubt as to what bearing they may have on politics.

Studies of human intelligence, as measured by I.Q. tests, might appear to make it possible to categorise rigidly social or racial groups, such as American Negroes, and further to indicate widely different levels of intelligence reached by selected human groups within any one state – and this could clearly have political implications of many kinds. But, as Arthur Koestler showed (*The Observer Review*, 9 December 1973), while some contemporary psychologists, notably N. J. Eysenck and Richard Herrnstein, have claimed on the basis of statistical data that intelligence is eighty per cent determined by heredity, others reach a figure of forty-five per cent for the genetic element in intelligence. Some scientists, however, have shown what positive, stimulating effects have been achieved on the physiological development of the brain of young rats by exposing them to stimulus-rich environments. Moreover, 'intelligence', in the context of these studies, relates to only one (admittedly very important) aspect of the human brain, and we must conclude that, given the conflicting results of current research, little is certain about the mental equipment of racial and ethnic groups that is helpful in political geography. And we are well aware how selected data drawn from ethnology was perverted by Adolf Hitler and by others who believed in the White Man's superiority as a racial attribute and how they were used to support political attitudes and policies as ill-grounded as they were ill-intentioned. Thus, in so far as, in this sense, ideas about race and ethnic types have entered into the decision-making of government policies, they have lacked scientific validity and have been clearly unhelpful to rational political behaviour.

However, the term 'race' is conveniently used in another sense where it calls attention to situations and problems of considerable importance in the internal and external relations of states. The economic policies pursued by President Amin in Uganda, where Indian residents were denied citizenship and indeed expelled, clearly implied racial discrimination, and the United Kingdom had to grapple with the difficulties of a sudden mass immigration of Indians who held British passports. Similarly, the activities of so-called terrorists or guerrillas in Rhodesia are properly described as racially inspired, as are also the revolutionary efforts of the Negro freedom-fighters of neighbouring Mozambique against their Portuguese rulers. Again, in yet another sense, the term 'race' is conveniently and not misleadingly used, for example, with reference to the three 'races' of Malaya, namely, citizens who are respectively of Malayan, Indian and Chinese origin and culture. So also is it used with reference to the inhabitants of the South African Republic, which are made up of Bantus (Negroes), Kaffirs, Hottentots, Indians, 'Europeans' of mixed descent, and Whites. In each instance the population forms what is best called a 'plural society',* drawn from different racial sources, yet the political problems which arise through their association within a single state are, in fact, primarily social. In the United States, too, the 'colour problem' relates less to race than to social considerations resulting from the original enslavement and subsequent inferior status of Negro citizens. In short, while on the one hand 'race' appears a little knowable phenomenon to challenge science, on the other it reminds us continually that in a world where it is widely held that all peoples should enjoy freedom to develop along their own lines, grave international dangers lie ahead of a violent collision between Negroes and Whites.

* For a short study of a plural society in Sri Lanka (Ceylon), in which language and religion are the main sources of division, see Farmer, B. H. [1968]: 'Some problems of a plural society', in C. A. Fisher, ed., *Essays* in *Political Geography*, London, pp. 147–59.

Race apart, other characteristics of population – notably language, nationality, cultural level, numerical scale and spatial distribution – beyond doubt have direct relevance to politics, and to
these we now turn.

2 Language Differences

That the peoples of the world speak with many tongues is a strong
divisive force which tests the skills of the interpreter and the trans-
lator on those occasions when nations speak formally to nations. The
fact that languages can be grouped into families and subgroups is of
academic and not of practical value, since the differentiation within
the same family has produced languages as different as English and
French or German and Russian. It is clear that the prolonged loca-
lism of life in earlier days fostered the development and differentiation of languages which may originally have been broadly
common to a people before their dispersion. It is clear, too, that
during history peoples at times changed their speech by adopting
that of those which they conquered or of those which conquered
them: thus the Celtic speech of Gauls gave way to Latin speech from
which the French language emerged, and Arabic gained dominance
in North Africa during the centuries which followed the Moslem
Arab invasions and conquests of the seventh century AD. The language patterns throughout the world vary much in their complexity.
For example, the language map of North America, where English is
used by the bulk of the population, is relatively simple, although
French persists in parts of eastern Canada. So also in South America
Spanish is very widely spoken, with Portuguese in Brazil. In contrast
to the Americas, Europe and Asia are remarkably polyglot.
Although the acceptance of certain languages, notably English and
French, for use at international conferences and for treaties is convenient, and although English, French and Spanish have come to be
used widely, far away from their original homelands, for most citizens language remains a serious obstruction to communication with
those of other lands.

To a considerable extent language is a distinguishing and emotive
attribute of nations, although it would be wrong to claim the simple
identification of one language, one nation. Certainly many national
groups, in the effort to establish their national individuality, were at
pains, by publishing grammar books, dictionaries and other litera-

ture, to show that their languages stood apart from those of their neighbours. So also others, like the Irish and Welsh, strive to teach and preserve languages which would otherwise fall steadily into disuse and, like Cornish, die out. But if the norm is for a language to be special to one particular nation and state, there are many cases where nations exist with more than one national language or with one that is shared with other nations. It is English that Americans, Australians and New Zealanders mainly speak, although they have modified this language in certain respects; yet none would deny that they have come to constitute separate nations. The Spanish-speaking Chileans, Peruvians, Argentines and others of South America present themselves as national groups even though in some respects these may show immature features. The Austrians are German-speaking yet nationally distinct from the Germans of the two German republics. Although most of the Swiss have German as their native tongue and four languages in all are formally recognised, the Swiss constitute a nation.

The existence of two or more large language groups within a state usually reflects, however, the association of distinct national groups. The political attitudes of these may be, but are not necessarily, at variance, for the political systems may be so devised and the social cohesion so strong as to overcome any separatist tendencies. To such factors which affect the unity of a state we shall turn later. Meanwhile, let us note how common it is that states incorporate a number of linguistic groups which are more or less well-adjusted to each other. In Spain which, in respect of both its physical and human geography, is made up of heterogeneous parts, Catalan and Basque are spoken as well as Spanish derived from Castilian. The United Kingdom has a dwindling fraction of citizens who speak Welsh and Gaelic but, although Welsh and Scottish national feeling is at times sturdily asserted, weakness to this state derives mainly from Northern Ireland, as a result of politico–religious sentiments, although, as in Scotland, English is the dominant speech. By contrast, in both Belgium and Canada, which have two official languages, these, as we shall discuss later, clearly reflect centrifugal tendencies. In possibly less degree this might appear true of Yugoslavia which has three principal languages – Serbo-Croat, Slovenian and Macedonian – which among them use both the Roman and a Cyrillic alphabet. In Sri Lanka (Ceylon) communal tensions were sharpened in the 1950s when Sinhala was established as the national language by a government dominated by Sinhalese, who make up nearly three-quarters of the total population, and these tensions were not relaxed until after 1966, thanks to a law which accorded to the Tamil minority the right to use their own language in their own areas, notably in the schools and the courts. An extreme case of linguistic diversity which does not, however, threaten the strength and unity of the state, is provided by the Soviet Union, where more than one hundred languages are recorded in the censuses, although one – Russian – is dominant, being spoken by about fifty-five per cent of the population.

It is not difficult to understand why use of a language other than that of the rulers of a state was continually taken in the past to imply disloyalty to the state and often occasioned attempts to suppress it and repression of many kinds. Consider, for example, a citation made by George Borrow [1846] with reference to Spain and to a law enacted in 1566, in which the king forbade the use of Arabic to the Moriscos (*sc.* Moors) as 'the use of different languages amongst the natives of one kingdom opens the door to treason, and is a source of heavy inconvenience; and this is exemplified more in the case of the Gitanes (*sc.* Gypsies) than of any other people'. And of the German-speaking province of Alsace, which France recovered from Germany in 1918 and had doubts about its loyalty, it has been written [Brogan 1940], 'by no means all Alsatians who habitually spoke German were disloyal to France, but all who were habitually disloyal spoke German'. Certainly stern and repressive action was continually taken by governments against linguistic minorities in the attempt to reduce tendencies thought to be politically centrifugal. The Tsar Alexander II attempted russification, suppressing other languages in favour of Russian; the Magyars after 1848 tried to force their own language on their Slav-speaking subjects; and the Italians, having incorporated South Tyrol into the Italian kingdom after The First World War, changed German place-names, stipulated that only Italian should be used in the Courts, and disallowed (in 1924) German teaching even in kindergartens. The objective of such policies, like others involving religious persecution, was an increasing degree of uniformity and unity within the state.

3 Nations and Nationalism

To the origins of nations and to the development of the political sentiment 'nationalism' we have already referred (see pp. 16–17).The growth of nations as relatively large and mature communities and, even more, the phenomenon of nationalism have been responsible in modern times, not only for positive progress in some fields of human endeavour, but also for wars and the increasing political division of the world.

For many centuries the existence of nations both in Europe and Asia carried with it no strong implication that they should be separately organised as national states. The long-lasting Roman Empire, for example, during periods of relative success and partial failure, preserved numerous groups, for the most part tribally organised yet not without elements of national character, within one civilised political unit. In the centuries which followed the fall of the Roman Empire in the West, when immigrant peoples settled down and slowly differentiated into national groups, empires, which associated peoples of many nations and tongues, were thought to be, and succeeded in being, normal forms of political organisation, many surviving, though not necessarily flourishing, into the twentieth century. In the main, therefore, the so-called nation state is a relatively recent innovation, marking revolutionary change.

Nations evolved in the course of history to become powerful political agents of change, their strength resting on their 'common sympathies which make them co-operate with each other more willingly than with other people, and desire that they should be governed by themselves, or a portion of themselves exclusively'. And as John Stuart Mill also emphasised, 'good government is no substitute for self-government'. Consciousness of nationality or nationalism is the sentiment and will that make a nation: 'it is more than a political contract; (it is) a union of hearts, once made, never unmade . . . a spiritual conception, unconquerable, indestructible' [Rose 1916]. Since, therefore, nationality, once consciously perceived and evaluated, has such a special character – it is unlike the state which can change its limits and even disappear – it is easy to see that nationalism, to which it gave rise, had such striking effects on the world pattern of states. Whereas patriotism is the love of country and the will to defend it and could be aroused with some success against invaders of multi-national empires, nationalism has a deeper and tougher emotive strength as would appear to have been expressed, mixed as it was with communist ideology, in the effort of North Vietnam in its protracted war against American-backed South Vietnam.

4 National Homogeneity and Heterogeneity

National sentiment ensures a proper pride in national achievement as it provides encouragement for its continuance. No less it commonly nourishes exclusiveness and may give rise to xenophobia and even chauvinism – belief in one's country right or wrong. Above all, it makes an appeal to men's minds comparable to that of a religion and serves to unify a national group and to fire it towards common action, both within the state in relation to those of other nationalities and outside it in its dealings with other nations. Hence a state with a single or dominant national group tends to acquire a high degree of integration: indeed, 'in the national State the strongest organisation and loyalty areas coincide' [Schwarzenberger 1964]; a nationally homogeneous population, politically organised, shows a high degree of cohesion and can be capable of generating a virtually explosive power. Certainly, the effect of nationalism varies according to the stage of development of the state, since maturity may overcome some of its more violent and unattractive features. But it is noteworthy that nationalism has proved an enduring force – even among the socialist countries of Eastern Europe, including the Soviet Union, although communist ideology hoped and expected that this allegedly bourgeois sentiment would prove obsolescent.

Few states are, strictly speaking, coterminous with nations so that, in respect of their populations, they exhibit national heterogeneity: normally one preponderant group is associated with minorities of other nationalities. And this heterogeneity can prove weakening to the structure and activities of the state unless its coercive powers are used to overcome the lack of consensus among the citizens.

When a geographical analysis is made of the national composition of a state, the nature and extent of its territory, its history, its language and other cultural characteristics, much may be learnt about its special character, problems, relative strength and viability. Here it is revealing and helpful to enquire into a state's *raison d'être* and its state-idea, two related concepts which can be usefully distinguished although they overlap. For every state it is possible to provide a *raison d'être*, an explanation of how it has come to exist and why it manages to operate and to survive, and at the lowest level this explanation points to a monopoly of political power held and exerted by a ruling group. A state-idea is a more complex concept since it not only explains a state's existence but offers a justification of it. Not all states have a state-idea, difficult as this may be to discover and define, while others may be searching for one. The state-idea goes back to Friedrich Ratzel, the father of political geography, whom we have quoted in this context at the head of this chapter. As Ratzel believed, a state is strong to the extent that the idea for which it exists and which distinguishes it from all others is understood and accepted by the mass of its population throughout the whole of its territory. The state-idea concept clearly relates to relatively recent times, since it involves the notions of popular acceptance of, and participation in, state purposes. It is related to, but in these respects stands apart from, the 'images' held about a state [Kristof 1968] and its 'iconography' [Gottmann 1952], which may be conceived of by only a minority of citizens, as for example by the intellectual élite and the ruling class in eighteenth-century Russia.

We shall discuss later in this chapter how far the concepts state-idea and *raison d'être* apply to four selected states. Here it is enough to note that, while the lack of a broadly accepted state-idea may involve internal weakness in one state, this may not apply to others, such as Rhodesia and the South African Republic, where governments, wielding all the powers of the state, can preserve unity and strength despite the disaffection (or would-be disaffection) of certain communities within it. Such states exhibit, without doubt, clear *raisons d'être* but lack state-ideas widely accepted, since the bulk of the population have little or no share in making political decisions. We may note, too, that the force of a state-idea can vary considerably. That of Israel, to which Judaism and the return to the Holy Land of the descendants of Jews long dispersed contribute emotive elements, is clearly strong. That of Bolivia [Fifer 1972] appears weak, involving only elements, such as the desire, which unites all Bolivians, to recover coastlands of which they were deprived in war by Peru and Chile. The reader will be aware that the state-idea is a modern notion most applicable to Western democratic countries. It might appear to have had its roots in the philosophy of Rousseau, who believed that a nation should decide collectively its own destiny, and in that of John Stuart Mill for whom government existed, with the participation of individual citizens, for their well-being. In fact, over a large part of the world states are found largely to lack state-ideas. This is most notable in Africa, where social and political development are widely immature and national communities do not exist to provide one solid basis for newly emergent states which, as a result, are dubiously viable as they search for symbols of their identity as a basis for unity and strength.

5 Manpower Numbers and Trends

Towards the understanding of states, a qualitative analysis such as has been attempted above may be supplemented by a quantitative review of their populations. Here we are on more measurable ground, being able to make use of the precision that statistics afford, although mindful of their limitations. Impressive as is the work of the demographer – the expert who handles and interprets statistics relating to population – he is necessarily restricted by their occasional absence or unreliability. For certain countries it still remains true that precise information, even about their total numbers, is often largely lacking: this would apply, for example, to Saudi Arabia and Mongolia, and even to China, for which, with nearly one-quarter of the world's population, 1970 estimates vary between 685 and 811 million. Such difficulties, however, are not enough to impair the usefulness of such an approach to the demographic aspect of states.

For many obvious reasons, including tax collection and military service, governments need to know many numerical things about the populations for which they exist and are responsible. Above all, they wish to know the birth and death rates, from which natural increase becomes known; the number of children per woman of child-bearing age; infant mortality; the age distribution and also the geographical distribution and the proportions of urban and rural population; the numbers of emigrants and immigrants, the balance of which clearly affects population numbers. Most states carry out enumerations of their populations with some regularity (e.g. every ten years) by censuses which yield a varying amount of data for refined analysis. Most countries, too, have reasonably reliable estimates available each year. From these it is possible to learn not only the total population of a state and of its administrative divisions but also the trends, whether towards slow or rapid increase, stability or even decline. Such figures are valuable in permitting estimates of 'manpower' – that is, the population, by sex, of those in their working years, leaving out of account those normally too young or too old to be so classified. With these figures interesting comparisons can be made which tell something of the changing relative economic and military strength of states in this dynamic world.

The term 'manpower' was invented long ago by the geographer Sir Halford Mackinder [1905] and has proved its worth as an index of economic and political potential. Given that nations vary substantially in their birth and death rates, as also in their gains and losses resultant from migration, it follows that some get stronger and others weaker in respect of the manpower which they command. Thus trends can be measured and compared that give a clear indication of the relative economic strength of states, which clearly lies behind their ultimate political and military strength.

If other things were equal – they never are – a list of state population totals, which included their predicted levels in the next decade or so ahead, would throw a clear light on the likely changes in power and policy of the principal actors in the international drama. Such lists have value for the present and future alike and with reference to the past, even though many important qualitative considerations would need to be borne in mind. One factor, for example, in the defeat of France by Germany in the war of 1870–1, as also of its collapse before the German attack in 1940, is clearly demographic. By the time of the earlier war France had lost its manpower superiority over Germany and, in the nineteenth and twentieth centuries, France experienced low birth rates which fell to 15.1 per thousand between 1935 and 1939 [Beaujeu-Garnier 1966]. So also, the remarkably rapid rise of Japan as a powerful mercantile and military power was clearly related to the growth of its population from a hitherto stable level, estimated at thirty millions in 1868, to ninety millions in 1941. But it will be made clear later (see chapter 5) that manpower is only one among a number of indices of national strength. If the economic and military power of states depended solely on manpower numbers, China and India would predominate and such countries as Brazil and Indonesia, the first with a population closely approaching the hundred million mark and the second with one in excess of this, would also occupy leading positions.

Four Representative Examples

The above general discussion can be extended and illustrated if close attention is now given to a selection of four states, chosen not at random but because in their different ways they show how, in particular cases, the national, linguistic and numerical characteristics of state populations, when considered in relation to the nature of their territories and their histories, tell us much about their special character and distinctive problems.

(i) Switzerland

This small country recognises three offical languages – German, French and Italian – and (since 1937) Romanche* as a fourth national language. These are spoken by 69.3, 18.9, 9.5 and barely 1 per cent respectively of the population. Some of the Italian-speakers are, in fact, Italians, and other tongues are heard among resident foreigners and seasonal workers, who account for more than ten per cent of total numbers. Although German is the official language it is *Schwyzerdeutsch* (Swiss-German) that is widely heard, while Franco-Provençal dialects are spoken by about one million citizens in western Switzerland. Many Swiss are bilingual in German and French, but their number is declining and English is becoming virtually a fifth national language. Linguistically divided, so Switzerland is also divided (almost equally) between Roman Catholics (52.7 per cent) and Protestants (45.4 per cent), for it was the home of the reformer, John Calvin. Yet no one could deny the reality of Swiss national feeling as also the strength and stability of the Swiss Confederation. This achievement invites explanation.

The germ of the Swiss state can be traced back to the thirteenth century, although political independence, virtually won by about the year 1500, was formally granted only in 1648 by the Treaty of Westphalia. The beginnings of the Swiss state are seen in the military success of the three Forest Cantons of Uri, Schwyz and Unterwalden against their feudal overlords, not least of whom were the Counts of Hapsburg. These hardy Swiss shepherds certainly exploited their geographical environment, well-suited as it was to defensive war and commercial profit: the Forest Cantons fronted Lake Zürich and commanded the approach from the north into Italy by the St Gotthard Pass, access to which was greatly improved in the early thirteenth century. Situated on the borderlands of the three kingdoms of France, Burgundy and Italy, and within the Holy Roman Empire, the Forest Cantons formed a free German league which sought, by

* This is the Latin-derived or Romance language spoken in the thinly populated Alpine canton of Graubünden where people are mainly trilingual.

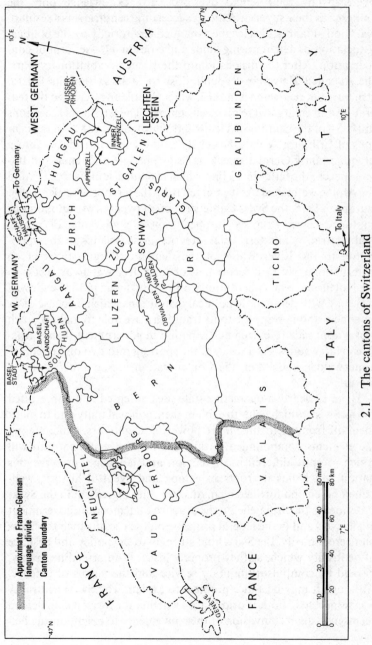

2.1 The cantons of Switzerland

overthrowing their feudal overlords, to acknowledge only the emperor as their superior. During succeeding centuries, as a result of wars and alliances, this league expanded territorially by the political association of neighbouring lands and cities in a loose form of confederation. After the dislocation of the French revolutionary wars, the so-called Helvetian Republic lost for a short time its federal structure but recovered it in 1803, when Napoleon re-created the federation and enlarged it to nineteen cantons. The territorial accessions in 1803 – of the cantons of Ticino and Vaud – and in 1815 of the cantons of Fribourg, Valais, Neuchâtel and Genève introduced into a predominantly German-speaking league people of French and Italian speech, the latter in Ticino, which extended southwards beyond the Alpine watershed. As it emerged from the territorial settlement of Europe in 1815, the Swiss Confederation of twenty-two autonomous cantons received from six European powers a guarantee of 'perpetual neutrality' and territorial integrity. Also, thanks to the application to the River Rhine of the then novel legal status of an 'international river', it secured, as of right, free waterway access to the North Sea. New constitutions in 1848 and again in 1874 endowed this state with democratic political institutions which, because of its smallness and in response to its traditions, are able to make a much closer approach to citizen participation in government than is feasible in large states. As a result of the splitting into two of Appenzell, Unterwalden and Basel, the Confederation now numbers twenty-five units.

There is clearly a distinctive state-idea accepted and appreciated by the Swiss, which helps to explain their political unity and to mark them off from their three more powerful neighbours. Chief among the elements compounded in this idea are the sentiment and will which, despite differences of religion and language, preserve this nation which has its roots in a long and eventful history, well-remembered and fortified by myths. Another ingredient in the Swiss state-idea is the firm belief in the practice of democratic government at all levels and in the federal principle, in the use of which the Swiss pioneered. Lastly, the Swiss hold strongly to the policy and practice of neutrality which, as they properly insist, is an armed neutrality, backed by compulsory military service and the means of defence. Although it may be a nice problem to explain why Swiss neutrality was respected in both World Wars – whether the Swiss will to defend themselves against invasion or the convenience to neighbouring bel-

ligerents of this neutral buffer state was the overriding consideration
– the fact remains that its neutrality, unlike that of both Belgium and
Luxembourg, has never been violated. By avoiding membership of
the United Nations and by refusing to join power blocs such as NATO,
the Swiss government affirms its neutrality to which, however, it
gives a positive meaning by its active support of humanitarian organisations. Nor should it be forgotten, as one factor in the strength and
vitality of Switzerland, that its citizens have built up, and successfully
sustain, a vigorous economy and a high standard of living.

(ii) Belgium

Smaller but much more populous than Switzerland, Belgium compares closely with the latter in certain respects, notably in its location
between Germany and France and in the fact that, while mainly Ger-
manic in language, it includes also French-speaking citizens. However, in contrast to Switzerland, Belgium appears to be sharply
divided and politically weakened by differences of nationality and
language.

The territory of the present Belgian kingdom occupied a frontier
position in the Roman Empire as the most northerly part of Gaul,
and within it immigrant Germans – Franks especially but also
Saxons – settled among a scanty Romano–Gallic population. As a
result this territory became a borderland between French and
German speech, combining populations which, on the one hand,
spoke Flemish, a dialect of Dutch, and, on the other, Walloon, a dialect of French.*

Another marked geographical feature of the lands which became
Belgium was that they included, seawards of the Ardennes plateau,
part of a routeway across Europe leading to the English Channel,
which has been used since prehistoric times. These lands thus
acquired international importance, one result of which was their industrial and commercial prosperity in the Middle Ages, while
another was their entangled political and military history right down
to recent times. They did, it is true, include a core area of national development – settled lands along the middle Scheldt and its tributary

* 'Walloon' (cf. 'Wales' and 'Welsh') contains the Teutonic element 'wahl' meaning 'foreigner'. Thus immigrant Germans – Franks and others in Belgium and Anglo-
Saxons in Britain – appear to have applied the label of foreigners to a pre-existing
population.

2.2 The language divisions of Belgium

the Lys, bordered by wide forests – but it was the Flemish nation, not a Belgian nation, that found its cradle there. And this was not large enough or strong enough to control its own destinies, for history records that, divided into secular and ecclesiastical fiefs, the southern Low Countries were subjected to continual changes of political allegiance: just as Mediterranean islands fell to the control of successive sea-powers, so the Belgian lands found themselves tied politically to outside continental powers. Parts of the southern Low Countries were long bound by feudal ties to the Kingdom of Germany, itself part of the Holy Roman Empire; to a lesser extent, parts were tied to the Kingdom of France. They were as much separated from, as drawn towards their neighbours to the north, the northern Low Countries, represented today by the Kingdom of the Netherlands. For a while – in the fifteenth century – the whole of the Low Countries, north and south, were united under the rule of the Dukes of Burgundy, who were vassals of both France and the Empire. This unity occurred again, under King Charles I of Spain, who also became Emperor in 1530. At this time the Low Countries were merely parts, yet economically valuable parts, of the Burgundian 'circle' of the Empire, which included *inter alia* the County of Burgundy, based on the Saône Basin, with its capital at Dijon. A few decades later the whole of the Low Countries found themselves freed from the Empire but dependencies of King Philip II of Spain. After the long wars of independence (1568–1609), only the northern Low Countries succeeded in shaking off Spanish rule and in establishing their own federal state (the so-called United Provinces), and the southern Low Countries remained dependencies of Spain, to become 'the chosen fighting ground of European armies, the chosen plaything of European diplomacy' [Freeman 1881]. In 1713 the southern Low Countries passed to the imperial rulers of Austria; in 1792 they were annexed to France and later, united with the northern provinces by the emperor Napoleon, became part of a short-lived Kingdom of Holland.

In accordance with the peace settlement which followed the fall of Napoleon in 1815, the southern Low Countries were merged into the Kingdom of the Netherlands which, in respect of the Grand Duchy of Luxembourg, became a member of the new Confederation of Germany. However, after their revolt in 1830, the Belgians seceded, winning independence under their own king, and in 1839 their country was neutralised when the United Kingdom, France, Prussia, Austria and Russia undertook 'severally and individually' to guarantee its independence and neutrality in the hope that it would act as a buffer, in the interests of peace, between its powerful neighbours, Britain, France and Prussia.

Like Europe, of which it is a microcosm, Belgium might appear to have experienced too much history. While its international importance is still affirmed by the presence in Brussels of the headquarters of the European Economic Community, as an independent state it is a relatively youthful creation. It has failed to create a single nation, conscious of its own identity, and thus, although it has a *raison d'être*, it lacks a clear-cut state-idea to unite and invigorate its two linguistic groups, the Walloons and the Flemings. Although during their long history these groups have been continually, and often profitably, co-operative on the economic plane, and although they express no desire to merge politically with their linguistic partners on either side (the French and the Dutch), they have come increasingly in recent years to stand apart as separate and self-conscious communities. French acquired prestige during the period of Austrian rule as also during the short French occupation; French-speaking citizens were numerically dominant during the last half of the nineteenth century when, within their area of the country, the coal, iron and steel industries of the Sambre-Meuse valley were flourishing. But the Flemish movement, which regarded language as the basis of Flemish nationality, had begun as early as 1832, very soon after the birth of the Belgian State, and fostered self-assertion against the dominance of French as the language of the ruling class. Since the birth rate of the Flemings has been consistently higher than that of French-speaking Belgians (18.5 per thousand and 13.5 per thousand respectively), they are now in the majority: fifty-five per cent, a figure which is expected to rise to sixty per cent by 1975. The acceptance of Flemish, now correctly and officially known as Dutch, as one of the two official languages was won only in 1932, and economic changes in recent decades have markedly favoured the Flemings and the area astride the Ghent-Antwerp axis where they are mainly concentrated. Notably the commercial and industrial growth of Antwerp and the development of the Kempenland (Campine) coalfield have brought prosperity to Flemish Belgium, while at the same time coal mines and iron and steel plants have been closed under Common Market auspices in the Walloon area of the country. The provincial capital of Liège in French-speaking Belgium sees its commercial supremacy passing to Antwerp, provincial capital of the Flemings, so that the turn has come for the Walloons to feel oppressed. Religious differences, too, exist for, although Roman Catholics are in the majority of those who profess religion, there are vocal anti-clericals; even so, religious liberty, as in Switzerland, is ensured so that religion is less important politically than are national, social and economic divisions.

It is unhelpful to the cohesion of Belgium that the two principal language groups are compactly arranged: the language boundary, dividing Walloons to the south from Flemings in the north, was virtually established in the eighth and ninth centuries and runs from Dunkirk to Maastricht, passing a little south of Brussels which is a predominantly French-speaking enclave in Flanders; there is also a small area of German-speaking citizens near the German border (figure 2.2). It might perhaps have been thought that Belgium's association with other states – with Luxembourg since 1922, with the Netherlands as well since 1947 and, since the fifties, with the European Coal and Steel Community and the European Economic Community – would have served to reduce internal disunity by engaging Belgians in wider interests and loyalties. Rather it would seem that the relaxation of external dangers and pressures have diverted Belgian political energy to their internal problems and quarrels. There are now two mini-Belgiums, more strictly three because of the multilingual capital of Brussels with its Flemish-speaking suburbs, and the country nourishes many political parties, some of which adopt extreme pro-Flemish and pro-Walloon attitudes, while others are splintered into Flemish and Walloon subgroups. The number and instability of Belgium's governments have become notorious. There were fourteen political crises between 1945 and 1972, five governments in 1936, four in 1946, three in 1958, while in 1968 the country was without a government for 136 days. Although the underlying governmental weakness of Belgium springs from its ethnic and cultural dichotomy, it is clear, as Dr Eric Williams [1973] argues, that the system of proportional representation applied at Belgian elections is partially to blame for these shortcomings.

Under proportional representation the conflict between French-speaking, anti-clerical and urban industrial Walloons, and Flemish-speaking, Roman Catholic, agrarian Flanders, with the multi-lingual Brussels region in between . . . has produced the disintegration of the traditional large parties, years of violence, demonstrations and riots, the break-up of the 500-year-old Louvain University with its international reputation, and led to Cabinet crisis after Cabinet crisis, each one taking longer to resolve.

The basic disunity of Belgium, and the range of conflicting political interests and parties which it presents, account for successive coalition governments which strive to survive by continual compromise. So acute are the differences that curious compromises are reached. To eliminate the dominance of French-speaking Belgians in high office, it was enacted in 1968 that top ministerial posts should be duplicated, so that government departments should have both a Flemish and a French minister. So also parity is sought in the number of top posts held by the two communities in the army, the civil service and the foreign service. Indeed, the central government has come to have 'a unilingual, parity perception of the state that satisfies no one' [Stephenson 1972]. The unitary organisation, adopted by the Belgian state at its inception, clearly fares badly: although it is symbolised by the monarchy, it has no roots in the popular will. Since Belgians share no positive state-idea, sectional interests outweigh common interests in the welfare of the country as a whole. It is by no means clear that federal structure would better serve Belgian needs. This is espoused by only some of the political parties and makes no widespread appeal. Nor can it be assumed that such organisational changes would rid Belgium of its disunity and supply it with a unifying state-idea of its identity and purpose.

(iii) The Soviet Union

Although clearly this state contrasts strikingly with Switzerland in many respects, it compares with it in at least two ways – in its stability and viability and in its adoption of the federal system. The Soviet censuses record over one hundred ethnic groups, eighteen of them numbering more than one million, and many of which form national groups. There are also as many languages, most of which belong to the Indo-European, Turkic and Finno-Ugrian families.

The Union of Soviet Socialist Republics (U.S.S.R.) is clearly not a national state, except in so far as the principal national group – the Russians, constituting rather more than half of the total population – occupy a special and superior position in relation to the many others. The federal constitution of the Soviet Union recognises the existence of national groups and indeed accords to them, according to their numerical scale and cultural standing, special places in the federal system. Thus the fifteen constituent Soviet Socialist Republics (S.S.R.s) which make up the Soviet Union acknowledge large and developed national groups, such as the Ukrainians, Georgians and Uzbeks, while smaller national groups, such as the Tatars, Yakuts and Buryats, usually have the status of Autonomous Soviet Socialist Republics (A.S.S.R.s). Smaller and usually less culturally advanced groups are also separately identified and function within the political –territorial system as *okrugs* and autonomous oblasts. By these means the Soviet constitution allows national institutions to operate regionally and thus to enjoy a measure of autonomy within the whole federal structure. Yet the Soviet federal system compares only formally with that of Switzerland since the full powers of the State are, in fact, centralised and exercised by the Central Committee of the All-Union Communist Party, membership of which comprises less than ten per cent of the adult population.

Although the hope and expectation of Soviet leaders was that national sentiment would prove an outworn, bourgeois creed and fade away in favour of wider international interests, uniting workers as such, this has not come about. Doubtless the concept of a Soviet citizen, fired with pride in, and loyalty to the Soviet system has acquired some reality inasmuch as the working population of the Soviet Union, regardless of nationality, have shared in the revolutionary changes which have produced an increasingly urbanised and industrialised society. Even so, the Soviet rulers have always had to be keenly aware of the vigour and claims of specific nationalities and have been at pains, by encouraging internal migration and by actually transferring national groups, to weaken the force of national feeling as a possibly separatist and thus disruptive force within the state. A policy of russification, which has involved the promotion of the Russian language and the movement of Russians widely into areas peopled by national minorities, has meant that, in most of the Union republics (both S.S.R.s and A.S.S.R.s), Russians are present in at least sizable numbers or even (as in Kazakhstan) actually form the major group. Also, by formulating and applying policies for the entire Union territory, which may have much justification on purely economic grounds, the Soviet rulers have increased the degree of interdependence of the national units, as, for example, by specialising in cotton cultivation in Uzbek S.S.R. at the expense of food crops. Some success in these unifying policies may be claimed on the score of economic advances and the raising of living standards generally – as also, by the spread of the Russian language at the expense of others. Thus an increasing proportion of some of the non-Russian nationalities record Russian as their native language, especially in the towns and among the younger age groups.

The multi-national Soviet Union maintains strength and stability not as a result of an integrating national sentiment but thanks to its governmental system which concentrates political power, including the control of the police and armed forces, the press, radio and courts of law, in the Presidium, which is a group of twenty or less leaders of the Communist party who have managed to reach the top. Like the old empires with which it has been compared, the Soviet Union wields coercive powers so that the broad consensus of citizens, on which the governments of Western democracies depend for their strength, is a matter of less importance and can be replaced in part by mere acquiescence.

(iv) Canada

Canada and the Soviet Union have geographically much in common: their northerly location, vast territorial scale, coasts on the Atlantic, Pacific and Arctic oceans, great resources of minerals, water-power, farm land and forests, multi-national populations, federal structure, and those common problems of remote, virtually empty expanses, much of them in Arctic and sub-Arctic latitudes. For all its size, however, Canada measures only forty-five per cent of the Soviet Union's area and, in respect of the population numbers which it supports, contrasts sharply with the Soviet Union, having only twenty-two millions, less than ten per cent of the latter's 241.7 millions as enumerated at the 1970 census. Further, another contrast which specially concerns us here is that Canada has become painfully aware in recent years of internal strains and stresses, involving danger to political unity, which are related above all to its national and linguistic components. Certainly it is a remarkable historical fact that states should have been established embracing the peoples of such extensive and difficult territories as those of Canada and the Soviet Union. Given that this has been achieved, why is Canada clearly less politically unified than the Soviet Union, so much so that, as it enters its second century as a federal state, it is confronted by the problem of countering separatist tendencies if it is to survive?

A brief glance at Canada's history invites the comment on its unification in 1867 that, as Dr Johnson said of a dog walking on its hind legs, it is surprising that it was able to effect this at all. With a scanty native population of American Indians and Eskimos, and a total population in 1867 estimated at only 1.5 millions, Canada's lands were then as now, virtually unsettled, as they were remote, difficult of access and subject to long and harsh winters. It was mainly within the St Lawrence basin, and then only in areas close to this river, that immigrant Europeans, and United Empire Loyalists who had moved north when the United States first emerged, had succeeded in creating sizable settlements and organised communities, with ports and towns, routes by water and by road, and an economy to sustain them. And the cardinal facts of Canada's statehood, when it was launched into self-government as a confederation, were that it combined two distinct national groups, British and French, that, given the territorial scale, regionalism was bound to be strong, and lastly, that it neighboured a much more populous and powerful country.

In retrospect it would appear that policies of high statemanship, both in Britain and in Canada, made possible the initial confederation of the former colonies of Ontario, Quebec, New Brunswick and Nova Scotia by the British North America Act of 1867. This achievement owed much to the adoption of the federal principle which allowed the sharing of the powers and functions of government between institutions at the centre and in the provinces: but for this, unification then would have been impossible. The proximity of the United States, strong and expansive, against which Canadians, backed by the United Kingdom, had warred successfully in 1812, certainly prompted confederation as an alternative to eventual absorption: the more so, since, with minimal armed forces stationed in Canada, this was 'an unguarded prize, ripe for plucking' [Graham 1950]. Also, thanks to technological progress, which brought not only the electric telegraph, but also the steam locomotive and the railway – means of transport superior to those provided by the river steamer, covered waggon and the horse – it was possible to envisage the effective government of widely spaced communities. Lastly, Canada's success in self-government after 1867 depended on the retention of the imperial link: it did not, as did the revolting American colonies a century earlier, renounce Britain, but retained with it

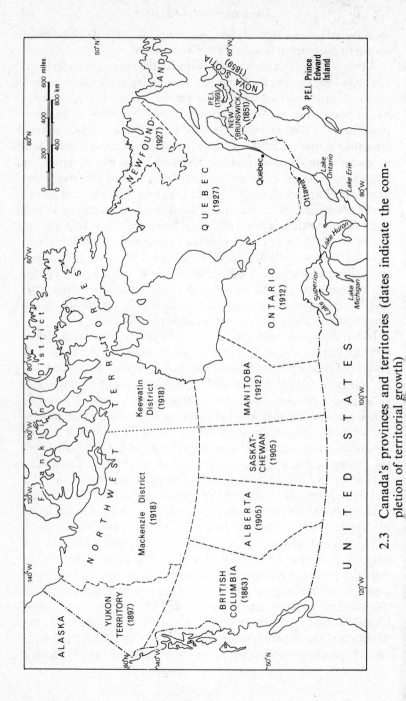

2.3 Canada's provinces and territories (dates indicate the completion of territorial growth)

close bonds necessary to safeguard its peaceful growth to maturity and strength. It was not until 1888 that the Canadian Pacific Railway, as a single-track line, connected Halifax, Nova Scotia, via the Kicking Horse Pass through the Rockies, with Vancouver, British Columbia. During the decades which followed confederation immigrants from Europe and investment capital from Britain and the United States greatly stimulated the settlement, agriculture, industry and trade of Canada. Population losses by emigration to the United States, however, until the 1960s very largely equalled the number of immigrants into Canada, so that it is natural increase – to the extent of five-sixths – that has produced the population growth of the Confederation. This grew with the additions of British Columbia in 1871 – in anticipation of the trans-continental railway – Prince Edward Island in 1871, Manitoba in 1870, and the two other prairie provinces – Saskatchewan and Alberta, formerly spheres of the Hudson's Bay Company – in 1905. Canada assumed its present form only in 1949 when Newfoundland was admitted as its tenth province.

Doubtless all states seek to achieve a unity which transcends diversity, although they apply different policies to this end and may face failure if the diversities of culture and attitudes are too marked. From colonial days onwards it was seen to be necessary to conciliate the large and compact French community which now stands at only 28.6 per cent of the total population. The Quebec Act of 1774 guaranteed to French settlers security in their religion and language, their customs and tenures, under their own civil law. From the start of the Confederation efforts were consistently made to ensure that French leaders took their share in the federal government and that the English-speaking majority in the two-house legislature did not use its numerical superiority to enact laws, on matters such as conscription, to which French-speaking Canadians were clearly opposed. Ottawa, as federal capital, which now appears very excentrally placed with reference to most of Canada, was carefully chosen near the line of contact between English-speaking Upper Canada and French-speaking Lower Canada. Although Canada has continued during the present century to admit immigrants, mainly from Europe and, in the 1960s, from the United States, and although it lists thirty-two ethnic groups in its census, citizens according to their ancestry are still predominantly British and French, who numbered 9.6 and 6.2 millions respectively in 1967. Other ethnic groups, however, now make up fully a quarter of Canadians and have for much the greater part settled in provinces other than Quebec.* In this province most of the French Canadians, who now share in the dynamic growth of the Canadian economy, preserve their own cultural traditions, although one million of them live elsewhere, mainly in neighbouring eastern Ontario and New Brunswick, both of which were originally explored and held by France.

Canada's task of nation-building has certainly some successes to record: by its role in the two world wars, by securing complete independence of Britain by the Treaty of Westminster in 1931, as also by its high standing as a trading nation and its own distinct foreign policy, Canada has demonstrated its national maturity. Even if assimilation between the different ethnic groups appears slow, and is little evident between English and French-speaking citizens, there is little doubt that a Canadian is a new kind of national. Yet regionalism has tended to grow stronger and even to challenge national unity. Certainly the scale and physical geography of this country, which tries to integrate large contrasting components such as the Appalachian Highlands of the maritime provinces, the St Lawrence and Great Lakes region, the prairies and the Pacific West beyond the Rockies, not to mention the desolate Shield areas to the north, necessarily invite the growth of regional interests and attitudes. It is not surprising that the provinces are unequal in their standards of living and in demographic weight as they differ in their economic interests and achievements. Ontario and Quebec form the core of the Confederation, with 13.7 million inhabitants (in 1971) – more than twice as many as in the four western provinces and more than six times as many as in the four most easterly ones. In 1965 Canada held its fifth general election in eight years, only one of which returned to power a majority party. In the provinces, in contrast, majority governments are the norm. Thus, while Canadians show strong political interests provincially, they show apathy towards federal politics. Also the provinces vie with each other in baiting, and in extracting concessions from Ottawa, and one of them – Quebec – harbours a political party which, supported by some of the leading economists and intellectuals, seeks separation from the Confederation.

For a few years the danger appeared real that Quebec would vigorously pursue a policy aimed at secession. President de Gaulle sensed

* Only 7.4 per cent of the population born outside Canada live in Quebec Province as compared with 25 per cent in British Columbia, 21.7 per cent in Alberta, 16.2 per cent in Saskatchewan, 18.4 per cent in Manitoba, and 21.7 per cent in Ontario (*Statesman's Year-Book 1971–2*, London, p. 179).

this mood in July 1967 when at Montreal, the second largest French city of the world, he made his famous appeal, rated 'unacceptable' at Ottawa: *Vive le Québec libre!* Two years later violence broke out in the streets of Quebec and Montreal, attributed to the Front pour la Libération du Quebec, urban guerrillas of questionable motivation, who murdered a Quebec minister and kidnapped the British Consul. Although there was widespread revulsion from these actions, the Parti Québécois (P.Q.), a moderately left-wing party, strongest in the towns, was committed to the goal of independence by democratic and non-violent methods. In the provincial elections to the Legislative Assembly of April 1970, this party secured twenty-three per cent of the popular vote [*Canadian News Facts* 1973], which was thought to reflect the views of nearly a third of the French-speaking population of Quebec. Support for the secession movement appears to be based less on the historical and cultural affinities of the French-speaking majority than on the fact that, since most of these speak only French, they are falling behind and lack the opportunity to share in administration and in big business which a minority of English-speaking citizens control at Montreal (*The Times*, 8 April 1974). However, the efforts of the federal government which required the use of French throughout Canada, recognition that constitutional changes in the Confederation, in line with the new idea of 'co-operative federalism', might be fruitfully discussed, and the realisation that pressure to squeeze more from Ottawa is a profitable policy – all these seem to have brought about a changed climate of opinion in Quebec which was reflected in the October elections of 1973.

At these elections, although P.Q. received thirty per cent of the votes, its own leader (René Lévesque) was not returned and the party secured only six seats in a house of 110, with the triumphant Liberal Party returning to power with no less than 102 seats.

To conclude, Canada has, at least for a time, averted political fragmentation since, if the more extreme claims of Quebec separatists were successful, other similar claims by other provinces might well arise. Whereas the *raison d'être* of Canada is clear enough – it was a group of colonies that had learnt self-rule and earned the right in turn to autonomy and independent statehood – its state-idea has not yet fully emerged since it awaits the process of the making of a nation. Canada cannot, and has no wish to seek unity by applying the apparently successful policy of coercion that the Soviet leaders apply in their country, so that the preservation of Canadian unity will depend on statesmanship by consensus which may need to take account of provincial ambitions. There is no longer the healthy fear of the United States, which brought with it a sense of patriotic unity against danger from outside. Although in some measure this survives in the fear of financial, economic and cultural subjection to this its chief trading partner, Canadians are willing to accept a standard of living ten per cent below that of Americans as a price to be paid for preserving their identity. The link with the British Crown, which for older Canadians may symbolise detachment from the republican United States, now counts for little. Yet, with the challenge of a vast, unspoilt continent to exploit and with a dynamic and basically flourishing economy, Canadians, robustly distinctive from both British and Americans whose language they mainly share, should confidently continue to seek their national identity.

3 The Territories of States

Then if we are to have enough for pasture and ploughland, we must take a slice from our neighbours' territory. And they will want to do the same to ours, if they also overpass the bounds of necessity and plunge into reckless pursuit of wealth.

(Plato, *The Republic,* Book II)

Although states are alike in their basic requirements – a politically organised population occupying a specific territory – they present remarkable variety in many respects: notably in forms of political organisation, systems of government, levels of material culture, population numbers and territory. This last requirement of states shows no simple norm; indeed the territories of states stand in such sharp contrast as to deserve separate analysis.

Note first that 'territory' is a technical term in political geography. It refers to the three related elements which make up the terrestrial environment which a state controls, namely, land, sea and air. The land areas of states, as usually measured, themselves include inland waters which in some instances are extensive: thus nearly one-tenth of Finland's land area is accounted for by inland waters while swamp and water make up a seventh of Uganda's area. For over eighty per cent of states their territory includes a varying zone of 'territorial seas' extending offshore, where states claim and can exercise jurisdiction. Also the air space above both land and territorial sea is rightly conceived to be part of a state's territory, and here, too, it has political rights of control. The air space consists of a segment of the atmosphere, and beyond this a share of outer space. International lawyers have attempted, without much success, to reach an agreed figure for the height of a state's air space, but this clearly depends on its technological ability to control passage through it. In short, territory is three-dimensional; it is even four-dimensional if account is taken of the duration of time it has served as the basis of a state.

When the territories of states are looked at comparatively, they are found to show sharp differences of many kinds, which can be reviewed under the headings: size, shape and location.

1 The Size of States

In sheer area states show an irregular gradation from the hugeness of the Soviet Union, which occupies 22.4 million square kilometres (8.65 million square miles), to the tininess of the Vatican City State which measures only 44 hectares (108.7 acres). Clearly independent states can be of any size: although they inevitably occupy more or less clearly defined land areas, they appear indifferent to areal extent. This is simply to say that states derive from historical processes and are man-made structures.

Before drawing any further conclusions about the relation of states to sheer area, it is worth noting how many and which are the outsize states and how others are graded down to areas almost minute. Independent states, outstanding for their areal scale are listed in table II where their populations are also given.

Thus eleven states, the territories of which range between over two million and twenty million square kilometres (7.8 million square miles), control more than half of the land surface of the earth. Their totalled populations also exceed more than half that of the world.

What is the political significance of territorial hugeness? What advantages and disadvantages may be expected to derive from this? Clearly there is no simple and direct relationship between the size of its territorial base and the political strength and status of a state. This follows for two reasons. First, political strength and power depend on people or more specifically manpower – its numbers, skills, organisation and technological level – and this does not automatically increase as area increases. As table II shows, six of the eleven outsize states are only lightly settled, even though four of the others contain very large populations. But manpower alone acquires economic and political weight only if it is skilled and effectively directed towards modern economic production: thus the superior manpower numbers of both China and India do not achieve, still less exceed, the economic and political power of the United States. The second reason why areal extent alone provides no clear measure of a state's strength and stature is that area alone takes no account of the very variable nature of land and the very different opportunities

which it offers for human exploitation. While it might seem right to
believe that the larger its estate, the more likely are a state's chances

TABLE II

THE LARGEST INDEPENDENT STATES IN 1974

Name	*Area* (million sq km)	*Population 1972* (millions)
Soviet Union	22.4	246.3
Canada	9.2	21.8
China	9.6	800.0
United States	9.1	209.0
Brazil	8.5	94.5
Australia	7.7	13.0
India	3.0	547.0
Argentina	2.8	23.5
Sudan	2.5	14.8
Algeria	2.3	14.6
Saudi Arabia	2.4	7.7
Totals	79.5	1992.0
World	146.0	3500.0

SOURCE: *The Statesman's Year-Book 1973–4*, Macmillan, London.

of discovering minerals of many kinds and of diversifying agricultural production, it remains true that land varies sharply in respect of
climate, landforms, location, soils and much else. Thus it is a common though varying feature of the territories of the eleven largest
states that a large, and in most a very large, part does not produce
much of value through being excessively cold, dry, mountainous,
swampy, or inaccessible. For example, sixty-one per cent of Australia has a rainfall of less than 38.5 centimetres (fifteen inches), and the
tundra areas of Canada comprise twenty-two per cent of the state.

Extra-large states also enjoy a certain advantage in respect of
defence in that, as was true of the Soviet Union during The Second
World War, defence in depth is practicable. China in the 1930s was

able to employ similar tactics against Japan and, nearly a century earlier, Mexico had bought time by yielding territory to the United States' armies in 1848. It is also an advantage for those large states which have long coastlines, such as Australia, Canada, China, the Soviet Union and the United States, that they can claim extensive areas of the world's continental shelf. The Sudan and Algeria are much less fortunate in this respect.

There are also political and economic disadvantages associated with huge extent. Several governments have experienced difficulty in adequately administering the whole of their territory. The problems of transport have been much reduced during the past few decades, but there can be no doubt that in the past, remoteness from the political core of an empire facilitated successful secessionist movements. The fluctuating frontier of China during the eighteenth and nineteenth centuries provides an example of this situation. The various movements for the creation of new Australian states have been most vigorous in those areas, such as northern Queensland, New England and the Riverina, remote from the state capitals of Brisbane and Sydney. Transport costs, indeed all development costs including labour costs, rise high in areas which suffer remoteness and extremes of climate unattractive to settlers. In short, the vigour and status of a state depend on many things other than territory. Thus, although table II includes the two superstates of today and China as a possible third of tomorrow, it includes others of middle status, such as Canada and India, as well as some of minor standing, like Algeria and Sudan.

The points made above about the relation of manpower and of physical geography to the standing of outsize states apply also to the more numerous states of large to small extent which pattern the world political map. States of large extent characterise the so-called New World, which was discovered and opened up only in modern times. While North America and Australasia include three of the giant states, the states of Africa and South America tend to be of large scale, this being explained largely in terms of their relatively early stage of development, their low population densities, and the difficult character of much of their interior lands. However, the oldest continent, Asia, has many large states, such as Iran, Mongolia and Indonesia with more than 1.3 million square kilometres (500,000 square miles) of territory. It shares, too, with Europe the vast Soviet Union. Apart from the Soviet Union, and three-quarters of its territory lies in Asia, Europe has states of modest to small size, although, in strictly legal terms, Denmark is very large: with its outlying self-governing county of Greenland, it can claim a territory of over 2,201,500 square kilometres (850,000 square miles), although six-sevenths of this is a permanent ice cap. But if Europe's largest states are small as compared with those of the other continents – the areas of the three largest, France, Spain and Sweden being only 556,850, 490,546 and 448,160 square kilometres (215,000, 189,400 and 173,035 square miles) respectively – it has also many quite small, like Switzerland, the Netherlands, Belgium, Albania, Cyprus, Luxembourg and Malta, and others so small as to be best styled microstates. It is worth tabling the world's smallest states to show how utterly they contrast with those given in table II.

These small and tiny states owe their survival to the chances of his-

TABLE III
EUROPE'S SMALLEST INDEPENDENT STATES IN 1974

Name	*Area* (sq km)	*Population 1970*
Cyprus	9251	633,000
Luxembourg	2586	345,000
Andorra*	465	20,550
Malta	316	322,070
Liechtenstein	160	21,350
San Marino	61	17,000
Vatican City State	0.44	1000
Monaco	1.89	23,400

* Andorra is not, strictly speaking, a sovereign state.
SOURCE: *The Statesman's Year-Book 1973–4*, Macmillan, London.

tory and bear witness to the modern notion that, where the will to independent statehood exists, it should be satisfied. But even though Europe houses a strikingly large proportion of the world's states – nearly one-quarter in only one-fifteenth of its total area – it is not the only continent with quite small states: witness the territorial scale of recently emerged states shown in table IV.

Hong Kong, a surviving colony from the nineteenth century, boasts an area of little more than 1000 square kilometres (400 square

miles), while Macau, Portugal's old foothold in China nearby, occupies only about fifteen square kilometres (six square miles).

TABLE IV
SMALL STATES OUTSIDE EUROPE IN 1974

Name	Area (sq km)	Population 1970
Gambia	9301	383,000
Qatar	11,000	160,000
Trinidad and Tobago	5128	1,010,100
Western Samoa	2842	146,635
Mauritius	1843	830,600
Tonga	700	92,360
Bahrain	598	216,815
Singapore	582	2,074,507
Barbados	430	243,741
Maldives	298	115,000
Nauru	21	6768

SOURCE: *The Statesman's Year-Book 1973–4*, Macmillan, London.

Small states and the fragments of empires which may eventually
become independent, suffer from a variety of political problems exa-
cerbated by their small size. Such territories generally offer only a
very limited range of resources, and have difficulty in promoting a
prosperous economy which offers their citizens the promise of a
rising standard of living. Malta, for example, has a programme of encouraging emigration of citizens to Canada and Australia. Mauritius
has not been able to reduce its serious level of over-population by
exporting labour, as Lesotho has done in southern Africa, and successive Mauritian governments have tried various economic policies
to reduce the country's dependence on sugar production and the high
level of unemployment. Some of the small states have developed as
important tourist centres, while others, such as Pitcairn Island
export postage stamps, and still others, such as Bermuda and Liechtenstein benefit from favourable tax structures. Small states find it a

major financial burden to support the paraphernalia of nationhood, which involves a diplomatic corps and representation at the United Nations. Small states generally are very difficult to defend from either nuclear or conventional attack, and it is often easy to apply sanctions against them through blockades. Hong Kong was once particularly vulnerable to water restrictions by China. Small states, and the debris of empires scattered around the world, are also sometimes subject to irredentist claims by adjoining states. For example, Spain claims Gibraltar; Morocco and Mauritania claim parts of Spanish Sahara; Guatemala considers Belize, formerly British Honduras, to be one of its provinces; Argentina covets the Falkland Islands, and Somalia and Ethiopia have an obvious interest in the Territory of Afars and Issas. It is not beyond the bounds of possibility that in the future some of these small areas will suffer annexation by a larger neighbour, as happened to Goa in 1961.

One of the risks faced by small states is that natural disasters, associated with storms and earthquakes may affect them very seriously. The effects of hurricanes on the economies of some West Indian states and Mauritius are relatively much more severe than on, for example, the economies of China or the Philippines.

Some small states have tried to overcome these disadvantages by federation with other small states, or through some form of association with larger states. The federation of Trucial States, and the abortive West Indian Federation provide two examples of the former situation, while Singapore's brief membership of the Malaysian Federation, and the association of Gibraltar and Surinam with the United Kingdom and the Netherlands respectively, illustrate the second case. Maude and Doran [1966] have written an interesting account of problems associated with the Gilbert Islands, which have a total area of only 430 square kilometres (166 square miles).

2 The Shape of States

The widely varying shape of state territories is the second characteristic which must receive attention. It might have been thought that geological structure and landforms, the result of non-human, natural forces, would indicate in some measure convenient frameworks for states. This hypothesis finds virtually no support, for states owe their territorial shapes, as also their areas, to the outcome of continuing historical processes – in other words, to human efforts

and contrivance which have often overcome the restrictive limits set
by climate, landforms and vegetation obstacles. The fact that some
states occupy such natural frameworks as islands of different scale
should not mislead us. Certainly at the giant scale Australia has
become a single state, as Cuba, Ceylon, Taiwan and Jamaica have
done at minor scales. But the large island of Borneo is divided between three political units, and New Guinea has three, although two
share a common administration. Hispaniola, Timor and Ireland are
divided between two states and the tiny island of St Martin, one of
the Windward Islands, although scarcely thirty-nine square kilometres (fifteen square miles) in area, finds itself unequally shared,
since 1648, between Overseas France and the Netherlands Antilles.

More commonly, and for obviously good geographical and political reasons, many island groups, like the Shetland Islands and the
Balearics, as also larger single islands, like Corsica and Man, have
come to form outlying parts of states with relatively close mainland
territories. In much the same way peninsulas and isthmuses are more
usually divided between states, according to their complications of
physical geography and international history. Thus the isthmus of
Central America, which is very small compared with the two continents which it connects, contains nine political units. Although the
large peninsula of Asia Minor now falls wholly within the Turkish
Republic, such simplicity is exceptional and a long list could be given
of politically divided peninsulas: Iberia, with two states plus Andorra; the Italian, formerly much divided politically before unification
in 1870, still contains the two microstates of San Marino and the
Vatican City; both the major and minor peninsulas of Scandinavia
are shared by two states; the Balkan peninsula has six, and the
Korean two, while the Malay peninsula contributes territory to
Malaya, Burma and Thailand.

There has been a number of attempts to classify the shapes of
states into several categories, but a simple division into three classes
seems adequate. The classes are *compact, irregular* and *divided*. There
can be no doubt about which states have a divided shape, because
their territory must consist of at least two discrete areas. It is more difficult to provide a precise distinction between compact and irregular
shapes, which form a continuum from a country such as Uruguay, as
a very compact state, to a country such as Chile, which has an irregular shape. It would be possible to give a mathematical definition in
the following manner. The most compact shape of any area is a

circle, the circumference of which represents the shortest boundary for that particular area. A comparison between the actual length of a state's boundary, and the circumference of a circle having the same area as the state, gives an index of the compactness of the shape. For example, if it is known that a state has an area of 813 square kilometres (314 square miles) contained within a boundary measuring 133.2 kilometres (82.8 miles) long, its index of compactness is calculated in the following fashion. First it is necessary to find the radius of a circle having an area of 813 square kilometres (314 square miles). A simple calculation gives the radius a value of 16.09 kilometres (ten miles). The circumference of a circle with such a radius equals 101 kilometres (62.8 miles). The ratio between 133.2 kilometres (82.8 miles) and 101 kilometres (62.8 miles) is 1.3, which is the index of compactness.

This calculation was performed for a number of countries, measuring the length of the boundary on maps at a scale of 1:1 million, and the following results were obtained. Uruguay was found to have the lowest index of 1.05, and it was followed in succession by Nigeria with 1.13, Rumania, with 1.37, France with 1.42, and Hungary with 1.47. The highest values, indicating the most irregular shapes, were obtained for Chile with 3.1, Thailand with 2.82, and Mexico with 2.58. Obviously if this index were constructed for each country, it would be possible to fix an arbitrary limit to distinguish compact from irregular states. But such an exercise would pretend to a greater precision than political geography can justify. It is not possible to assert that in every situation shape is politically significant. It is generally true that states with compact shapes experience fewer problems because of undue expense of communications, and that the risk of secessionist movements seems to be greater in irregular states, where some regions are remote from the state's core. But these generalisations do not carry the force of laws. For example, Nigeria, with a very compact shape, has experienced a particularly bitter secessionist movement. It is sufficient for political geographers to be aware that the shape of a state's territory may be significant, and to explore any possible relevance in each particular case. For example, the original shape of Israel in 1948, with the very narrow waist of territory between Jordan and the Mediterranean, was long considered a liability by many Israeli strategists. It is this fact more than any other which encourages some factions in Israel to continue the occupation of the West Bank of the Jordan, which was started in 1967.

A well-known case of a state that seemed to have adjusted its territories with some closeness to a unit of physical geography, is the Austro-Hungarian Empire during the fifty years or so before its collapse in 1919 [Hoffman 1967]. Its territories included, but tended also to extend beyond, the basin of the middle Danube River, but from its collapse a number of small states of variant shapes have emerged. The range of state territorial shapes, both past and present, is readily seen in the political maps of atlases and little more need be said. Beyond doubt the most irregular shape, and one very difficult to map effectively, is that of Chile, which has a length of about 4022 kilometres (2500 miles) but a breadth averaging only 177 kilometres (110 miles), with which, on a smaller scale, Norway compares. A territorial oddity of several states, for which reasons must be sought in both physical geography and political history, is the long and relatively very narrow tract known as a panhandle. The Alaskan territory of the United States presents such a panhandle where, in the south, it separates Canada from the sea; Afghanistan has a similar feature in the east where its panhandle in the Hindu Kush approaches China's Tibet and separates the Soviet Union from Pakistan; similarly the Caprivi Strip extends eastwards from South West Africa for about 483 kilometres (300 miles).

The evolution of the Afghan panhandle is described in chapter 4. It took place in the 1890s at about the same time as Britain and Germany concluded agreements establishing the Caprivi Strip. This territorial appendage of South West Africa is 434 kilometres (270 miles) long, and contains two clearly distinguished areas. West of the Linyanti or Kwando River, the Strip has a width of only thirty-two kilometres (twenty miles), and the surface deposits consist of characteristic Kalahari dune formations. This arid section supports a population of about 500 Bushmen. The eastern region has the heaviest and most reliable rainfall of the whole of South West Africa, and apart from 80 kilometres (fifty miles) along the northern boundary, its limits are marked by the perennial Kwando and Zambezi rivers. The soils in the east consist of sandy loams interspersed with black turf soils, and they support a population of about 20,000 members of the Masubia and Mafue tribes. These people live mainly along the river courses or at waterholes and pans on the interfluves.

In 1883 a German merchant acquired a leasehold on some land at Lüderitz Bay, and the following year a German protectorate was declared over part of the coast. On 30 December 1886 the German

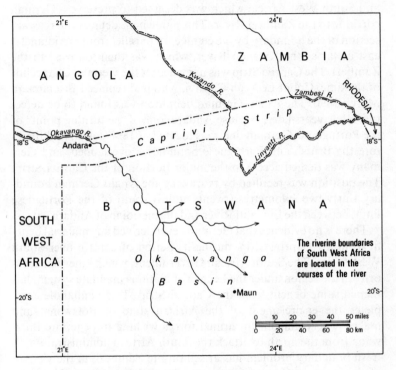

3.1 The Caprivi Strip

and Portuguese authorities agreed on a boundary separating their possessions of Angola and South West Africa; the description of this boundary from the coast to the Zambezi at Katima Mulilo is quoted in chapter 4 (p. 80). On 1 July 1890 Britain and Germany agreed on a boundary between their respective protectorates of Bechuanaland and South West Africa, which was designed to preserve a German corridor to the Zambezi River. This agreement defined the relevant section of the boundary by the eighteenth parallel from meridian 21° east as far as the Kwando River, which was then followed to the Zambezi. The Caprivi Strip was named after the German Chancellor of the time, Count Leo von Caprivi, who had replaced Bismarck in March 1890. The Anglo-German definition was found to be defective a few years later, because Andara, one of the turning points of the Portuguese–German line, was located at 18°4' south, and therefore the British and Portuguese boundaries overlapped, and Germany was denied access to the major portion of the Caprivi Strip. The position was rectified by redrawing the Anglo-German boundary thirty-two kilometres (twenty miles) south of the Portuguese limit, between the Linyanti River and the meridian of Andara.

There is no evidence that Germany ever derived any material benefit from the Caprivi Strip, during its period of control over South West Africa. The South African Government, which inherited authority in the region under the League of Nations mandate system, has reaped some benefit from the Caprivi Strip. This panhandle completes the encirclement of the African state of Botswana, and makes it very difficult for armed forces wishing to penetrate Botswana from the north to attack the South African administration. A fresh boundary problem has arisen on the Zambezi, in the vicinity of the junction of the territories of South West Africa, Rhodesia, Zambia and Botswana. The Zambian Government insists that it shares with Botswana a common boundary some hundreds of yards long; the South African Government is convinced that the four territories meet at a point in the Zambezi. The resolution of this disagreement has obvious implications for the ease of communication between Zambia and Botswana.

Curiously non-geometric as are the shapes of state territories, it appears that many achieve a certain measure of compactness, notably in Europe and Africa. But this compactness may be a cartographic rather than a geographical reality for, to return to a point made above, all is by no means equal where land surfaces are concerned. The specific territories which states have come to control – or try to control – are made up of very different geographical components, each offering opportunities and limitations unequal in degree and in kind. For example, facts of physical and vegetation geography necessarily affect the ease and cost of internal transport. The difficulties of movement of people and goods within Peru and Bolivia whose territories lie astride and below the lofty Andean mountain system are clearly considerable, even in days of cheapening air transport. In other words, shape alone has little direct relation to the ease and costs of internal transport and administration.

As might be expected, the territories of states show a high degree of geographical continuity. This is true for many states because they grew over the centuries by a process of settlement and expansion outwards from an original core area and sought to control access throughout their own lands. For those states which were formerly the colonies of empires, as for colonies which still exist, territories are normally continuous, even though their limits were the somewhat arbitrary result of international agreements. The prime purposes of states include the defence and administration of the populations established within their territories, and for these purposes a continuous land area might seem to be the most convenient; however, in a strict sense, states with a divided shape are not uncommon and this does not necessarily create much difficulty. Such discontinuities are in some cases due to the fact that states include in their territory islands off their mainland as does the United Kingdom, Norway, Spain, Italy and Greece, to cite familiar cases. Some states, like Indonesia and the Philippines, are virtually 'sea-states' in that their territories are groups of islands. These two states have developed the archipelago concept, by which they claim authority over all the sea lying between their islands (see chapter 8). Denmark's territory is made up of peninsular Jutland and several nearby islands which are separated by the sea channels which link the North and Baltic seas. Northern Ireland, an integral part of the United Kingdom, is separated from Great Britain by the North Channel. Separation of major areas of state territory by the intervening land of a neighbouring state is little found, although Alaska's detachment from the United States' mainland will be recalled and the more curious case of Pakistan, with its larger and less populous western part separated by 1609 kilometres (a thousand miles) of Indian territory from its smaller but more populous part, has disappeared with the emergence of Bangladesh as an independent state [Tayyeb 1972].

Another type of territorial discontinuity exists which rests on the legal provisions of a state whereby overseas territories, formerly colonies, are integrated into the metropolitan country. In this way, Portugal, the Netherlands, Spain and France have politically organised overseas territories, usually at great distances away, which enjoy, in varying degree, regional autonomy and representation in the governing bodies of the home country. Thus Overseas Portugal included the Cape Verde and Madeira island groups as well as enormous territories in Africa, the populations of which were accorded Portuguese citizenship and which formed part of a customs union with Portugal. Similarly, the Netherlands Antilles, together with Surinam (formerly Dutch Guiana), are integrated into the Netherlands and its government. The Balearic and Canary Islands are conceived of, and organised as parts of Spain. France as a state and in its government at Paris includes a surprising number of geographically detached parts. Until it secured its independence in 1962 Algeria, which France had fought hard to acquire in the 1840s and had become the home of a million Frenchmen (*colons*), was regarded as part of France, in the central government of which it shared. The following territories, widely dispersed along the seaways, are in the legal sense parts of France, sending their deputies and senators to its national assemblies: French Guiana, the islands of Miquelon and St Pierre which lie off southern Newfoundland, the island groups which make up French Polynesia, and the Territory of Afars and Issas in North East Africa, which has its coast and the port of Jibuti on the Red Sea.

The separation of fragments of territory as enclaves within another state is a fairly common situation which interests political geographers. Robinson [1959] has written the best systematic account of exclaves and enclaves, which describe the same area of territory from the respective points of view of the state which owns the area and the state in whose territory the area is embedded. He distinguishes three types of enclave. The first is a true enclave, where a fragment of the territory of one state is entirely surrounded by the territory of another. This situation was extremely common during the feudal period of European history, and some of these territorial curiosities survive today, although the most familiar European enclave is West Berlin, which has been the subject of a good study by Robinson [1953]. The second type is described as a pene-enclave.

These areas are continuous with the territory of the state that owns them, but because of adverse physical circumstances, such as high mountains, can only be reached by passage through the territory of another state. There are a number of Austrian pene-enclaves on the border with Germany. The third type is styled quasi-enclave, to indicate an area which is technically an enclave but which does not function as such, because the state whose territory intervenes allows unfettered access between the two parts of the divided state. Robinson quotes the case of a German enclave, cut off by a section of Belgian railway, as an example of this situation.

Probably the greatest number of enclaves in any area are found along the boundary between India and Bangladesh, in the vicinity of Cooch Behar. There are 121 Indian enclaves in Bangladesh totalling sixty-seven square kilometres (twenty-six square miles), and they contain twenty-one Bangladesh enclaves measuring twenty-three square kilometres (nine square miles)! There are ninety-two enclaves belonging to Bangladesh on the Indian side of the boundary, totalling forty-four square kilometres (seventeen square miles), and they contain three Indian enclaves which occupy seventeen hectares (forty-two acres). These complex territorial arrangements were created in the period 1661–1712, during conflict between the Mughal Empire and Cooch Behar, and confirmed by the peace treaty which ended the war. The situation was not altered during the period of British rule, and therefore Lord Radcliffe, who defined the boundary between India and East Pakistan in 1947, had no alternative but to perpetuate the arrangement. The efforts of the Indian and Pakistan authorities to exchange these slivers of territory were not successful, and it will be interesting to see whether the more cordial relations between India and Bangladesh will allow the matter to be simplified.

3 The Location of States

Apart from area and shape, the territories of states are differentiated by their location on the earth's surface. Together with many other features of physical geography, the location of a state, as perceived by its inhabitants and their government, affects attitudes and policies towards other states, especially towards those nearby. It may also increase or reduce the opportunities for cultural contacts, trade and travel.

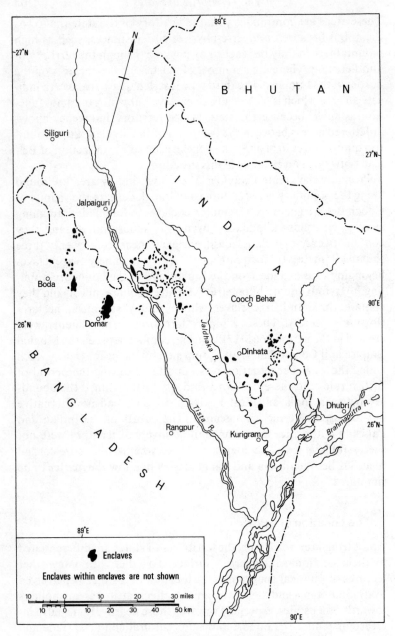

3.2   Enclaves along the India–Bangladesh border

It has been customary for political geographers to examine a state's location from two viewpoints [Pounds 1972; Weigert *et al.* 1957]. First there is the absolute location, which is its permanent place on the earth's surface, and this can be accurately expressed in terms of latitude and longitude. The importance of this location is that it determines which climatic systems will influence the state, and the seas to which the state has easy access. Second there is relative location, which is determined by the country's proximity to other states; over a period of time these will vary in their strength and importance.

It seems more realistic that the relative viewpoint should dominate, and that the analysis of location by political geographers should be made relative to changes in the political power and the economic wealth of states, to changes in the techniques available for the exploitation of resources, and to changes in world patterns of production and trade.

The significance of fluctuating patterns of political power to the location of particular areas can be illustrated by reference to the cases of Outer Mongolia and Tibet. These two countries shared a common peripheral location in the Chinese Empire, and the onset of the Chinese revolution in 1910–11 created a situation where the people in each area were able to establish their autonomy. In both cases the local rulers were able to engage in negotiations with the Chinese, deriving valuable support from the adjacent Great Powers, Russia and Britain respectively. When the Chinese Communist Party established its hegemony over the Chinese mainland in 1949, the power situation for Mongolia and Tibet had changed in different ways. Mongolia's separate existence from China was still underwritten by the very powerful Soviet Union, and China had no sensible alternative but to accept the loss of this area. Britain had been replaced on the Indian subcontinent by two independent Asian governments, neither of which had the strength, even if they had the will, to resist China's reconquest of Tibet.

Afghanistan and Thailand also illustrate the influence of changes in political power and economic wealth upon locations. At the end of the nineteenth century they were both buffer states. Afghanistan separated the spheres of Britain and Russia, while Thailand stood between the Burmese province of British India and French Indochina, apart from a short section of the upper Mekong valley. With the termination of the British and French Empires in Asia, Thailand

and Afghanistan have lost their buffer role, and have therefore shed the problems and forfeited the advantages of that position. Thailand's location in the post-colonial period has presented new and serious problems related to the civil wars waged in Khmer, Laos and South Vietnam. By contrast the introspective nature of modern Burma has caused no problems but has offered no opportunities for profitable relations. New power situations have developed around Afghanistan during the post-colonial period. The Soviet Union has become increasingly powerful, and modern Iran is wealthier and better armed than Persia was during the first half of the twentieth century. In contrast, the powerful British presence along Afghanistan's eastern and southern borders has been replaced by the weaker Pakistan, which is beset by friction and conflict with India. This change in the power patterns of the area has encouraged the Afghan authorities to raise the question of the creation of a Pathan-speaking state out of the western hill districts of Pakistan.

The need to revalue a state's location, as techniques of production, transport and war change, has long been known. The power of steam-driven ships allowed them to escape from the great wind belts and this meant the beginning of a more prosperous period for certain islands such as Hawaii, which were located off the trans-Pacific routes of sailing vessels. The ability of aeroplanes to fly longer distances means that Iceland is no longer a transit point for flights across the Atlantic. Changes in the techniques of production have reduced the adverse effects of some locations. States possessing large areas of their territory in the world's arid zones have been able to offset this disadvantage by the use of water for irrigation, by the tapping of artesian basins by deep drilling, and by the breeding of plants and animals which are adapted to such conditions. Canada and the Soviet Union, whose location means that they possess considerable areas with short growing seasons, have benefited by the introduction of grains that will grow and mature quickly. The extension of mineral exploration and exploitation on to the world's continental shelves represents a particular advantage to some peninsular states. South Korea, South Vietnam and South Africa are able to lay claims to wide areas of the submarine continental margins according to the prevailing international conventions.

The development of very large oil tankers has restored the commercial and strategic importance of the Cape of Good Hope, which had been diminished in the nineteenth century by the cutting of the

Suez Canal. In 1967 the Suez Canal could be used by tankers of 60,000 dwt fully laden, and tankers of 150,000 dwt in ballast. In December 1972 thirty-seven per cent of the world's tanker fleet consisted of vessels too large to pass through the Suez Canal as it existed in 1967. This figure will rise to fifty-four per cent within three years, because three-quarters of tanker tonnage on order consists of ships in excess of 150,000 dwt. Couper [1972], notes that if the canal is widened to accommodate larger tankers, transit dues will have to rise to a level which will confirm the advantage of the Cape route for vessels larger than 200,000 dwt.

The development of nuclear submarines capable of delivering nuclear warheads, and the possibility of using weapons launched from satellites has meant that some locations, such as central Asia, have lost some of the defensive advantages which their remoteness seemed to confer on them. These new military techniques also mean that the need for foreign bases has been reduced, and the strategic importance of some island locations, such as Malta, Sri Lanka and Singapore, has been sharply reduced.

Revaluing the significance of the location of states according to changing patterns of production and world trade is now largely an historical exercise. Examples are provided by Turkey's role as a bridge for land routes linking western and northern Europe with the Near East, before the eleventh century, when Venice and Kiev were the main trans-shipment points. After that period, direct trade via the Italian peninsula and the Mediterranean became more common. The discovery and eventual commercial development of the Americas transformed the political and economic significance of the British Isles. In modern times the patterns of production and the principal trade routes do not seem capable of such dramatic change, although the importance to Cape Town of the closing of the Suez Canal has been noted. However, it would be a mistake to believe that significant changes will not occur in the future. For example, one of the major disadvantages of Japan's location is that its oil supplies are drawn from the Persian Gulf, and must pass through the territorial waters of Indonesia or Malaysia if they are to avoid the much longer route through Bass Strait. Restrictions have been placed on the passage of giant tankers through some straits controlled by these two states. The discovery of major oil fields in the off-shore areas of eastern Asia will significantly reduce Japan's disadvantage.

Conclusion

States vary in the size, shape and location of their territories, and it would be possible to create a classification of states based on the varying combinations of these qualities. It is predictable that this would be an arid process, because the combination of these characteristics is unique to each state, and there is no guarantee that the same characteristics will have identical levels of significance to the state's political and economic development. All that the political geographer can do is to be aware that the size, shape and location of territory may play a very important role in influencing the attitudes of people living in different states and the policies that their governments develop.

4 Frontiers and International Boundaries

We could not have a coterminous frontier with France in Burmah. That would involve vast expenditure on both sides, and lines of armed posts garrisoned by European troops . . . We had proposed the buffer state in the interests of both countries, for it was evident that if our boundaries were contiguous, any fussy, or ill-conditioned frontier officer, whether English or French, would have it in his power to magnify every petty incident into a grave international question, which would be transferred to Europe, and thus grow into a cause of exacerbation between the two Governments; whereas if a country like China were in occupation of the intermediate territory, neither England nor France would ever hear a word of any little troubles of the sort.

[*British and Foreign State Papers*, volume 87, 1894–5, pp. 272 and 379]

Historically, the zones and lines which separate sovereign states have always been a fruitful source of dissension, and the contemporary disputes between China and the Soviet Union, India and China, Iraq and Iran, and Israel and the Arab states show that the situation has not really changed. This chapter examines frontiers, which are zones of political transition, and international boundaries on land, which are lines, theoretically without any width, marking the territorial division between states. Maritime boundaries are examined in chapter 8.

1 Frontiers

In political geography the term 'frontier' has two different meanings: it can refer to either the political division between two states or the division between the settled and uninhabited parts of a single state. Popular usage interprets the term in two senses – as a zone or as a line

– but political geographers should always use the term to refer to zones. This distinction, between frontiers and boundaries referring respectively to zones and lines, was made clear by Fawcett [1918] and East [1937] in a manner which should have placed the issue beyond doubt. Unfortunately some authors still use the terms as synonyms. To distinguish between the two meanings of the word it is helpful to consider frontiers within a state to be *settlement frontiers*, while designating those between states as *political frontiers*, and each category is now considered separately.

(i) Settlement Frontiers

There are two types of settlement frontier. The primary settlement frontier marks the limit of a state's authority as it enters into possession of territory which it has acquired by treaty or purchase or succession. The American and Canadian frontiers of the eighteenth and nineteenth centuries provide the best examples of primary settlement frontiers. Secondary settlement frontiers coincide with the division between inhabited and uninhabited areas, and are found in most countries today. The Highlands of Scotland, the Everglades of Florida and the Simpson Desert of Australia contain secondary settlement frontiers. There are a number of important differences between these two kinds of settlement frontier.

Primary settlement frontiers are now entirely historical features, while secondary settlement frontiers are found in many countries where an adverse physical environment, or inadequate techniques, hinder the further extension of land-use and settlement. During its existence, the primary settlement frontier marked the effective limit of the state's authority, whereas today states, such as Australia and the Sudan, which have large unoccupied areas, provide medical and security services there. The range of actual and potential economic activities in a primary frontier was generally greater than the range found in secondary frontiers. Fur trapping, timber cutting, semi-subsistence cultivation, grazing, mining and manufacturing and service industries were all found at some point on the American frontier, or developed after it had passed. The advancement of modern secondary frontiers usually involves a small number of activities, such as mining in western Australia, extensive ranching in Argentina, and irrigated farming in Mali.

The limited range of economic activities available on secondary frontiers is usually reflected in low population densities, although there have been exceptions to this situation in West Pakistan. Some primary settlement frontiers possessed high population densities, and the American Census Bureau's definition of the frontier zone – areas having a population density of less than 2.3 persons per square kilometre (two to six persons per square mile) – would have excluded many of the early frontiers of Georgia. The high population densities on some sections of the primary frontiers, together with their 'rudimentary socio-political relations marked by rebelliousness, lawlessness and/or absence of laws' [Kristof 1959], often resulted in a rapid advance of that frontier. For example, in 1783, 1.62 million hectares (four million acres) of the Cumberland Valley were sold in seven months, and during two months of 1795, 26,000 migrants crossed the Cumberland River in search of cheap land [Billington 1960]. In contrast, the advance of secondary frontiers is normally carefully planned, often involving government agencies where major capital works are concerned and where adverse effects on the physical landscape are feared, and the numbers of immigrants is usually low.

Political geographers are interested in the location and width of the settlement frontier at any particular time, and the processes by which these characteristics change during any period. The frontier's location can be partially established by reference to detailed population maps, but consideration of the economic and political organisation of the frontier is also essential. Any change in the location of a primary or secondary frontier will reflect the balance between forces of attraction generated by the nature of the frontier environment and forces of pressure from the frontier hinterland. The role of unusually favourable soil groups, such as those found in the Blue Grass country of Kentucky and the cotton lands of the Gulf plains, in promoting the rapid advance of the American frontier, are well-known. Rapid advance in other cases has been prompted by the discovery of precious metals and stones in the frontier. Government policies regarding land tenure also played a role in some areas in creating favourable conditions for settlement. In a very good paper about the American frontier in the Shenandoah Valley, Mitchell [1972] demonstrates that the Virginian authorities were anxious to develop this area in 1710, in order to protect the settled areas east of the Blue Ridge from French and Indian incursions. They achieved this aim by relaxing the traditional limit of 405 hectares (one thousand acres) per grantee, enabling rich men to acquire much larger areas. Such grantees then sold off most of their land at a profit, and this encouraged land speculation, which fortuitously coincided with the first major influx of settlers from Pennsylvania.

Blakemore and Smith [1971] have shown how the promulgation of new laws in 1845 and 1851 paved the way for the settlement of migrants, particularly Germans, south of the Bio-Bio, which for more than three centuries had separated Spanish and Indian Chile. They note that this area, between the provinces of Concepcion and Cautin, is appropriately called La Frontera. Turner [1953] and Billington [1960] have shown that many frontiersmen were moving westwards to avoid high land-prices, punitive taxation, and political and religious disabilities, imposed either by the first, well-established settlers or by the governments of their homelands. It is also probable that the rate of advance of any frontier was a function of the previous experience of frontier conditions and the presence of alien populations beyond the frontier. As the American frontier moved westwards, the early experience gained in preparing mining laws, land legislation and Indian treaties was applied in a way which allowed these problems to be settled much faster. Periods of standstill along the frontier often coincided with difficult terrain, especially where this was occupied by well-organised indigenous groups. Paullin [1932] prepared a map showing the location of battles against the Indians in North America, which reveals that the fiercest resistance often coincided with broken terrain, which offered excellent strategic opportunities for defence. It should not be assumed that primary frontiers always advanced. At times the frontier retreated due to a variety of factors, which included a succession of unfavourable seasons, defeat by indigenous forces, preoccupation of the hinterland government with internal organisation, and the greater attraction of another frontier.

Secondary settlement frontiers are found in all states which include areas of unfavourable environment, such as tropical or temperate desert, heavily dissected uplands, and thick tropical rain forest, or areas which require the use of advanced and often costly techniques if they are to be used for purposes other than mining. Such areas are bypassed by the primary frontier, because frontiersmen were usually concerned with rapid exploitation and profit. These less favoured regions will be subject to later settlement if circumstances require or invite it, and new techniques or discoveries make it possible to revalue the environment. But Wyman and

Kroeber [1957] recorded that in the mid-nineteenth century the expansion of the Canadian frontier ran up against the rocky Pre-Cambrian Shield, which diverted the frontier southwards, where it joined the American westward advance. Australia has one of the longest secondary frontiers in the world around its central desert, and comparable frontiers are also found in northern Canada and the Soviet Union, bordering their tundra regions. Attempts to thrust forward secondary frontiers normally depend on some incentive, such as shortage of food in wartime, strategic needs, the discovery of new minerals and the shortage of land. In Java population pressure on available land resources has caused the cultivation of slopes with a high erosion hazard. Similar causes have resulted in the extension of grazing and cultivation in southern Matabeleland, by Rhodesian Africans, into areas where there is a high drought risk. The spectacular advance of cultivation in Soviet Asia was stimulated during the Second World War by the need to replace food supplies formerly produced from major supply areas captured during the German attack. A century ago the threat of a Russian advance into Hokkaido encouraged the Japanese Government to foster the rapid colonisation of that island. Under a system of government subsidies, 65,000 immigrants entered the island in the decade following 1869 [Harrison 1953].

The discovery of new mineral deposits, or changes in the price of minerals that make development of known deposits a commercial possibility, have also allowed the advance of secondary frontiers at particular points. The sharp rises in the price of gold during 1973 and 1974 resulted in some abandoned mines in the Australian frontier being reopened. In May 1973 the Algerian and Moroccan Governments finally agreed jointly to export 700 million tons of iron ore from the Gara-Djebilet district of southwest Algeria over the next sixty years. The establishment of a settlement at the mine, and the construction of a railway to the Moroccan port of Tarfaya, will push back the secondary frontiers of this region. Conversely, the exhaustion of mineral deposits or sharp falls in price can cause the retreat of a secondary frontier, which can be caused in marginal farming areas by a succession of bad seasons or declining returns on products.

(ii) Political Frontiers

Beyond the settlement frontiers lies territory that legally belongs to the state, and these frontiers can be pressed back until the limits of the state are reached. Beyond political frontiers lies an unclaimed zone and then the territory of another state. Political frontiers disappear when states compete for the unclaimed territory and delimit a boundary separating their areas of sovereignty. Strictly speaking political frontiers have everywhere given way to boundaries, but there are some international borderlands where the location of the boundary is not clearly marked, and where the jurisdiction of national authorities is not coterminous. This situation obtained in the Aksai Chin between India and China, in 1956 and 1957, when the Chinese built a road through the area between Sinkiang and western Tibet; 180 kilometres (112 miles) of the road crossed territory claimed by India, although this was not discovered for some months. Wilkinson [1971] has written an account of the political geography of Oman in which he shows that a frontier between Oman and Bahrayn was first noted in the eleventh century AD. This frontier persisted, although varying in width, until 1955, when Britain unilaterally proclaimed the boundaries of Abu Dhabi. The dispute over this zone, including the Buraimi Oasis, has continued between Saudi Arabia and Oman.

The geographer's interest in political frontiers centres on contemporary situations, where states dispute the location of a boundary in a former frontier, and on historical situations, where the frontier disappeared after the establishment of a boundary. The characteristics of political frontiers which hold the most interest are their physical characteristics, their position, the attitudes and policies and strength of the states lying on either side, the influence of the frontier on the landscape, and the manner in which boundaries were drawn within them.

A useful distinction has been made between frontiers of contact and frontiers of separation [East 1937]. Some frontiers, either by the attraction of their resources or the ease with which they can be crossed, allowed contact between distinct political groups. This contact involved migration, trade, inter-marriage and conflict. Other frontiers possessed physical characteristics which made them unattractive to exploit and very difficult to traverse. Yet it must not be easily assumed that the geographic nature of the frontier determined the degree of intercourse between states. The attitudes and policies of the rulers of those states would be generally decisive. For example, when Chile achieved independence its limits coincided with the Atacama Desert to the north and the Andes to the east, both physical barriers that inhibited contact with neighbouring groups. Yet, during the last century, the policies of Chilean governments carried the country into war with Peru and Bolivia over the Tacna-Arica districts of the Atacama, and into a dispute with Argentina concerning the trans-piedmont slopes of the Andes, which were in some cases settled by Chilean emigrants. Conversely, during the second half of the nineteenth century the forested frontiers of the Kingdom of Benin, on the Niger coast, were no more difficult to traverse than many similar frontiers in that area. But no trade was conducted across this frontier because the Benin rulers actively discouraged their citizens from trade with Europeans.

Political frontiers often experienced less intensive economic development than the territories they separated. This is easily understood since the physical environment was often less favourable and the frontier usually insecure. Deserts, mountains, rivers, marshes, forests and woodlands have all formed frontiers at some stage of human history. Predictably, political frontiers were less densely populated than the flanking states, and inhabitants of the 'no man's lands' usually suffered a much lower standard of living. Tacitus described the debased condition of the Slavic Venedi, who occupied the mountainous frontier between the Peucini and Fenni. In more recent times the wretched Bedde pagans occupied the marshes between the Bornu and Sokoto kingdoms in the western Sudan and were raided for slaves by both of these states [Prescott 1967, p.43]. States welcomed frontiers which could be easily defended, and mountains were approved because the defence could often be restricted to a few passes. In Lord Curzon's view, deserts formed the best defensive frontiers, but such a view discounted the mobile and warlike tribes which occupied some deserts, and which made unfriendly neighbours. Davies made this point very clearly about the northwest frontier of British India. 'So long as hungry tribesmen inhabit barren and almost waterless hills, which command open and fertile plains, so long will they resort to plundering incursions in order to obtain the necessaries of life' [Davies 1932].

Many states tried to mark their edge of the frontier with some permanent structure. The famous Chinese and Roman walls are the best examples. The Great Wall of China served not only to exclude nomadic barbarians but also to restrict the number of Chinese who adopted a modified agricultural system, and thus became more difficult to control from the Chinese capital. The walls of the Roman Empire, unlike the Great Wall of China, did not mark a major divide in the environment and seemed to be built solely for the defence of the Empire, by permitting some control, if not exclusion, of the barbarians. Such linear features approximated to boundaries, but they were only part of a defensive zone around the state. Primitive counterparts of these Roman and Chinese structures were identified by Huntingford [1955] in the Ethiopian highlands. There the Kafa constructed deep and wide ditches, reinforced by pallisades, to mark the edge of the uncultivated and unoccupied areas which separated them from their neighbours.

Frontiers were generally replaced by boundaries by one of two processes. In some cases the flanking states incorporated the frontier into their territory, until it became necessary to draw a boundary between them. In other cases a subsidiary political organisation was created within the frontier. Annexation of part of the frontier was often initiated by land hunger in the state, or through the development of new techniques, which allowed the frontier resources to be revalued. If the frontier existed because of the internal weaknesses of the flanking states, or their preoccupation with threats from another direction, the resolution of internal weaknesses or the removal of the external threat allowed part of the frontier to be appropriated. In some instances the frontier was invaded to satisfy strategic requirements. After the Roman successes in Gaul, the eastern flank of this advance was protected by the annexation, as new provinces, of Noricum, Pannonia, Moesia and Dacia, all within the Danube Basin. This advance also removed the scene of conflict from the Mediterranean centres of the Empire [East 1962].

During the last century, when colonial powers were competing for territory in Africa and Asia, they often resorted to the device of proclaiming spheres of interest or of influence over unclaimed territory, which separated their firm claims from the undisputed territory of another state. The responsibilities assumed under these concepts were never made clear, presumably deliberately. They were both arrangements whereby a portion of territory was reserved from interference by another competing colonial power: it was as though the claimant state had secured a political option which it might choose to exercise sometime in the future. The degree of interference with indigenous organisations in the sphere of influence or interest varied enormously. At one end of the scale, the European state claimed only the exclusive right of its nationals to trade in the area; at the other end, there was a high degree of political control approximating to the condition of a protectorate.

The subsidiary political organisations created within frontiers included marches, buffer states and protectorates. A march is a border territory organised on a semi-permanent military system to defend the frontier. The Carolingian Empire was protected from the Slavs and Avars by a series of marches stretching from the Baltic Sea to the Adriatic Sea: Sorbia, Bohemia, Moravia, Pannonia and Friuli. Sometimes marches became the seats of new empires as is shown by the history of the Mark of Brandenburg.

Buffer states have been constructed between powerful states to reduce the chance of conflict between them. Technically it was usual to define buffer states as those that were created and guaranteed by major powers, but this is probably unduly restrictive. It is also useful to class as buffer states those which were allowed to continue in existence during periods of colonial competition. Afghanistan, Nepal and Thailand were left as indigenous states in Asia, largely because the British authorities wished to avoid common boundaries with Russia, China and France. East [1960] noted the interesting coincidence that many landlocked states were located in apparent buffer positions. Protectorates, which are one form of colony, were sometimes constructed in frontiers. The British authorities in southern Africa surrounded the Boer Republics of the last century with the protectorates that today form the independent states of Botswana, Lesotho and Swaziland. They did this to prevent direct access from the Republics to the sea.

2 Boundaries

As noted earlier these have replaced political frontiers throughout the world, although there are some areas, such as those in eastern Arabia and the Himalayas, where the exact position of the boundary, in an area of overlapping territorial claims, has not been settled. Political geographers have studied international boundaries more intensively than any other branch of their subject, and the literature from Ratzel [1897], through Fawcett [1918], Lapradelle [1928], Ancel [1938], Boggs [1940], Jones [1945] to Prescott [1967] shows a continual refining of old concepts and the exploration of new avenues of research. In these books, and in the thousands of papers studying particular boundaries, two themes have appeared more than any others. The first deals with the evolution of the boundary, and explains why boundaries occur in particular locations. The second concerns boundary disputes which have enlivened international relations throughout history. These twin themes help us to understand the influence which boundaries exert upon individual and national behaviour, which in turn produce consequences for border landscapes.

(i) The Evolution of Boundaries

The classical model of an international boundary emerging after a political frontier had been whittled away by encroachments from either side, probably applied in comparatively few cases. It would only happen where there was a long period of historical, continuous, indigenous political power, such as occurred in Europe. Genicot [1970], in an interesting article, has shown how, after the eleventh century AD, the uncontrolled forested lands, which separated the various political units, were cleared, appropriated, sold and disputed, until there were no areas where political authority of some description was not exercised. But outside Europe the intervention of colonial powers created a political discontinuity in the evolution of boundaries from frontiers between indigenous groups. It is very difficult to identify any international boundary which has not involved European states directly at some stage of its evolution. The Sino-Korean boundary seems unique in this respect, and that involved Japan in a colonial role.

The selection of a precise boundary to replace an indefinite frontier occurs because one or both of the flanking states is dissatisfied with an uncertain border. The precise reasons for this dissatisfaction will vary. For example, Britain and France drew a boundary between Nigeria and Dahomey in 1898, because their military posts were interlocked and there was the danger of local fighting. Britain suggested that the boundary between Persia and Baluchistan should be defined in 1870 for two reasons. First, Britain wished to pacify the coastal areas of Baluchistan in order to construct a telegraph line, and second, it was thought that a clear boundary would save the British-protected state of Kalat from further attack by Persian forces. In some cases governments wished to construct a boundary to avoid an uncertain and irregular administrative situation, which was being exploited by fugitives from justice. Thus in 1899 Britain and Germany decided to partition a neutral zone in the hinterland of Togoland and the Gold Coast, because of the administrative problems it created. In 1965 Saudi Arabia and Kuwait divided the neutral area which had previously separated their territories. Boundaries have been carefully defined when states wished to develop the borderland without creating disputes with neighbours. Laws [1932] and Peake [1934] have described how the boundaries separating the former Belgian Congo from Northern Rhodesia and Tanganyika respectively remained undemarcated until copper and tin deposits were discovered in the borderland. Fifer [1966] has discussed the role which the development of rubber plantations, in the upper Amazon basin, played in the evolution of the boundary between Bolivia and Brazil. Some boundary negotiations were initiated because one of the states concerned was fearful of the further advance of a more powerful neighbour. Thailand, in 1893, secured a boundary and a treaty with France which it hoped, in vain as it turned out, would end the risk of any future French advances.

The period of decolonisation since the Second World War has also witnessed the construction of some new international boundaries. The boundaries between India and Bangladesh and Pakistan were fashioned to separate opposed religious groups. In French West Africa many internal boundaries were elevated to the international rank, and the approaching independence of Papua New Guinea convinced the Australian Government of the need to place the location of the boundary with Indonesia's West Irian beyond any doubt.

Three aspects of boundary evolution are appropriate for geographical analysis: evolution in definition, evolution in position and evolution in the functions applied at the boundary.

Jones [1945], following Lapradelle, identified four stages of boundary evolution: allocation, delimitation, demarcation and administration. Allocation refers to the first political decisions on the allocation of territory; delimitation involves the selection of a specific boundary site, which is then marked on the ground during the stage of demarcation; and administration provides for the maintenance of the boundary markers. This is really an ideal scheme and not all boundaries have passed through each stage in this orderly manner. Some original lines of allocation have remained unchanged and unmarked, especially in African deserts; other boundaries were immediately delimited without any preparatory allocation, and in other cases there were a number of delimitations before demarcation occurred.

The allocation of territory was usually defined by one of two types of lines. The first type consisted of straight lines connecting known points or geographical co-ordinates, and the second coincided with features of the physical landscape. The Portuguese–German Declaration of 1886, dealing with the boundary between Angola and South West Africa, illustrates both kinds of boundary.

> The boundary follows the course of the River Kenene (Cunene) from its mouth to the waterfalls which are formed south of the Hunbe by the Kenene breaking through the Serra Canna. From this point the boundary runs along the parallel of latitude to the River Kulingo (Okavango), then along the course of that river to the village of Andura (Andara) which is to remain in the German sphere of influence, and from thence in a straight line eastwards to the rapids of Catima (Katima) on the Zambezi. [Hertslet 1909, p. 703]

At that time this borderland was imperfectly explored and the boundary followed known river courses and connected known points. There was always the danger that subsequent exploration would reveal that the described boundary could not be matched to the actual landscape. The assumption that the crest of the Andes, between Chile and Argentina, also coincided with the watershed caused serious problems between the two countries.

The allocation of territory by some arbitrary boundary generally solved immediate territorial conflicts and allowed states to proceed with the development of their economies in security. The need for the delimitation of the boundary emerged subsequently, if the borderland was shown to have intrinsic economic value, or if disputes with the neighbouring states developed. The retention of the original line of allocation occurred where the borderland lacked any economic or strategic value; where the boundary separated the colonial possessions of a single power; where the administrations were more concerned with developing areas other than the borderland; and where the two flanking states could not agree on any new line.

A glance at the world map shows that the original geometric boundaries have been maintained in the tropical deserts of Africa and Arabia, and in Antarctica. The delimitation of a boundary, which is generally decided by agreement between two states, or at conferences after wars, takes one of three forms. The first is a complete definition, which merely requires the demarcation teams to identify the named points on the line and the course of the boundary between those points. Such precise definition is possible only when exact, large-scale maps are available. In most colonial situations such maps were not available; indeed the need to construct boundary maps accounts for much surveying and cartographic work during the latter part of the nineteenth century. The second means of definition includes power to deviate. In these cases the site of the boundary is described in considerable detail, but the demarcation commissions are authorised to vary the line slightly, in order to create a better boundary. Usually the maximum deviation is laid down as one kilometre (.62 mile), and it is sometimes stipulated that deviations must transfer roughly equivalent areas to the two states. In both these methods of definition the boundary may be described in different ways. A common method is to provide a series of courses and distances, so that the surveyors plot the boundary in the same manner as a ship's course. The bearings and distances should always be as accurate as possible, and it is important to specify whether bearings are from true or magnetic North. When the country through which the boundary is drawn is imperfectly known, the line is described by a series of turning points, and the demarcation teams are left to select the course of the boundary between them. The turning points used include physical features such as mountains and river confluences, and cultural features such as road junctions, bridges and estates. Astronomic co-ordinates have also been used in deserts, and cases have occurred where the letters on a map have been designated as turning points.

Very often on the maps available to the boundary draughtsmen, the features which were most clearly marked were rivers and mountain ranges, and not surprisingly they frequently used such features to describe the boundary. With the exception of some precise landforms, such as arrêtes, physical features often have two characteristics which make them unsuitable for boundary definition. They possess area and they are impermanent. Again and again difficulties have been created between countries because of the problem of interpreting the location of a boundary along a watershed, or a river which changes its course.

The third form of boundary delimitation is definition by principle. In these cases the treaty-makers indicate to the demarcation teams the result which they wish to achieve, and leave the surveyors to identify the correct line in the landscape. Usually the territory is distributed on the basis of some human features of occupance. For example, in 1878 the Treaty of Berlin defined part of the boundary between Montenegro and Albania by reference to tribes, such as the Klementi, Grudi and Hoti, which were to remain with Albania. In 1815, a Territorial Convention between Austria and Prussia defined the boundary by reference to the lands belonging to towns and cantons.

Generally, the document which delimits the boundary also contains instructions for the demarcation of the line. Sometimes these instructions are carried out with dispatch, in other cases they are never fulfilled, perhaps because a new disagreement and delimitation make them unnecessary, or because matters of higher priority occupy the available survey teams. If the diplomats and negotiators have done their jobs well, the demarcation commissions face only technical surveying problems. Unfortunately, in many of the boundaries drawn in Africa, South America and Asia during the nineteenth and twentieth centuries, the delimitation was not done as carefully as it should have been. This has meant that those charged with identifying the boundary in the landscape have had to interpret the terms used. The problems of interpretation were most acute when the treaty contained imprecise or ambiguous terms, contradictory terms and inaccurate descriptions including the use of false or non-existent place-names. Even Holdich, perhaps the most famous British boundary engineer, once produced a boundary description which did not accord with the landscape (India Record Office, Secret External, 8 September 1896, Number 4). In 1896 he represented the British Government in negotiations to fix the boundary between the Mashkid River and Koh-i-Malik Siah, separating Baluchistan from Persia. On the basis of existing maps, in which he expressed complete confidence, Holdich persuaded the Persian Commissioner to accept a line which he deemed most suitable. The boundary ran north along the Tahlab River, to its junction with the Mirjawa River, then passed along the watershed of the Kacha Koh range to the Kacha Koh peak, from which it went direct to the Koh-i-Malik Siah. In fact Holdich was so pleased with this line that he wrote: 'No more perfect boundary than that afforded by mountains and river combined could be devised.' The description contained two flaws. First, the names Mir-jawa and Tahlab both refer to the same river, and therefore there is no junction as stated in the description. Second, the Kacha Koh peak is not on the watershed; headward erosion has shifted the watershed 9.7 kilometres (six miles) west of that peak. This means there are two problems of interpretation to be solved: first to pick a point on the Tahlab River which corresponds to the junction, and second, to convey the boundary from the watershed to the Kacha Koh peak. It is not clear whether this problem was solved by the Pakistan and Iranian Governments in 1958, because neither Government will disclose the new boundary line which was agreed then!

Smith [1907] records the use of a false place-name on the Tanganyika–Kenya boundary. The name Atorigini, given to one of the mountains used as a turning point, represents the Masai expression for 'I forget'. Hinks [1921] notes a contradictory definition on the boundary between Peru and Bolivia. A specific confluence was named as a turning point, and to make sure that its location was clear the definition noted that it lay north of latitude 14°S. Unfortunately the surveyors found that the confluence lay south of the latitude and had to decide whether they could draw the line to a point south of that parallel.

During the process of defining a boundary more closely, changes in position may occur. The areas transferred from one side to the other normally decrease as the definition proceeds from the stages of allocation to demarcation. This point is illustrated by the history of the Anglo-French boundary between the river Niger and Lake Chad. When the second allocating boundary of 1898 is compared with the first of 1890, it is noticed that the maximum movement of the boundary was 145 kilometres (ninety miles), and that Britain had gained 38,332 square kilometres (14,800 square miles) and lost 11,785 square kilometres (4550 square miles). This situation was reversed in 1904, by the delimitation of the boundary, when 51,696 square kilometres (19,960 square miles) were transferred to France, and the maximum boundary movement was 112.6 kilometres (seventy miles). When this delimited boundary was demarcated in 1907, the Commission made only nine small changes involving 44 square kilometres (seventeen square miles).

Geographers are interested in the different locations of any boundary precisely because such movements involve the transfer of territory from one side to the other, and this change may produce

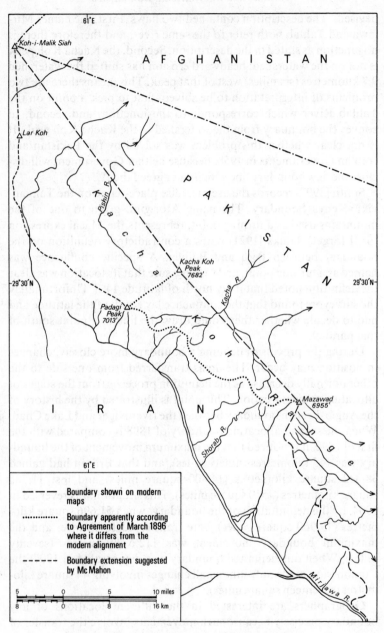

4.1 Part of the Iran–Pakistan boundary

geographical consequences. For example, when the Turkish Empire lost control of the Balkan States, boundary changes in the area were frequent, and Pallis [1925] has described many of the mass movements of Greeks, Turks and Bulgarians. Wiskemann [1956] has written of the large-scale movements of Germans from those areas east of the Oder-Neisse Line, which were transferred to Poland at the end of the Second World War. It is also possible that major economic changes will occur in the transferred area, not only because of population transfers, but also because of tariff barriers erected at the new boundary, and the internal economic policies of the new country to which it is attached. The changes are likely to be less marked in cases where the altered boundary only existed for a short time; where few state functions were applied at the former boundary; where the groups formerly separated by the boundary have a strong cultural similarity; where the economy of the transferred area used to be oriented across the boundary; and where the economy of the transferred area was of a self-contained nature. The converse set of conditions would create a situation where the impact of the boundary change would be most severe.

There does not seem to have been any research by geographers into the way in which the application of state functions at the boundary evolves. It seems probable that as the boundary's position becomes more precisely known as it passes through the stages of allocation, delimitation and demarcation, the state will be able to apply functions connected with migration and trade more effectively. It is also true that many colonial administrations in Africa and Asia adopted a policy of laissez-faire towards the boundaries with adjoining colonies; but that the independent governments, which have replaced them since the Second World War, have revealed a new sense of nationalism by policing transport across the boundaries with considerable diligence.

(ii) Boundary Disputes

Jones [1945, p.3] once wrote that a boundary 'like the human skin, may have diseases of its own or may reflect the illnesses of the body'. The symptoms of the disease or illness are friction between governments in their common borderland and boundary disputes. There are four kinds of boundary dispute. The first is a positional dispute, which arises because of uncertainties concerning the delimitation or

the demarcation, which allow the opposed sides to make different interpretations most convenient to their own purposes. The second
may be described as a territorial dispute. Such disputes arise from
some quality of the borderland, which encourages a state to lay claim
to part of its neighbour's territory. The third type of dispute concerns
the use of transboundary resources, such as a river or mineral
reserves, and may be called boundary disputes over resource development. The last type, which probably occurs less often than the
other kinds, arises over state functions applied at the boundary, and
are conveniently called functional disputes.

Positional disputes occur because of imperfect boundary evolution, and they are particularly likely to occur when there are long
intervals between succeeding stages of boundary evolution. The crux
of positional disputes will be either the legal interpretation of some
term used in the boundary delimitation, or the geographical argument that the line does not properly correspond with the terrain. An
example of the legal positional dispute is provided by the Anglo-
German Agreement of 1886, which drew a boundary between Nigeria and Kamerun, terminating 'at a point on the right bank of the
River Benue, to the east of and as close as possible to Yola as may be
found on examination to be practically suited for the demarcation of
the boundary' [Hertslet, 1909, pp.880–1]. Britain argued, when the
time came to select the point, that the term 'practically' had both
political and economic meanings. Politically Britain found it inexpe-
dient to draw a boundary within sight of the walls of Yola, since the
Emir of that important town was losing a considerable proportion of
his territory to Germany. Economically Britain argued that the
boundary should be drawn sufficiently distant from Yola to leave the
people an adequate supply of firewood and pasture. For Germany,
of course, the term 'practically' had only a technical meaning, and
they wanted the terminus very close to Yola.

The coastal section of the same boundary provides a very good
example of a positional dispute based on geographical grounds. In
1885 the boundary between Nigeria and Kamerun was defined as following the Rio del Rey from the coast to its source, and then a direct
line to rapids on the Cross River. Three years later it was discovered
that the Rio del Rey was a broad estuary, only twenty-nine kilometres (eighteen miles) long, and that two rivers entered the head of
the estuary. To the west was the river Akpayafe; to the east was the
river Ndian. This discovery raised a vigorous dispute over which of

these rivers should be considered the proper continuation of the Rio del Rey. Germany pressed for the western river and Britain the eastern river, and for some time neither Government was disposed to make concessions since the disputed territory might prove to be 'an Eldorado or a swamp'.

Many international boundaries coincide with rivers, and probably no other type of feature has produced so many positional disputes. The disputes arise for two reasons. First, on wide rivers with islands, a particular course for the boundary must be selected through the various channels available. Unfortunately these channels do not remain constant, and some peripheral islands become attached to the river bank by the deposition of sediment. This particular problem caused difficulties along the Franco-Thai boundary which followed the Mekong. For the first quarter of this century there were frequent disputes as the Mekong's course changed, and in 1926 France was able to persuade Thailand to agree to a convention, which interpreted the boundary, and any subsequent changes, in France's favour. Second, the course of the river can change, either slowly by the imperceptible movement of meanders across a flood plain, or abruptly, when the neck of a meander is cut through or when major floods occur producing new drainage patterns. Unless this problem is considered beforehand, it is necessary to decide, once the change in course occurs, whether the boundary follows the new course or whether it continues along the abandoned course. This difficulty occurred along the Burma–Thai boundary in 1938. An exceptional flood on the Meh Sai cut deeply into the Burmese bank, near the confluence with the Meh Ruak. It was decided by the British and Thai authorities that it was easier to control this borderland if the inhabitants knew that the river marked the boundary. Accordingly the boundary was transferred to the river's new course, and Thailand gained 648 hectares (1600 acres), 10,000 teak trees and some good pasture. An additional agreement made provision for the repatriation of persons transferred from one country to the other by the changes in the river's course.

The most famous case of this type of problem occurred in the Rio Grande, which forms the boundary between the United States and Mexico. In 1895 Mexico claimed an area of 242 hectares (598 acres), known as El Chamizal, which the southward shift of the river had transferred to the northern bank near El Paso [Hill 1965]. The Mexican claim was based on the view that the course of the river had changed abruptly during floods in 1864. The United States Government rejected this interpretation and insisted that the change had been gradual, through the normal process of erosion and deposition. In 1905 both countries signed an agreement which authorised the exchange of parcels of territory transferred to one side from the other by movements of the river, and this was done regularly in cases where the land was not developed for residential or industrial purposes. But development had occurred in El Chamizal and this prevented an easy solution. In 1964 the two Governments agreed on a new boundary in this area, which transferred 255 hectares (630 acres) to Mexico and 78 hectares (193 acres) to the United States of America. Under the terms of the agreement a new permanent channel has been constructed for the Rio Grande in this area.

Territorial disputes occur when a state lays claim to areas under the sovereignty of a neighbouring state. The basis for such claims often rests on the fact that the boundary does not coincide with any significant division of the physical or cultural landscape. Now since most boundaries represent a compromise between the conflicting strategic, economic and ethnic claims of the adjoining states, it follows that most boundaries will show some degree of unconformity with lines which relate to only one of these aspects. If, therefore, a state wishes to make a territorial claim, it is usually possible to produce favourable arguments, however weak. Because the initiation of a territorial claim requires a definite act, it is usual for a state to launch its claim in the most favourable circumstances. It is, therefore, not surprising to discover that such claims are made when there are marked shifts in the relative strength of states, such as occur after a war, during the immediate post-colonial period, or after the settlement of a civil war. For example, after the defeat of Germany in 1918, Portugal reclaimed an area on the east coast of Africa, ceded to Germany under duress in 1894; Somalia's claim against Ethiopia and Ghana's territorial claim against Togo were launched during the process of decolonisation; Afghanistan's support of secession movements in western Pakistan in 1948 was designed to take advantage of Pakistan's domestic problems and its disagreements with India; lastly, China's claims to areas of the Himalayas along India's northern borders followed the establishment of internal hegemony in China and the reconquest of Tibet.

Hill [1945] has usefully distinguished the arguments supporting territorial claims into two categories. First, legal claims assert that the claimed territory should belong to the claimant state. Second, other arguments assert that it would be more appropriate or satisfactory if the territory was ceded to the claimant state, but where there is no claim that the territory is illegally held.

One of the best contemporary examples of a legal claim was provided by that of the Philippines to areas of Sabah, when the Malaysian Federation was first being created. The background to the claim concerns a treaty signed by a British syndicate and the Sultan of Sulu in 1877–8. According to the treaty's English version, the Sultan ceded the land in question to the syndicate, forever and in perpetuity. In due course the area became a British protectorate in 1883, and a Crown Colony in 1946. The Philippines' claim rests on two grounds. First, it is asserted that the Sultan had no right to sign such a treaty because Spain was the sovereign power. The British authorities disposed of this argument by pointing out that Spain renounced its rights in this area in a treaty of 1885, and that when the United States replaced Spain in the Philippines, Britain secured American recognition of the position. Second, the Philippines' authorities claim that the Malayan word *padak* in the treaty does not mean 'grant and cede' but rather 'lease'.

The second type of territorial claim deploys a much wider range of arguments, which may be classified as geographical, historical, ethnic, cultural, strategic and economic. The geographical arguments are normally designed to show the desirability of extending the state's territory to make the boundary coincide with some physical feature, such as a river or watershed. These arguments are related to the concept of natural boundaries, which implies that the best boundaries follow major physical features of the physical landscape. Pounds [1951; 1954] has shown how the natural boundaries of France in the seventeenth century were considered, by some Frenchmen, to be the Atlantic and Mediterranean coasts, the Rhine, the Alps and the Pyrenees. Note that states always wish to advance to natural boundaries, but never to retreat to them! The Indian Government, during its dispute with China, has laid considerable emphasis on the superior qualities of the main watershed as the proper boundary, even though the problem of identifying the main watershed in the Himalayas is probably an impossible task. Geographical arguments also turn on the proposition that some areas, which are divided, or which are threatened with division, have a basic, regional unity. After the First World War, when Rumania and

Yugoslavia were disputing an area known as the Banat, Rumania argued that the area formed a unit and should be preserved within Rumania. This meant that the Rumanian authorities were discounting its ethnic variety of Magyars, Rumanians and Serbo-Croats, and emphasising the suitability of the surrounding rivers as natural boundaries, the complementary nature of the products of the plains and surrounding hills, and the opportunities for the employment of hill-dwellers on the plains.

At the same time Greece and Yugoslavia were making claims based on strategic ground against Bulgaria. In each case the claims were made to areas from which the German and associated forces had launched rapid and successful attacks. The delegates to the peace conference accepted these arguments, but they were careful to avoid reversing the situation by giving Greece and Yugoslavia pronounced salients from which Bulgaria might be attacked. The area of Cambodia, known at The Parrot's Beak, which thrusts a salient towards Saigon between the East and West Vaico rivers, figured prominently during the war in South Vietnam. Originally, at the end of the last century, that salient was much wider and deeper, and at that time it was known as The Duck's Beak. French authorities insisted in 1871 that Cambodia should cede territory in order to make French Indochina less vulnerable.

Historical arguments often refer to periods that are not well-defined and which predate modern national states. France, in particular, has shown a partiality for such arguments. They were used effectively in 1892–3 against Thailand. France had occupied the area of modern Vietnam, and was pressing for a boundary along the Mekong on historical grounds, as explained by a French official to the British Ambassador in Paris.

> He said, in reply, that the French Government were still of the opinion expressed by their predecessors two years ago (February 1891), to the effect that the left bank of the Mekong was the western limit of French influence, and that this opinion was based on the incontestable rights of Annam, which had been exercised for several centuries. He added that these rights were too important to be abandoned, and too well established for the Siamese to persist in contesting them. [*British and Foreign State Papers*, volume 87, 1894–5, p.210]

Not surprisingly, when French control of Indochina passed to the

Japanese in the early part of the Second World War, Thailand was able to use its own historical arguments to effect, and for the duration of the war it repossessed certain territories lost to Burma, Malaysia and French Indochina before the First World War.

The post-colonial period has witnessed the emergence of many territorial claims based on ethnic grounds. The colonial boundaries were generally drawn on the basis of the best information available, but the information about tribal distributions was often inaccurate. This meant that several tribes were divided by the boundary into two countries. This situation created few difficulties during the colonial period, because few restrictions were placed on movements across the boundaries. The much stricter supervision of boundaries by the newly independent states of Africa and Asia, has created some difficulties, which they have tried to solve by territorial claims. The Somali claims to the Ethiopian areas of the Haud and Ogaden are possibly the best known, but there have also been ethnic claims by Ghana against Togo, by Cameroun against northern Nigeria, and by Guinea and Senegal against Portuguese Guinea.

The economic arguments in support of territorial claims are usually designed to show the economic integration of the claimed area with a region already held, the need of the area claimed as a routeway, or the value of the area as reparation for damage suffered during war. Czechoslovakia's claim to the Teschen district of Silesia rested on two main arguments. First, the Freistadt area was regarded as being inextricably linked with the industrial complex of Ostrava, where metal foundries depended upon the Karvina coking coal. The coal was also needed to a lesser extent in Bohemia and Moravia. Second, the Czechoslovakian Government claimed that the Olderberg-Jablunka-Sillein railway was of vital importance, since it formed the arterial line connecting Slovakia with Bohemia-Moravia. The railway through the Vlara Pass, which Poland claimed could be further developed, was not considered suitable by the Czechs because of the steep gradients and sharp curves. At the end of both world wars, German territory was awarded to other states as compensation: in 1919 Belgium obtained the area of Rwanda-Urundi from German Tanganyika, and in 1945 Poland secured the area of Germany which had lain east of the Oder-Neisse Line.

The initiation of a positional or territorial dispute implies the desire of at least one state to move the existing boundary. By contrast, disputes over resource development and functional disputes reveal a desire to create some mechanism for overcoming the problem without moving the boundary. The two most common transboundary resources which might create difficulties are water, whether contained in rivers, lakes or artesian basins, and minerals which can be extracted in a liquid or gaseous form, such as petroleum, natural gas and sulphur. There are two situations when problems may arise over the use of waters straddling a boundary. The first occurs when the boundary is drawn along the course of the river, or through a lake. Such waters are properly called boundary waters, and very often treaties governing such boundaries stipulate that neither riparian state can use the waters in a manner which interferes with the rights of the other. This means that these waters cannot be dammed without agreement, which must also be sought if it is desired to dredge them, to draw water for irrigation or the generation of hydro-electricity, and to construct piers or landing stages into a river which may alter its regime. Presumably, today, there are also provisions to prevent one country from allowing the discharge of toxic wastes into boundary waters. On boundary lakes used extensively for fishing, such as Lake Victoria, it may also be necessary to reach agreement about the mobile schools of fish.

The second situation occurs when a river flows across an international boundary, as the Nile does on its course through Uganda, the Sudan and Egypt. It is obviously possible for the upstream state to interfere with the river's discharge, to the detriment of the downstream state's supply; and it is possible also for the downstream state, by building a barrage, to cause flooding in the upstream state. There have been disputes in both these situations, but happily, they seem to be solved fairly quickly. Even such bitter opponents as India and Pakistan reached agreement on the Indus and related rivers which were divided by the partition of the Punjab, and in several other cases, including the Mekong and the Niger, the machinery exists for mutual consultation and development of such international resources. The risk of disputes over oil fields seems much greater on shared continental shelves, and most recent agreements on boundaries in such areas restrict drilling within specified distances of the boundary.

Functional disputes, as mentioned earlier, are comparatively rare. Two are recorded on the Somali–Ethiopian and Afghanistan–Pakistan borders. In each case the international boundaries crossed the transhumance route of pastoralists based in Somalia and

Afghanistan. The disputes arose when the Ethiopian and Pakistan authorities began to place restrictions on these movements, in retaliation for territorial claims by the other two countries. A problem also arose between Iran and Iraq over the Shatt al Arab. The northern bank of this river forms the boundary between the two countries under an agreement of 1936. From time to time Iraq, which has other differences with Iran over the trans-boundary Kurdish population and the division of the continental shelf at the head of the Persian Gulf, has interfered with the right of Iranian vessels to travel via the Shatt al Arab to the Iranian port of Khorramshah. Iran finally abrogated the 1936 treaty in 1969.

A Representative Example: The Evolution of the Russo-Afghan Boundary

The boundary drawn between Russia and Afghanistan during the last three decades of the nineteenth century illustrates many of the general points made in the two earlier sections of this chapter.

In 1864 Russia signed the Treaty of Chuguchak with China and established their common boundary from the Altay Mountains to the Tien Shan Range, on the borders of Kokand. At that time, this boundary, in its southern section, lay well south of the areas of Russian authority, which was effective north of the forty-fifth parallel, except in the Syr Darya and Chu valleys. This meant that there was a zone varying from 885 kilometres (550 miles) in the west to 644 kilometres (400 miles) in the east between Russian possessions in central Asia and British possessions or areas of influence in India and Afghanistan. The western political frontier, lying east of the Caspian Sea and south and east of the Aral Sea, was a desert crossed by the Syr Darya and the Amu Darya. It was occupied by loosely organised Turcoman tribes, who frequently fought among themselves and often raided southwards into Afghanistan, and by the well-organised Khanates of Khiva and Bukhara. The eastern section of the frontier was composed of the high ranges of the Pamirs and Tien Shan, occupied by valley kingdoms such as Kokand, Zeravshan and Ferghana. The next four years witnessed a spectacular Russian advance into the frontier, along the Syr Darya and Zeravshan River, which ended with the annexation of Zeravshan and Ferghana. This advance meant that in the east only the Khanate of Bukhara, less than 161 kilometres (100 miles) wide, separated Russian and Afghan territory, and it prompted British

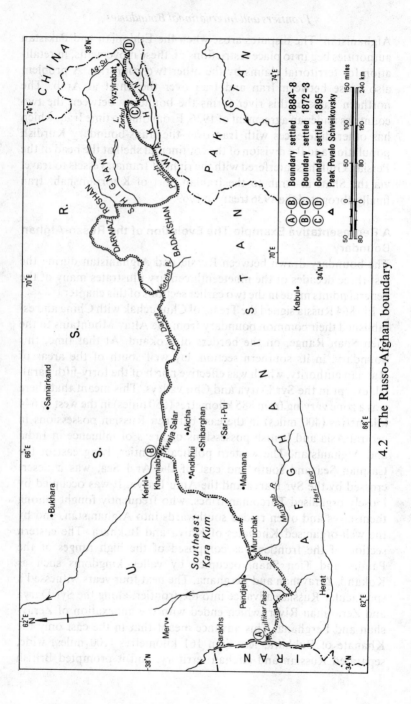

4.2 The Russo-Afghan boundary

moves to reach a definite territorial arrangement with Russia, to avoid any risk of conflict. A warning had also been sounded about the western frontier in 1867 by the British representative in Persia. He correctly predicted that Russia would attempt to open a road between central Asia and the tenuous footholds on the eastern shore of the Caspian Sea at Krasnovodsk and Gasan Kuli, in order to make the newly acquired territories commercially profitable. The route which the Ambassador thought most attractive to Russia followed the Atrek valley, skirted the Golul Dagh and then crossed the desert via Merv, which in 1867 was only 100 miles north of territory claimed by Afghanistan.

Britain opened the negotiations in 1869 and it was immediately apparent that both sides favoured the establishment of a neutral zone between British and Russian possessions, but there was no agreement on the width of that zone. Britain wanted the zone to be very wide and to include all the Turcoman country and Khiva and Bukhara; Russia wanted the zone to be narrow enough to allow a satisfactory connection between Transcaspia and central Asia. Now it is obvious that the definition of a neutral zone there required the establishment of two boundaries: namely those of the neutral zone with Russian and British areas. Remarkably, the British Government offered Russia an agreement which defined only the northern boundary of Afghanistan, and which made no mention of a neutral zone!

The boundary, agreed in an Exchange of Letters in 1872–3, stretched from Zorkul Lake, in the Pamirs, to the Persian border. Westwards from the lake the boundary followed the Pyandzh River to its confluence with the Amu Darya, and then along this river to the port of Kwaja Salar. From this point the boundary was defined in principle along the outer boundaries of the Afghan districts of Akcha, Sar-i-Pul, Andkhui, Shibarghan and Maimana, and then the agreement stated that the boundary between Persia and Afghanistan was too well-known to need definition. It is evident that this line, allocating territory to Afghanistan, became vaguer in definition as it proceeded westwards. It will come as no surprise to learn that the river boundary survived, but the boundary west of Kwaja Salar was only defined and demarcated after a long and bitter debate. Both sides recognised that the rivers did not coincide with political divisions in the area. Bukhara held Darwaz south of the river, and Afghanistan laid claim to the Roshan and Shignan districts of Badakshan north of the river, but both sides considered that the need for a

clear boundary outweighed the desirability of preserving the indigenous political fabric intact. Thus in 1873 the position was that a line
had been drawn, along rivers, in the most critical section of the frontier, where a potential clash seemed most likely. East of Lake Zorkul
the Pamirs seemed to remove any risk of collision, and west of Kwaja
Salar, the Kara Kum desert seemed to be an effective political frontier.

As in so many other cases, once a boundary had been agreed relations between the two countries improved, and the previous political dangers seemed to disappear. The British Government was
shocked six months afterwards when Russia, despite previous pro-
testations, annexed Khiva, but for a decade there were no other
serious alarms. In 1882 the British Government raised the question
of defining the boundary west of Kwaja Salar in more detail, but
without any urgency. Indeed, so complacent was the British Government that it turned down a Russian offer to negotiate a boundary
from Kwaja Salar almost due west to Sarakhs on the Hari Rud, apparently convinced it could secure a boundary lying north of this
line. That was the best offer the British Government received, and
the history of the negotiations, which lasted until 1888, was characterised by Russian military advances towards Afghanistan and
British diplomatic efforts to halt them. In February 1884 Russia
accepted the surrender of the Merv tribes, and the occupation of
Sarakhs followed soon after. This meant that Russian troops were
now established on the three main rivers which traversed the arid
southeastern Kara Kum: the Hari Rud, the Murghab and the Amu
Darya. Following earlier precedents in the Syr Darya valley, the
Russian forces worked their way southwards to Pole Khatun and
Zulfikar on the Hari Rud, to Pendjeh on the Murghab, and to Kerki
on the Amu Darya. The British authorities did not fail to protest on
each occasion, but there was no Russian withdrawal, and by April
1884 boundary negotiations began in earnest to fix a line between
Afghanistan and Russia. There were no more British illusions about
a neutral zone or a Persian wedge – the political frontier was about to
disappear through annexation.

The two Governments disagreed about the basis on which the
boundary should be drawn. The British Government thought that
the line should be based on 'the political relations of the tribes which
inhabit the country'. This would enable Britain to press for a northerly line which encompassed groups over which, at some recent

date, Afghanistan had exercised suzerainty. The Russian representatives believed that the boundary should coincide with the ethnic and geographic divisions of the borderland. This meant that Russia could, and did, claim that all the Turcoman and Saryk tribes, some of which they controlled, should be placed under Russian authority. The Russian view held sway and the negotiators were faced with the difficult problem of drawing a boundary in a very complex situation. It was complex for many reasons. First, there were three strategic points, which the British Government insisted must remain in Afghanistan. They were the Zulkifar Pass and Kwaja Salar respectively at the western and eastern extremities of the line, and Maruchak, on the Murghab, in the centre. Between Zulkifar and Maruchak the rivers drained northwards, whereas east of Maruchak they drained eastwards. In both areas there were zones where a mixture of Saryk and Afghan occupation occurred. The valleys were used for irrigated cultivation and the interfluves, known as *chul*, were used by both groups for pasture. In the valleys Saryk lands were often watered by canals that originated in Afghan farms; to give the heads of the canals to Russia would be an injustice to Afghan farmers, and to leave the heads of the canals in Afghan hands made the Russian subjects fearful for their supplies of water. Finally, owing to Turcoman raids there had been significant population movements in recent years as Afghans retreated southwards and were replaced by Saryks.

Despite these difficulties an agreed delimitation was completed by September 1885. From Zulfikar to Maruchak the line was completely defined by turning points and rivers, and only a few minor differences arose during the demarcation in 1885–6. East of Maruchak the boundary was defined as a line north of the Kaisar and Sangalak rivers, which left Andkhui to Afghanistan and terminated at Kwaja Salar. This vague line, nearly 322 kilometres (200 miles) long, confirms a British Government's admission to one of its representatives, a year before.

> As to the further line of boundary from the Murghab to the Oxus (Amu Darya), Her Majesty's Government have not sufficient information to form any decided opinion upon its details. [*British and Foreign State Papers*, volume 76, 1884–5, pp.1156–7]

Two problems arose in this sector of the boundary. First, the British and Russian commissioners could not agree on the identity of the Kaisar and Sangalak rivers; and second, they could not agree on the

location of Kwaja Salar. There is no doubt that the British view of
the two rivers correctly interpreted the spirit of the agreement, but
the Russians tried to advocate an interpretation that pushed the
boundary well south of its intended location. The matter was eventually resolved when the British authorities began to enlarge on their
claim, in order to deny Russia access to any wells south of the desert.
Access to a watered route near the boundary was a prime aim of
Russia's strategy, and so the British view was accepted.

In view of the ease with which Kwaja Salar had been proposed and
accepted in 1872–3, it was amazing that it should be discovered, in
1886, that there were serious doubts about its location. The commissioners discovered that the name Kwaja Salar applied to a ferry, a
tomb, a house, a narrow portion of the river, and a district east of
Khamiab, and the termini claimed by Russia and Britain were thirty-
four kilometres (twenty-one miles) apart. A separate conference was
convened in Saint Petersburg to deal with this question, and there it
was found that whichever terminus was selected, Russia would
acquire authority over some Afghan territory. In fact the local governors had marked the boundary between Afghanistan and Bukhara in
1873, when the first boundary was settled by Russia and Britain, and
that low earthern wall lay north of the extreme British claim. Obviously Russia had the right to insist on the letter of the 1885 agreement, but to have done so would involve accepting responsibility for
border areas, occupied by Afghans, where friction with Afghanistan
was possible. Rather than do this Russia made concessions over the
terminus in exchange for some additional lands for the Saryks west
of Maruchak. The final demarcation was finished in January 1888,
completing a classical case of boundary evolution, which began
with the vague allocation in 1872–3.

Thus, by 1888, the only section of the boundary to be defined
stretched eastwards from Lake Zorkul to the Chinese border about
193 kilometres (120 miles) away. This line was settled very quickly
and without difficulty, and this contrast with the other sections is
perhaps a measure of the rugged nature of this country and its lack
of intrinsic wealth, although it had a negative strategic value in the
plans of the British and Russian Governments.

After 1880 Russian explorers began to penetrate the Pamirs
south of Lake Zorkul, and the need for a boundary became evident.
The north and south limits of the zone within which the boundary
would eventually be drawn were quickly established. The Russian

Government would not consider any boundary north of the latitude of the lake, and the British Government would not consider any line which would have given Russia access to passes leading to India. In 1895 a boundary was agreed which passed south from the eastern end of Lake Zorkul to the crest of the Nicholas Range which formed the northern watershed of the Ag Su River. It followed this crest through the Bendereskogo and Urta Bel passes so long as the crest lay south of the latitude of Lake Zorkul. Providing Kyzylrabat was south of the same latitude, the boundary was to leave the crest for the Ag Su River at that settlement. If the settlement was north of the lake's latitude, the boundary should be drawn to a convenient point of the Ag Su River just south of the latitude. Beyond the river the boundary was to be continued eastwards to the Chinese frontier. The vagueness of this description is evidence of the imperfect topographical knowledge of both parties. The latitude of the lake was not stated; the range containing the two passes was not named; the latitude of Kyzylrabat was not accurately known; and the location of the Chinese frontier was a mystery. This uncertainty placed a great responsibility upon the demarcation commission created by the agreement, and it is plain that if either side had decided that the boundary was inconvenient, there was ample opportunity for disagreement which would make the work of the commission impossible. The agreement also stipulated that Britain would hand over the land between this boundary and the Hindu Kush to Afghanistan, and that the Amirs of Afghanistan and Bukhara would exchange the territories which they controlled north and south of the Amu Darya respectively.

It was this agreement which produced in the Himalayas the Wakhan Strip, that curious extension of Afghanistan, which stretches to the Chinese border and separates the modern states of Pakistan and the Soviet Union. The line was demarcated very quickly, and the fact that the Russian representatives made no important difficulties, probably reflects the fact that it was generally accepted that Russia could move no closer to British India without risking a serious rupture in relations with Britain.

Conclusion

Boundaries are continuing to evolve in definition, position and function, especially in Africa and Asia, where the modern successors to colonial empires are making quite certain that their limits are clearly

defined. Boundary disputes are also a feature of modern international relations, especially between Israel and its Arab neighbours,
between China and India and between China and the Soviet Union.
It should be stressed that it is the attitudes of the states concerned
which are decisive in fixing the intensity of any boundary dispute. If
states have the goodwill to settle their disagreements over their
boundaries peacefully, this can always be done, but if one state
wishes to force a boundary quarrel, usually it will be able to find
some pretext. This simple fact was enunciated by Ancel between the
two world wars:

> Il n'y a pas de problèmes de frontières. Il n'est que des problèmes
> de Nations. [Ancel 1938]

> Il n'y a pas de 'bonne' ou de 'mauvaise' frontière: cela depend des
> circonstances. [Ancel 1936]

5 The Categories of States

'A nation', said Kossuth (in 1848), 'must have its own Government'.

'We do not go so far', said the head of the deputation (*sc.* of Hungarian Serbs). 'One nation can live under several different Governments, and again several nations can form a single State.'

[Cited by Temperley 1919]

Understanding is better than classification, yet beyond doubt an analysis that also includes an attempt to categorise assists understanding of our present states system. This can be done in a variety of ways on the basis of selected criteria. Criteria are provided by international law, by degrees of political power which reflect a combination of economic, military and diplomatic strength, by types of political structure, by geographical content and character, by systems of government, by national composition of the population and, not least in importance, by the levels of maturity attained. Other categories are indicated by the use of such terms, applied to states, as 'residual', 'successor', 'neutral', 'unaligned' and 'buffer', each of which throws one ray of light on their diversity. It need hardly be added that these various classifications are not mutually exclusive and that each embraces variant forms.

1 States in International Law

International law is primarily concerned with states that are 'sovereign' or independent, regarding them as legal personalities whose relationships it seeks to define and regulate. However, the distinction between sovereign and non-sovereign states is not neatly clear: 'sovereignty is more like a spectrum or continuum, with different states lying at different points on it' [Mendelson 1972]. Some political scientists and international lawyers believe that states, being subject to various restraints, are not in fact sovereign. Certainly many states appear to suffer from limitations of sovereignty as do the members of the European Economic Community, Czechoslovakia in respect of Soviet Union pressure, and both Switzerland and Austria which are subject to the duty of permanent neutrality (i.e. they have no legal power to make war except in defence of their own country). Such limitations do not, however, prevent these states from being classified as independent, if only because they stand in sharp contrast to those which are legally dependent, lacking the right to engage in certain political activities, notably in the field of foreign affairs. The category of dependent or 'client' states once included a wide range of subgroups, members of which were in different degrees of dependence on outside powers. British 'dominions' and some Crown colonies enjoyed full powers of self-government, being restricted only in respect of external relations, until, by the Statute of Westminster in 1931, they acquired full control of their own affairs. Some states, like Egypt and Bulgaria, were long subject to the 'suzerainty' of the Sultan of Turkey which, at certain times, weighed only lightly on their political freedom. States, described formally as 'protected' or as 'protectorates' of an imperial power were usually, in theory if not always in fact, governed by their own rulers but dependent in respect of foreign policy and defence. The Himalayan state of Sikkim, as a protectorate of the Indian Union, so remains today. Many dependent peoples were organised as colonies virtually controlled by the metropolitan power, as were Portuguese Africans until recently. Curious types of dependent states are represented by those organised as 'condominia', i.e. subject to the control of two powers: such today are the New Hebrides, for which the United Kingdom and France are jointly responsible, and the small Caribbean island of St Martin, held jointly by France and the Netherlands. In addition were the territories mandated by the League of Nations to either Britain or France in the Middle East (Palestine, Lebanon, Iraq and Syria) and others in Africa, notably the former German colonies of South West Africa and Tanganyika – for which, respectively, the Republic of South Africa still holds, and Britain held responsibility. Trustee territories of the United Nations form another and now much reduced group of dependent states: certain islands of Micronesia, originally German holdings, which were later mandated to Japan and are now administered by the United States, and Papua – New Guinea for which Australia had a similar responsibility.

As we have already noted (pp. 13–14), dependent states have greatly dwindled, especially in recent decades. Those that remain are of two different kinds. On the one hand, there are the remnants of empire, small once important strategic or commercial outposts like Gibraltar, Hong Kong, Macau, Afars and Issas and Spanish Sahara. On the other hand, and in sharp contrast, are the extensive dependencies such as Mozambique was until late in 1974 and South West Africa still is: the former was, and the latter is important strategically and economically to Portugal and the South African Republic respectively. On a numerical count it would appear that out of a total of about 160 states of both kinds, less than fifteen per cent remain dependent. And the continuing movement towards decolonisation reduces this figure: the end of 1974, for example, witnessed the advent of Papua New Guinea as an independent state. Similarly, while it is still the case that some countries of large territorial scale – notably Australia, Canada and India – contain politically dependent territories, clearly as they become developed and settled these will become members of the federations within which they lie. Exceptionally, and thus contrary to the modern trend towards eliminating imperialism, the largest of the states with one-party communist regimes have continued to follow imperialist policies, little though they would so present them. Such were the recovery and integration of Tibet into the People's Republic of China, as also earlier the recovery and incorporation into the Soviet Union of the Baltic republics of Lithuania, Latvia and Estonia.

2 The Hierarchy of States

Independent states as legal personalities are regarded as equals and thus the United Nations accords them equal voting rights in its General Assembly. However, it recognises the obvious fact that states wield widely varying political power by requiring that of the fifteen members of the Security Council the five that have permanent seats are five leading powers, namely, China, France, the Soviet Union, the United Kingdom and the United States of America. Since states can grow either weaker or stronger through time, their relative grading is far from stable. Thus in 1913, before the First World War, eight so-called 'Great Powers' then existed, six of which were European, although most of these controlled additional manpower and resources in their imperial holdings. These six were the United Kingdom, France, Germany, Russia, Austria–Hungary and Italy, and the fact that so much political strength was concentrated in Europe testifies to the ascendancy it still held in international politics. Of the other two 'Great Powers', Japan owed much to the adoption of certain features of material civilisation of which western Europe was the home, and the other, the United States, had been long the beneficiary of immigrant settlers and investment capital from Europe. The top standing of these states resulted from their political power which rested on their relative strength in respect of manpower, economic and financial potential, armaments, diplomacy, and perhaps too we should add, their unity and national morale.

While so many powers existed, attempts to maintain peace by alliances that sought to establish a 'balance of power' became objectives of foreign policy. The two world wars showed the failure of such policies and, as a result, produced a wholly new situation in which only two states, one outside Europe – the United States – and the other Euro-Asiatic – the Soviet Union – became so powerful as to justify the appellation 'superpowers'. After 1945 when the United States exploded atomic bombs in Japan and after 1949, when the Soviet Union exploded its first atomic bomb, it was clear that these two held an ultimate offensive power in war that no other state then possessed. In the years ahead the number of superpowers may well be enlarged, if and when China develops military and economic power commensurate with its enormous manpower, and if and when the European Economic Community evolves into a well-knit federal state of nine or more members. In contrast to the superpowers, the term 'great' cannot be widely applied; Britain and France, however, both with nuclear weapons, industrial strength and diplomatic skills, best occupy this next lower rung. The term 'middle states' has a certain usefulness to describe those countries which for a variety of reasons earn more prominence politically than do the bulk of states which, for want of better terms, are often called 'small' or 'lesser'. Among middle states may be noted Yugoslavia, Canada, Mexico, Japan and doubtless some others.

Yugoslavia appears to have achieved political stability and strength despite the divisive and composite character of both its physical and human geography. Its military vigour during the Second World War, well-attested by the Partisans led by Tito against the German army [Auty 1970], shows the difficulties which would meet an invader and, while enjoying political independence of

Moscow, it maintains good relations with non-communist countries and adopts a posture of detachment from the power blocs which divide the communist and non-communist world. Canada occupies a much higher status within the international community than might be expected of a country of twenty-one million inhabitants. Fortunate in having only one neighbour, powerful but well-disposed, it has no territorial claims on others, and stands surprisingly high among the world's trading nations, commanding ample hydro-electric power and being able to supply important products, notably grain, non-ferrous metals, natural gas and timber. Also, Canada manages to retain some freedom of action in external affairs and to avoid necessarily underwriting the policies of the United States, helped in this by her membership in the Commonwealth and her non-membership in the Organisation of American States (see p. 229). Similarly, in the Americas, Mexico is acceptable as a 'middle power' on the following grounds: its population (fifty millions), the second largest in Latin America, its political and financial stability, its oceanic accessibility, its special relation with its U.S. neighbour and chief trading partner, and its expanding but still underdeveloped economy. As the Second World War showed, Japan had the capability of considerable military and naval power. Today, given its very large manpower and remarkable industrial and commercial success, it clearly occupies the rank of a 'middle power' even though divested of its former military strength. Lastly, it would appear that the bulk of independent states fall into the category of 'small states', small, that is to say, in wealth and political power. Small powers in this sense are not necessarily small in either population or territorial extent. This epithet could well have been applied to the extensive Ottoman Turkish Empire in its last century, the weakness of which became widely apparent.

Such a classification of states on the basis of the power which they can theoretically exert on others, while generally helpful towards the understanding of international politics, allows of no precise application to international situations. Efforts to rank states according to some power formula have never been successful. Mathematical analyses by German [1960] and by Fucks [1965], using a variety of indices, were clearly unrewarding and at times surprisingly unrealistic in their results for several reasons. Many considerations that lie behind the power of a state, such as the quality of leadership, morale, territorial space and relative location, cannot be objectively measured; moreover, the power of any state is very variable according to the place where it is applied. Thus Britain's power to intervene in Ireland and Rhodesia clearly differ sharply in degree. Similarly, the Soviet Union's power to intervene in Cuba in 1962 was clearly less than its power to intervene in the Middle East, which, in turn, was less than it could have applied in Poland. The terrifying military power available to the superpowers has such destructiveness as to have excluded its use in all the conflicts in which the superpowers have become involved. Small states are not always compelled to accept the will of the stronger and can achieve some success in the pursuit of their policies. Stronger powers may be expected to get their way in their dealings with small powers by a combination of diplomatic means, financial arrangements, threats and persuasion, yet it has been a remarkable feature of recent decades that small states have often been able to attain their objectives, at least in part, at the expense of stronger states and even superpowers. 'Paradoxically', Fox wrote [1959] 'the small States in the 1950s seem to have found greater freedom of manoeuverability at the very time their military inequality vastly increased.' We recall that in 1948 President Tito was able to flout Stalin and follow his own socialist road independently of Moscow's direction; North Korea and the Vietcong were restrained but not defeated by the United States; and the states of Central and South America, although very weak in comparison with the United States, have been able to follow successfully policies far from welcome to Washington, as when American businesses have been nationalised or when (in 1949) President Perón established in Argentina a virtually fascist regime. Indeed, given the widely held view today that all peoples, regardless of race, colour and level of culture, should be left free to develop in their own way, the rules and objectives of international politics have changed. Thus it becomes exceptional, as in the case of the Soviet Union's relations with its socialist neighbours, for a state to use its superior power openly against others in pursuing its own particular interests.

The fortunes of Cuba offer a commentary on how superpowers can fail to achieve their policy objectives. This former colony of Spain, which is situated close to the mainland of the United States, only 150 miles from the coast of Florida, won its political independence by the Treaty of Paris in 1898. United States troops occupied it during the years 1898–1902 and, since the United States required that it should not enter into any relations with a foreign power that might endanger its own independence, Cuba's role became that of a client state. The revolution which broke out in 1953 under the leadership of Fidel Castro was wholly successful by 1959 and, backed by the Soviet Union, Cuba became in 1960 the focus of a confrontation between the two superpowers. The points to underline here are that, as an outcome of this critical situation, Cuba retained its independence of the United States, although it exchanged this for dependence on Moscow. No total victory was won by any one of the three parties involved. The Soviet Union secured a communist outpost in Central America but at continuing heavy financial cost for the support of Castro's regime, put by *The Times* (29.1.74) at £150 million a year. And the United States retains on Cuban soil – at Guantánamo – a military base, which it originally leased from Cuba as a coaling station in 1902.

Another small state, Iceland, which has a population of less than 200,000 inhabitants, has been very successful in fishery disputes by exacting concessions from much stronger powers, notably the United Kingdom and the Federal Republic of Germany (see p. 205). And the proliferation of new small states – no less than seventeen in Africa alone obtained membership of United Nations in 1960 – has given numerical strength and advantage to the Afro-Asian bloc which can at least air its views and challenge the policies of stronger powers in the U.N. General Assembly.

The sheer power which superpowers and some other states appear to control is thus, in practice, subject to a number of limitations – the changed attitudes against what used to be called 'gunboat' diplomacy, international law, and the non-use of the most destructive weaponry of modern war. Even so, it would be easy to list occasions in recent times when superpowers have used their strength to get the results desired. The Red Army in 1956, by invading Hungary, put an end to the revolution which threatened the Communist regime there, just as in 1968, the U.S.S.R.-led military occupation of Czechoslovakia disposed of the Dubcec government. So also the opposed attitudes of both the United States and the Soviet Union were sufficient to end swiftly the Anglo-French military adventure in support of Israel against Egypt in 1956.

3 Unitary States

In respect of their political structure, as distinct from their forms of government, states are either 'unitary' or 'federal', although between these two norms there are many gradations. The unitary state is the common type, accounting for about ninety per cent of all independent states. The term 'unitary' implies that there is a single depositary of sovereign power, at the discretion of which specified powers of government may be delegated to regions and districts within the state territory. However, such delegation of power may be reduced, increased or otherwise changed by the central government. That this kind of state has come to exist so widely results from the fact that many states are largely 'nation states', the product of efforts of a single national group. However, many states with mixed national populations are also unitary in structure and this kind of state organisation has proved the more attractive to political leaders in newly emerged states, such as, for example, Cyprus and Uganda, since it maximises the powers of government at the centre. The existence of so many unitary states doubtless reflects the success of unifying policies, although this success relies in some instances on a relatively considerable use or threat of coercion by government.

Some states have remained unitary in political structure although they might appear to lack sufficient social homogeneity as have, to cite two examples, Spain and the South African Republic. The acutely perceptive writer Richard Ford [1846] wrote: 'It would be far from easy to predicate any single thing of Spain or Spaniards which will be equally applicable to all its heterogeneous component parts.' Spain, in respect of its physical geography, is made up of many distinctive regions, some of which lie peripherally to, and seawards of, its large interior plateau. And to the differentiation associated with landforms, climate and vegetation, are added varieties of national and linguistic groups. The existence of four spoken languages – Spanish, Portuguese (in Galicia), Basque and Catalan – might in itself suggest that a federal rather than unitary structure suited Spanish conditions. Certainly two national groups – the Catalans and the Basques – both with developed strong industrial and commercial interests, have often sought autonomy. The political unity of Spain and its organisation as a unitary state came about through historical events. The late-medieval struggle against Moslem intruders provided a unity of purpose for the Roman Catholic population of the Iberian peninsula and the dynastic union of the kingdoms of Castile and Aragon, with a new capital at Madrid, made possible centralised government and the growth of Spanish patriotism, expressed in the expulsion of the Moors and Jews and remarkable imperialistic effort overseas. Yet, as the Spanish Civil War of the 1930s reminds us, this unity is somewhat fragile and has depended on the assertion of dictatorial powers by the central government.

The South African Republic, of relatively recent origin and strikingly lacking in social homogeneity, nevertheless adopted a unitary form of organisation. This Afrikaner republic dates from its Constitution of 1961 when it replaced the Union of South Africa which had originated as a British Dominion in 1910, and obtained full independence within the Commonwealth in 1931.

The South African Republic is about two-and-a-half times the area of Spain and it brought together in one unit four unequally sized provinces which represented the efforts of white colonists to establish settlement, farm the land and exploit the mineral resources of a country with a non-white population several times larger. The four components of this republic – Cape Colony, Transvaal, Natal and the Orange Free State – each had its own special interests and characteristics and their contacts with each other were loose, given the great distances and slow transport by road until the railway building of the 1880s and 1890s. Cape Colony and Natal, where British settlers were numerically greater than Boer, had strong commercial interests related to their seaports and to the sea route between western Europe and the Orient. Transvaal and the Orange Free State were Boer creations, dependent on livestock farming until, with the discovery of the scale of the Rand gold resources, the economy of Transvaal began to be transformed with the influx of Europeans and the growth of towns and industry.

Each of the four provinces had for different times been British colonies practising responsible government, and the two Boer units had enjoyed periods of independence – Transvaal as the South African Republic between 1853 and 1887, and the Orange Free State from 1854 until 1902. Cape Colony was so extensive – it is more than half the Republic's area – that it had long faced the possibility that it might have to divide into western and eastern separately administered parts. Physical geography, by presenting vast stretches of dry veldt and desert north of the Orange River, together with mountain structures, interposed physical difficulties to the easy association of areas undergoing settlement and development. A further obstacle to any process of unification was provided by the existence of the three

British protectorates of Basutoland, Bechuanaland and Swaziland.*

Each province of South Africa faced its own regional problems, including defence and relations with native peoples. Also, British and Boer rivalry and conflict in the late nineteenth century suggested that there was little common ground upon which a single state could be built. By their national origins, language, religion and legal systems, British and Boers stood culturally apart. Territorial ambitions had brought them at times into armed conflict, and the northward Trek of Boers, out of which grew the farm-based communities of Transvaal and Orange Free State, symbolised the divergence of their aspirations. They were, however, drawn together by awareness of their minority position for together they made up only twenty-one per cent of the total population in 1911. The bulk of the population consisted of Bantus (several distinct national groups), Cape Coloured, descendants of slaves by mixed marriages who had no national, tribal or linguistic identity of their own, and some Asiatics, mainly Indians, in Natal. Clearly South Africa presented that complicated racial and social mixture of peoples that is rightly termed a 'plural society'. The difficulties in the way of unification were the greater in that, although the East Coast Lowland and the Eastern Highland were almost wholly Bantu-settled, elsewhere Whites and non-Whites, in factories, mines and on farms, became closely associated.

As we have already noted, war commonly enters into the process of state building. The South African war of 1899 to 1902, by its results, made unification possible. Transvaal and the Orange Free State were reduced to the status of Crown colonies from 1902 until 1907 when they were granted responsible government (i.e. control of their own internal affairs through a house of assembly and their own ministers). Further, the operation of a customs union, thanks to the railway network, highlighted the community of interest between the two interior landlocked provinces and the two coastal ones – between the hinterland and the seaports. And, given the special conditions of South Africa, notably its heterogeneous population and its restriction of political power to the white minority, it is easier to understand why the structure of the new state adopted the unitary form. The new provinces were downgraded in political status, becoming dependent for their powers under the new constitution on the decisions of the central government. One federal feature, however,

* In 1966 Basutoland became the independent republic of Botswana, Bechuanaland the independent kingdom of Lesotho and Swaziland an independent kingdom.

characterises the South African Republic: its two houses of parliament meet at Cape Town while Pretoria (about 1287 kilometres or 800 miles away) is the seat of government and Bloemfontein is the seat of the judiciary.

4 Federal States

Although most states have a unitary organisation, sixteen or about ten per cent of those that are independent belong to the federal type. These, too, are regarded as persons in international law since, although composite in character, their international relations are solely the function of the central government. The units held together in a federal state, while exercising a range of powers over their own affairs, lack the power of external sovereignty, which involves making war and peace and conducting diplomatic relations with other states. In this way the true federation, or *Bundesstaat*, can be distinguished from other states made up of more loosely associated units, which used to and now only rarely exist, and in which international affairs are either retained or shared by members. Such loose confederations or *Staatsbünde* were the German Confederation of 1815–66 and the Swiss Confederation until 1848. A contemporary representative of this type would appear to be the United Arab Emirates, which was formed by the political association of seven Persian Gulf emirates in December 1971.

The federal state came to acquire a certain vogue in this century since, particularly to United Kingdom governments, it seemed to promise political integration in place of fragmentation. Certainly it does this, and can take many variant forms, offering a flexible structure capable, as part of a liberal and democratic system, of accommodating greater social and regional differences than can be freely integrated into a unitary state. A unitary state seeks to create a region of a high degree of functional unity and to achieve a considerable degree of uniformity. In some contrast, a federal state may be so designed as to permit fuller expression of the individualities of its component parts. It is of the essence of a federal state that centrifugal forces are strong and that, if it is to function successfully, they should be held in check by centripetal forces: the central government must have enough powers and engage enough loyalty and support to safeguard unity. On the one hand, the component parts seek to enjoy a large measure of autonomy but, on the other, they should be willing also to yield to the federation powers sufficient to make viable this larger economic and political unit, which can bring advantages to the component parts as to citizens in general. Centrifugal forces may be many and varied: national sentiment, historical associations, distinct forms of economic specialisation, remoteness from the federal capital, differences of culture and of population densities. Centripetal forces, on the other hand, which should prove strong enough to contain these separatist pressures and to sustain a wider unity and loyalty, include the desire for security, access to larger markets, better access to capital investment, and greater influence in the outside world. Clearly, wide disparities between the federating units – in area, population numbers and densities, resources and productivity – make it harder to achieve unification and successful functioning. If one unit stands far above the others in such respects, it may seek to dominate weaker partners and thus may threaten or undermine the bases for successful and democratic federation. Indeed, it may be generalised that federations are the more likely to operate smoothly where the component parts are of roughly similar scale of area and population, where there are no marked cultural or ethnic differences between the people of the different members, where transport and communication between them are easy, where no boundary problems between the units exist, and where there is no neighbouring state that has a special interest, be it ethnic, economic or strategic, in one member of the federation. Such a model for perfection, it need hardly be said, is a figment of the imagination rather than a reflection of reality. We shall see that, as they diverge from this model, existing federal states face a range of problems and difficulties which throw down a challenge to their viability.

Certainly, in two early cases, resort to federal political structure has worked well. Both the United States and Canada followed up their federation by achieving remarkable territorial growth. It is a common feature of federal states that they have as their basis a written constitution, modified, it is true, by subsequent amendments and by unwritten conventions. By such means are defined the powers and duties that are shared between the central government and those of the members, which are known variously as states, republics, provinces, *Länder* or even, as only in Switzerland, cantons. But it is important to recognise that federal states are not necessarily organised in accordance with democratic principles, and also that in practice their constitutions may prove misleading as a guide to their political behaviour. Certainly some federal states have been markedly successfully, although some of these were threatened with collapse as a result of civil war, as were the United States in 1861–4 and Nigeria in 1967–70. Certainly, too, there are failures to record, notably the federations of Ethiopia and Eritrea, Burma, Central Africa, Libya and the West Indies, to which we shall later turn.

Table v lists the federal states in 1973, giving their formal names, dates of origin as such, the number of components federated, as well as their territorial areas, population totals and capital cities. The federal structure of these states is indicated by use of the terms 'union', 'federation', 'confederation' and 'commonwealth', but these do not exactly define the nature of specific federal structures, which in any case change with time. The term 'confederation' suggests that the powers and functions of the central government are limited to the advantage of those of the members and this has a degree of truth when applied to both Switzerland and Canada. The term 'federation' suggests stronger power at the centre which applies to the United States where the federal government, and notably the President and the Supreme Court, have certainly increased their powers since earlier days. The term 'union' does not explain how powers are shared, but certainly in India the central power remains strong as also in the Soviet Union where, despite the federal constitution, predominant power is wielded by the Presidium of the Communist Party operating from Moscow. In some of the South American states, notably Argentina and Brazil, government has often taken the form of presidential one-party dictatorships despite basically federal constitutions. Of the sixteen federal states most are republics, two of them socialist states under the control of their Communist parties. One – the United Arab Emirates – is ruled by emirs headed by a president, and two – Canada and Australia – remain kingdoms, although this historical survival may not last much longer. Six are members of the Commonwealth.

Most of the federal states of today adopted this form of organisation when they moved to independence from former colonial status; not quite all, for Brazil, a federal republic since 1889, had formerly been independent but ruled by an emperor, and Switzerland has been independent since 1648. For others in the list, notably the Federal Republic of Germany, the Soviet Union and Yugoslavia, federal structure replaced earlier unitary organisation. A glance at the column in table v that records the dates when the federations were

TABLE V
FEDERAL STATES

Name	Date	Number of components	Area (million sq km)	Population 1970 (millions)	Capital cities	Form of government
America, United States of	1782/7	50	9.1	203.2	Washington	Democratic republic
Argentine, Republic of	1816	24	2.8	23.5	Buenos Aires	Presidential republic
Australia, Commonwealth of	1901	6	7.7	13	Canberra	Democratic kingdom
Brazil*	1889	22	8.5	94.5	Brasilia	Presidential dictatorship since 1930
Canada, Confederation of	1867	10	9.2	21.6	Ottawa	Democratic kingdom
Germany, Federal Republic of	1955	11	0.25	61.5	Bonn	Democratic republic
India, Union of†	1950	21	3.05	547	New Delhi	Democratic republic
Malaysia	1963/5	4/3	0.13	9.2	Kuala Lumpur	Democratic republic
Mexico	1824	29	2.0	48.2	Mexico City	Democratic republic
Nigeria, Republic of	1960	12	0.92	55.7	Lagos	Democratic republic
Soviet Socialist Republics, Union of	1922	15	22.4	241.7	Moscow	Socialist (one-party)
Switzerland, Confederation of	1848	25	0.04	6.3	Berne	Democratic republic
Tanzania, United Republic of	1964	2	0.94	12.2	Dar Es Salaam	Democratic republic
United Arab Emirates	1971	7	0.84	0.2	Dubai	Emirates, headed by a president
Venezuela, Republic of	1830	20	0.91	10.8	Caracas	Democratic republic
Yugoslavia, Socialist Federal Republic of	1946	6	0.26	20.3	Belgrade	Socialist (one-party)

* Formerly the United States of Brazil.
† India became an independent dominion in 1947 and a sovereign democratic republic in 1950.

SOURCE: *The Statesman's Year-Book 1973–4*, Macmillan, London.

formed, shows that the United States rather than Switzerland provided the earliest model for this type of state. Certainly the Swiss Confederation had its beginning in late medieval times, but it was for centuries a loose league of cantons rather than a federation as defined above. It was only in 1848 that the Swiss, reacting to external pressures and guided by ably constructive statesmanship, drew up a new constitution which created truly federal institutions and concentrated in the Federal Council foreign affairs which had been previously conducted by individual cantons [Bonjour and Offler 1952]. Clearly the Americas made a large contribution to the theory and practice of federalism, accounting for six states, four of them set up after successful revolution against their imperial masters between the 1780s and the 1820s; the other two – Canada and Brazil – achieved federation without armed conflict. The remaining federal states are all creations of the twentieth century, six of them dating from the end of the Second World War. Federations of the last hundred years or so, notably those with extensive territories, clearly owed something to the facilities of transport provided by railways, later supplemented by surface motor and air transport, which made more feasible than ever before the defence and administration of outsize states.

The number of units assembled in a federation can clearly be few (three in Malaysia) or many (fifty in the United States). In the federation by aggregation, which is illustrated by those of Switzerland, the United States, Canada and Australia, the units brought together had previously enjoyed autonomous existence. Indeed, some experts assert that the six states of the Commonwealth of Australia, like the fifty states of the United States are actually sovereign states, even though the constitutions to which they acceded do not accord to them the right of secession. Exceptionally, and doubtless theoretically only, such a right is available in the Soviet Constitution to the fifteen republics incorporated in the Soviet Union. Other federations spring from the reverse process of disintegration since they emerged as parts of formerly large unitary states: such are the Indian Union, part of the British Indian Empire, the Federal Republic of Germany, the western part of the German Reich, and the Soviet Union which, as successor to the Russian Empire, had to abandon control of a tier of nations on its western border. In such cases, the units of the federation are less stable geographically and the federation may be subject to change in numbers and extent. Thus the Indian Union, which comprised twenty-seven states at different ranks at its origin in 1950, has already been reshaped several times, having in 1972 twenty-one states of equal rank. So also Nigeria was reorganised after its civil war into twelve constituent states in place of the three regions outlined at its inception in 1960.

No simple generalisations can be made about the scale of populations and of areas of federal states (table v, columns 4 and 5). Populations range from the small totals of Switzerland, Malaysia, Venezuela and Australia to the huge totals of India, the Soviet Union and the United States. Similarly, areas show a very wide range – in square kilometres from the 41,440 (16,000 square miles) of Switzerland to the 22.4 million (8.7 million square miles) of the Soviet Union. Even so, it is noteworthy that most of the federal states attain considerable size: eight exceed 1,295,000 square kilometres (500,000 square miles) and of these seven exceed 2.59 million square kilometres (one million square miles). Further, it is a characteristic of these large federal states that they include, in addition to their member states or provinces, large territories administered by the federal government (see p. 14). This is not an exclusive feature of federal states, being mainly a function of extensive territories, geographical obstacles to settlement and stage of development. Given time and as they become developed and settled, these territories may come to qualify for membership of the federation, as did Hawaii and Alaska in 1959.

In their choice of capital cities most federal states deliberately broke new ground. Unitary states grew around capital cities selected in past times and these have tended to become outstandingly large and populous (like London, Paris, Lisbon and Stockholm), absorbing considerable shares of total population. Federal states were at pains to avoid using as capitals large cities with existing political commitments, and thus to avoid internal jealousies and friction that such might well arouse. Further, there was the desire, by concentrating the functions of federal government at a 'neutral', freely chosen and conveniently accessible site, to provide a symbol of political unity and a centre which could play a unifying role. Admittedly such federal capitals may show little or no geometric centrality today, although when first chosen in relation to a smaller state territory, they may have had some degree of centrality, as had Washington and Ottawa.

As illustrations of the above ideas, note that Ottawa stood between provinces respectively English and French-speaking. Berne for Switzerland stands at the frontier between German and French-speaking areas and at a point on the Swiss plateau, if not strictly central at least not excentrically placed. Washington, within the federal District of Columbia, approachable by road and coastwise shipping, stood at the junction zone between the industrial north and the agricultural and slave-holding south. Canberra, too, was built in federally administered territory within the most populous part of Australia, only after careful consideration of where the capital could best be sited. After the Second World War, when Hitler's *Reich* was partitioned and the western part under Allied military administration was being launched as the Federal Republic of Germany, the choice of capital fell upon the Rhenish town of Bonn, little notable then except as a pleasant residential and university town and the birthplace of Beethoven. One of the more recent and imaginative of federal capitals is the city of Brasilia, built to high architectural standards and at high cost, again within a federal district and inaugurated in 1960. This was deliberately chosen in avoidance of the two dominating cities of Rio de Janeiro and São Paulo to start the settlement and economic development of interior lands: it was accessible only with difficulty and seasonally by road and is essentially dependent on air transport. Not all federal states have sought to develop a neutral capital. The Soviet Union abandoned the imperial capital of Leningrad in favour of Moscow, the historic capital of the Russian people and now a 'primate' city. The use of Belgrade as Yugoslavia's capital, again the largest city of the country, reminds us of the special place which Serbia occupies in President Tito's federal state. Similarly for Mexico, Argentina and Venezuela, the largest historic cities provide the capitals. India was content to use the facilities offered by New Delhi which had been built by its former imperial ruler.

Let us complete this review of the category 'federal state' by considering in the light of specific cases why some federal states have proved so successful while others, especially in recent times, have failed. As to the first question, we note that the successful federations originated in two different ways: those of one group were achieved by free negotiation and have always operated on democratic principles, but those of the other group, in contrast, owed their advent to the coercive efforts of a Communist Party and resorted to systems of government by no means democratic. Lastly, we should note that a few of the federations, such as those of Tanzania and the United Arab Emirates, are so young that their viability may not yet be beyond doubt.

Successful federations by aggregation were freely negotiated by pre-existing political units which had had experience of responsible government and where the communities concerned, or at least their political leaders, stood at a relatively high level of education. These bases for federation existed to facilitate, and thus to explain, the successes in turn of Americans, Swiss, Canadians and Australians. In each case a set of circumstances favoured union. A will existed among the units of the would-be federal states strong enough to overcome the centrifugal pull of their divergent interests and cultural differences. More positively there was sufficient social homogeneity and experience of democratic government to make federal association feasible and workable in the common interest. Clearly also two other favourable factors were relevant. In all four cases geography offered the chance of integrating settled areas of varied character and of complementary productivity into one territorial continuum which could be linked together and to a chosen capital city. The other factor, less evident in the Australian case but obtrusive in the other cases, was the feeling of insecurity owing to external dangers which (in Dr Johnson's words) 'concentrate the mind wonderfully' and favour co-operative action on the principle that union is strength because divided we fall.

To the Swiss and Canadian federations and their problems we have already referred (pp. 32–5; 42–8). Here, as an illustration of how one federation by aggregation was lastingly achieved, we may glance at the United States, which has been called 'a political framework of contrasting but complementary regions held together in tension and reciprocation' [Whittlesey 1956; Hartshorne 1968].

(i) The United States of America

The thirteen British colonies of North America which, with some help from France, won their revolutionary war, occupied and controlled a continuous territory of lowlands and highlands which lay behind the Atlantic coast with its tide-water ports. Settlers in continuous colonies were in some contact with each other, sharing common problems of defence, trade and undetermined boundaries as they expanded inland. These colonies as a whole stood somewhat aloof from lightly settled European territories which lay beyond their imprecise bounds: French and English settlers astride the lower St

Lawrence valley beyond woodlands to the north, French within the Mississippi basin and Spanish outposts in Florida. As their combined stand and military operations against Britain showed, the British colonists were not only conscious of their common political culture, ideology, needs and hopes, but had learnt to co-operate successfully. Although there were a few Dutch, German and Swedish settlers, most had come from the British Isles and their use of English and of English law and institutions made for a substantial degree of social homogeneity and like thinking. Not least in creating a sense of togetherness was their experience of local and regional self-government by means of assemblies which represented at the least owners of property. Despite the reserve powers held by colonial governors on behalf of the Crown and the overall control of the British Parliament, the colonists had grown self-reliant as they had been able to practise a great deal of local autonomy. The colonists' attitude to the imperial power, their desire for political control of their own affairs, common interests in defence against Indian attacks and in trade and territorial expansion into and beyond the Allegheny Mountains – all these exerted a unifying force. On the other hand, differentiating factors related to different environments and differing economic and social problems, exerted centrifugal and divisive effects.

The New England colonies in the north, for example, occupied highland country, engaged in farming, lumbering, fishing and trade, and had developed a markedly democratic spirit. The four southern colonies – Virginia, Maryland and the two Carolinas – although, too, necessarily interested in overseas trade, were organised by an aristocracy of white settlers engaged in plantation agriculture based on a labour force of Negro slaves. Indeed, the so-called Mason-Dixon line along the northern boundary of Maryland already in late colonial days marked off two communities to the north and south which had differing and diverging attitudes and interests: less than a century later these clashed in the American Civil War which was fought to preserve the Union and also to end slaveholding in the South. On balance the centripetal forces proved strong enough for a novel federation to be made. Common interest was sufficient to express togetherness in this way; statesmanship skilfully contrived the division of political power between the federation and the individual and unequal colonies, which had become 'sovereign states' during the Revolution. Thus a new state, organised on the federal principle, succeeded in reconciling varied state interests and concerns and, as events proved, became strong enough to carry out a policy of settlement and territorial expansion which brought its limits to the Pacific coast.

(ii) Yugoslavia

This country also represents the application of the federal principle. At the end of the Second World War, as successor state, it replaced the kingdom of the Serbs, Croats and Slovenes which, organised on unitary lines, had existed uneasily for over twenty years, backed by the Serbian army. Although the Serbs had enjoyed independence in medieval times, they re-won this by stages during the nineteenth century, and fully in 1878, having successfully revolted against the multinational Turkish Empire, of which they had formed part since the late fourteenth century. With its capital of Belgrade on the Danube, modern Serbia was at first confined largely to the basin of the Morava River, but, successful in the Balkan wars of 1912–13, it expanded southwards deeply into the Macedonian basin of the Vardar River which flows through Greek territory to reach the Aegean Sea. The Kingdom of the Serbs, Croats and Slovenes was clearly composite nationally since, as constituted in 1919–20, following the collapse of both the Austro-Hungarian and Turkish empires, it included the western territories of Bosnia, Herzegovina and Montenegro. The peoples of these countries had been much involved in the Second World War as guerrilla fighters, mainly against the Germans, and had come to respect the leadership of Josip-Broz Tito and to accept the communist ideology and organisation as a unifying force and a military weapon. When one considers the great variety and difficulties that the physical and human geography of Yugoslavia present, it would appear that federal structure is highly appropriate as the means of effecting its unity. That this was achieved owes much to the policy and personality of Tito as a charismatic leader and to the efforts of the Yugoslav Communist Party of which he was and remains head. And in any attempt to explain the success of the Yugoslav federation, it should be remembered that its all-powerful Communist Party, like that of the Soviet Union, had a centralised, not a federal, organisation.

The centrifugal forces inimical to the unification of the Yugoslav lands and peoples appear formidable. Much of the country of Serbia, and much more of Bosnia, Herzegovina, Montenegro and Macedonia, is mountainous or at best highland, and the physical geography of the Yugoslav lands provided in early days a number of core areas within which were created in some isolation separate national groups, notably of Serbs, Croats, Slovenes and Macedonians. The relatively extensive lowlands and hills astride the Sava-Danube-Tisa rivers in the north (in Slovenia, Croatia and Serbian Vojvodina) and in the old military highways related to the Morava-Nišava and Morava-Vardar rivers, facilitated throughout history the intrusion into Yugoslav lands of strong military powers from outside, notably in modern times the Ottoman-Turkish and Austro-Hungarian empires. Another obstacle to unification due to physical geography is presented by the broad zone of arid and dissected highland which falls steeply to the Adriatic Sea (in Istria and Dalmatia) and makes difficult surface access to the seaports from the well-settled interior lowlands. The term 'Yugoslav' (i.e. South Slav) is a spurious indication of unity since, together with West and East Slav, it applies only to a geographical division of the broad area in Europe within which Slav languages are spoken; moreover, in its linguistic context, it includes Bulgaria, itself an independent state. In fact, the peoples of Yugoslavia are markedly disparate and the principal groups – leaving aside small minorities – reveal differences of nationality, religion, language, alphabet, historical associations and other cultural traits, and clearly at its inception the Yugoslav state in no sense embraced a Yugoslav nation.

The cultural disparities of the Yugoslav peoples may be briefly indicated. The five principal national groups (all Slav in language) are the Serbs, Croatians, Slovenes, Macedonians and Montenegrins (see table VI). The Slovenes and Croatians were traditionally Roman Catholic and lived under Austro-Hungarian influences and domination, whereas the Serbians and Macedonians were Christians of the Eastern Orthodox Church and had been for some five hundred years subjects of the Moslem Turkish Empire. One effect of this is that over one-tenth of the Yugoslav population, especially in Macedonia and Montenegro, is Moslem. Serbo-Croat is widely spoken – in Serbia, Croatia, Bosnia, Herzegovina and Montenegro – but whereas the Cyrillic alphabet (of Greek origin) is used in Serbia, Montenegro and Macedonia, the Roman alphabet is used in Slovenia and Croatia, and both are used in Bosnia and Herzegovina. Add to these divisive factors differences in customs and living standards, a reflection in

TABLE VI
THE SOCIALIST FEDERAL REPUBLIC OF YUGOSLAVIA

Member republics	Area (sq km)	Population 1971 (millions)	Capital cities	Principal national groups as percentage of total population in 1953	
Serbia, including Vojvodina and Kosovo-Metohija*	88,361	8.4	Belgrade	Serbs	41.7
Croatia	56,538	4.3	Zagreb	Croatians	23.5
Bosnia-Herzegovina†	51,129	3.7	Sarajevo		
Slovenia	20,251	1.7	Ljubljana	Slovenes	8.8
Macedonia‡	25,713	1.6	Skoplje	Macedonians	5.3
Montenegro	13,812	0.5	Titograd	Montenegrins	2.8
Totals	255,804	20.3			

* Vojvodina and Kosovo-Metohija are autonomous regions.
† Serbs and Croats make up the bulk of the population of Bosnia-Herzegovina.
‡ Some Macedonians are citizens of Bulgaria and Greece.

SOURCES: Areas and populations from *The Statesman's Year-Book 1973–4*, Macmillan, London. Percentages of national groups from Hoffman, George, W. and Neal, Fred Warner (1962): *Yugoslavia and the New Communism*, New York, p. 29.

part of different histories of alien domination, and it is surprising indeed that Yugoslav unity was ever achieved.

As already noted above, only a concatenation of favourable circumstances proved strong enough to make possible the creation in 1946 of the Federal Republic of Yugoslavia. These were the defeat of the German and Italian military forces which had occupied the country, effective and accepted leadership which controlled the army and applied Communist ideology and methods, and an acute awareness after centuries of foreign rule that political independence was worth the restriction of national claims which a federal system imposes. Even so, and despite substantial transfers of power by the constitutions of 1953, 1963 and 1971 to the six national units, it is clear that Yugoslavia achieves only an uneasy unity. The political upheaval in Croatia, the second largest republic, in December 1971 exposed the underlying sources of division and weakness. The pretensions of Serbia (see table VI), the largest member of the federation, were again challenged; national feelings in the member states were clearly stronger than Communist ideology, and their policy objectives, as in respect of capital allocations, cannot be easily reconciled since there is little or no Yugoslav nationalism [Cviic 1972]. Centrifugal forces still operate to preserve unity, notably the leadership of the ageing Tito and the Communist Party, which had a membership in 1968 of 1.14 millions; also, in the background, there is the watchfulness of the Soviet Union, which would seek to prevent Yugoslavia becoming either a loose confederation or, yet worse, a congeries of warring nations.

(iii) Recent Federal Failures

The above discussion suggests that federation provides a means of achieving political unity that can contain diversity without assimilation. It shows also that successful integration can be effected only where the social forces making for unity are sufficiently strong or, failing this, are supplemented by forceful means, as is illustrated by the making of the Soviet Union, which was aided and abetted by the presence of the Red Army and by Communist Party tactics. In the decades following the Second World War, a number of federal states were set up only to fall apart, thus indicating that federation offers no simple and dependable means of unification. A glance at some of these will suggest why they failed and also the limitations to the application of this principle of political organisation [Frank 1968].

Libya, freed during the Second World War from Italian imperial rule, was launched in 1951 as an independent federal kingdom made up of three units – Tripolitania, Cyrenaica and Fezzan. The federal system seemed fitting on geographical ground in that in this largest of the African countries (nearly 1.8 million square kilometres or 0.7 million square miles) the settled areas of the three units, which were unequal both in population numbers and cultivated area, were widely separated by great desert stretches. However, only twelve years later and six years before a republican system replaced the monarchy, a unitary system was introduced and ten administrative divisions were created. It might well seem that this change owed something to the discovery of petroleum sources in the late 1950s which transformed the economy of this agricultural country, and to the belief that the problems and projects to which these gave rise could be better handled by a centralised government wielding full powers.

The Central African Federation and the West Indian Federation were both shortlived because they were imposed from outside and lacked sufficient support from the peoples to which they applied. On economic ground, the integration into one federal state of the three British dependencies of Northern Rhodesia, Southern Rhodesia and Nyasaland had much to recommend it. The first is rich in metals (especially copper), the second has a mixed agricultural and industrial economy, while Nyasaland is primarily agricultural. However, while the concept of federation found favour with the United Kingdom Government and the small minority of white settlers, it had no appeal to the leaders of the African population which made up over ninety-five per cent of the total. Launched in 1953, it lasted only ten years. The West Indian Federation of 1958 attempted to unite as an independent federation the two former British colonies of Jamaica and Trinidad and Tobago [Dale 1962]. But these islands lie about 1609 kilometres (1000 miles) apart and, although they had cultural elements in common as a result of British rule, inter-island rivalries and jealousies were stronger than the will of the islanders and their political leaders to join together. In short, it can be said of such federal failures that no valid and integrative state-idea existed to make union desirable and viable to the peoples concerned.

5 Other Categories of States

The attempt to classify states on the basis of territorial contrasts, while it has an evident descriptive interest, does not help us much in understanding their complexities. The contrast, for example, between the former Russian and British empires, in that the one was continental whereas the other was clearly maritime, is easily grasped and indeed entered substantially into the politico-geographical thinking of Sir Halford Mackinder (see pp. 234–5). Earlier attempts to categorise states according to their main geographical characteristics were not very useful [Fairgrieve 1941; Weigert 1957]. Peninsular, archipelago, desert and coastal states, for example, rarely have a great deal in common. An examination of states by such criteria simply demonstrates the important but obvious point that peoples at different cultural and technological levels respond politically and economically in different ways to similar environments. This is not to imply that physical features, such as high mountain ranges and major rivers, will not vary widely in their political significance. A French political geographer [Goblet 1955] attempted a classification of states, using territory as a differential. He distinguished between states which were 'intensive', 'extensive', 'mixed' (i.e. 'intensive –extensive') and 'maritime': a fifth category the 'metropolis colony' state (or empire) was a 'mixed state' with normally some discontinuity between its intensive core (metropolis) and its extensive territories (colonies). For Goblet an intensive state is a 'quality' state with a high degree of stability and a rank 'highest in the scale of evolution'. Further, it enjoyed 'optimum limits' to its territory and, well-illustrated in the case of France, could be found also in states ranging in area from Denmark to the United States. In contrast, an extensive state occupies 'a maximum of territory, peopled almost inevitably, by heterogeneous human elements'. This type of state, Goblet argued, was a product of primitive civilisation in specially favourable environments, such as the steppe-lands of northern Asia and eastern Europe, which invited territorial expansion. Such empires as those of the Mongols, Russians and the Ottoman Turks well-exemplified the extensive state which was marked, claimed Goblet, by impermanence, instability or even the tendency to break up into a number of states more coherent and homogeneous in population. It is not easy to grasp exactly what distinguishes Goblet's third category – the 'mixed state' – from his 'extensive state', for this again applies to states of either an explicitly or implicitly imperial character which have expanded to include wide territories containing a variety of national groups which, for this reason, at least in the last 150 years or so, were threatened by instability and disruption. Much the same comment applies also to Goblet's last two categories. In short, the scheme of classification, while reminding us how relatively well or ill the populations of states are adapted to their territorial bases and while hinting at the different levels of maturity, stability and strength states have attained, provides categories too loose to explain satisfactorily the realities of existing states. Very many states, broadly intensive in Goblet's sense and thus stable and mature, nevertheless have features of the extensive state (i.e. minority nationalities not assimilated to the major national group, such, for example, as the United Kingdom has in respect of Northern Ireland and France in respect of Brittany).

The biological analogy of the state to an organism, which goes back to the pioneer work of Friedrich Ratzel and pervades Goblet's thinking, has also been used by van Valkenburg [1939], who suggested that states should be classified as 'young', 'adolescent', 'mature' and 'senile'. Such argument by analogy has no scientific validity, for states are structures made by and for human societies and, as Hartshorne [1954] reminds us, 'men collectively through successive generations are at no time older than their predecessors'. The fact remains that states, past and present, exhibit from time to time strength, weakness, resilience and the ability to survive, as also different degrees of maturity in their behaviour. Age as such does not directly explain why a state is strong, or weak or able to survive, nor is it so easy always to determine the age of a state: the Soviet Union, adolescent in its present organisation, is successor to the Russian Empire, which was old. Austria and Hungary, as 'residual' states, may be regarded as roughly the national core areas around which the Austro-Hungarian empire was built: are these states old or young? The unusual fate of eighteenth-century Poland, which was eliminated from the map of Europe by successive partitions, while related to its internal political weakness, was not due to senility but to the co-ordinated policy of its three powerful neighbours – Austria, Russia and Prussia. Although it would be generally agreed, for example, that France is a mature state and that, in contrast, Uganda appears immature, it is very difficult to establish a yardstick by which the maturity of states can be measured. De Blij's world map [1967], which attempts to distinguish states which today show youth, adolescence, maturity and old age, is an interesting but unsuccessful exercise. It shows, for example, that most of the states of South America are mature, which is a curious comment on their governmental instability and financial weakness, that old age has come to Turkey, Afghanistan, Ethiopia and Paraguay, that Morocco has reached maturity but Egypt remains still adolescent, that India and Pakistan combine youth with adolescence, and that the Soviet Union is both youthful and mature!

Conclusion

In conclusion, some mention must be made of the attempt by Russett [1967] to make completely objective groupings of the world's states. Using the technique of factor analysis, Russett identified international regions for each of five sets of data. The first regions were based on social and cultural homogeneity measured according to certain internal characteristics such as economic development, communist influence, intensive agriculture, size and Catholic culture. Common or similar political attitudes revealed by an analysis of voting during the 1963 session of the United Nations served to identify the second type of region. Regions of political interdependence were constructed by a mathematical examination of the membership of states in international political institutions. The fourth type of region was recognised by the degree of economic interdependence measured by the state's intra-regional trade as a proportion of its national income. Finally, regions of geographical proximity were constructed by manipulating the direct distances between the capitals of the world. Each of these regional groupings produced unique arrangements of states, and thus the results for the political geographer were rather disappointing, although they enabled Russett to go on and draw certain conclusions about conflict and integration, which will be of interest to political scientists concerned with the theoretical side of the subject.

Berry [1969] wrote an enthusiastic review of this book and urged political geographers to follow Russett's lead, but this clarion call has not been heeded [Prescott 1972]. There is a very good reason why political geographers have resisted the invitation of this distinguished proponent of the mathematical method in economic geography. Very few political geographers today work at the global scale; they are either concerned with individual countries or small, obvious groups of countries. Those individuals who, in the past, have written world political geographies, did not produce very satisfactory volumes. No single author has written a better global political geography than Bowman [1922], but there have been some better composite works published since the Second World War. The work edited by East and Moodie [1956] used several authors, and probably for that reason has never been re-published in a revised edition. It has been one of the strengths of political geography in recent years that workers have recognised the need for detailed regional studies, and this has meant that no one can write with equal confidence on all parts of the world. Even continental studies need several authors and the recent volume on the political geography of Asia [East, Spate and Fisher 1971] shows what can be done by a team of writers in regional political geography. This means that political geographers are generally concerned with regions that are easily identified, without recourse to complicated mathematical techniques. They may be concerned with countries having a similar location, such as landlocked or buffer states; countries experiencing similar political processes, such as those which have emerged from the disintegration of empires, or which are facing the threat of secessionist movements; or states which have certain common economic characteristics, such as the world's major oil producers.

6 The Economic Structure of States

An essential element of European construction is a regional policy designed to improve living standards in those parts of the Community where they lag behind, either because of decaying agriculture and obsolete industry or on account of other structural difficulties such as peripheral position in the Community, bad communications etc.

(Anonymous, *European Community*, September 1973)

In essence, the politics of regionalism have always been the politics of disparity.

(A. Raphael, *African Development*, February 1974)

The treatment of the economic structure of states by political geographers is more uneven than the treatment of any other aspect of the subject. Kasperson and Minghi [1969] and Jackson and Samuels [1971], who have edited volumes of readings in political geography, neglect the economic structures of states. One looks in vain for an adequate treatment of international trade and national resources from the viewpoint of the political geographer. De Blij [1967] and Weigert *et al.* [1957] both examine aspects of the economic structure of states from the point of view of the world's power structure. Weigert is particularly concerned with the power equations linking the Western World with the Soviet Union and its allies, and with the underdeveloped countries, and he believes the role of political geographers is to be concerned with estimating the quantities in these equations. Pounds [1972, chapters 6, 10] provides the fullest treatment of economic aspects of political geography. First he builds on the study of the availability of resources by Jones [1954], in an interesting analysis of the relationships between resources and national power. He gives particular attention to policies connected with promoting self-sufficiency and an integrated transport system. Second, the political significance of international trade is considered in a separate chapter.

1   The Economic Aspect of Political Geography

In view of the partial treatment of this subject, it seems worthwhile to explore systematically the interests of political geographers in this field, and to discover the ways in which such interests differ from those of economic geographers. Political geographers are interested in the political significance of a state's economic structure, the way in which the political significance varies in time and area, and the role of political policies in changing a state's economic structure. These interests are directed always towards a political unit at one of three possible levels. First there are states. Second, there are the subdivisions of states, such as federal units, planning areas, and the administrative divisions, ranging from counties or provinces to parishes or cantons. States may also decide to form multi-national organisations, such as the European Economic Community, which form the third political level.

It is evident from this description that the interest of the political geographer in this field complements rather than overlaps the work of the economic geographer, and this point can be illustrated by two examples. In the Gippsland plains of eastern Victoria there is an important dairying region. An economic geographer studying this area may well concentrate on such matters as the distribution of farm sizes, the role of mechanisation in changing the structure and output of the industry and the categories of products generated in the area and their marketing. The political geographer would be primarily concerned with this region as one of the dairying areas of Victoria, and the comparative advantage to such areas of the federal support programmes, compared with Queensland and New South Wales. The second example concerns the railway being constructed between Dar es Salaam and the Zambian copper regions of Ndola and Kitwe. The economic geographer will be properly interested in the influence which the construction of the railway has upon the agricultural landscapes through which it passes, and the impact of the increased volume of traffic on the structure of the port of Dar es Salaam. The political geographer will be curious about the effect of the railway upon the power relationships in central and southern Africa. These will involve the reduced dependence of Zambia on routes through Rhodesia and Angola; the increased possibility of contact between Botswana and African countries north of the Zambezi; the closer relations between Zambia and Tanzania which may have implications for the East African Community; and the possible role of the People's Republic of China in this area, in view of its pre-eminent part in the construction of the railway.

For a comprehensive examination of the economic structure of a state, political geographers must consider it in four ways. First it is necessary to investigate the occurrence and balance of groups of economic activities, such as farming, mining and manufacturing, which may be termed the *industrial structure*. From this examination much will be learned about the economic strength of the state, its degree of self-sufficiency, and its economic stability. It is evident that Nigeria, with its wide range of primary exports and a developing manufacturing sector, is in a much stronger economic position than Bangladesh; and that the United States with its wide resource base is better equipped to deal with the problems presented by fuel shortages than Japan. Second, consideration of the *regional structure* of economic activities will allow identification of underdeveloped and overdeveloped areas of the state. These areal distinctions will be important in understanding secessionist movements and policies designed to relocate economic activities. The desire of individual European governments to succour depressed areas, such as Northern Ireland and southern Italy, has led to difficulties in forming regulations to cover this subject in the European Economic Community. The third aspect focuses on the differing extents to which sections of the population are involved in the economy, and the benefits they derive from that involvement. This investigation of the *sectional structure* will discover groups which are under-privileged and over-privileged to an extent which begins to have political implications. For example, the expulsion of Asians from Uganda in 1972–3 was related to the important position this group occupied in the retail and manufacturing sector of the country. Finally, because the industrial, regional and sectional structure of each state provides a unique combination, states develop a complex series of relationships, which afford opportunities for conflict and co-operation. Thus the political geographer must be concerned with this *comparative economic structure* of states, in order to investigate relevant questions of commodity agreements, economic alliances and the distribution of foreign aid. Each of these aspects is now examined in turn.

2 Industrial Structure

Any investigation of the industrial structure of a country's economy must be concerned with two levels. First, it is necessary to identify the balance among the primary, secondary and tertiary forms of production, and then each of these categories must be examined, in turn, to discover the range of activities included. It is also essential that these analyses should be conducted over a period of time so that significant changes can be detected. These points can be illustrated by the examples of Gambia and Nigeria. In 1968, the agricultural sector of Gambia and Nigeria contributed 57.7 and 54.6 per cent, respectively, to the gross national product. But this superficial similarity was less important than the differences in the composition of the agricultural industry in the two countries. In Gambia the only export crop consists of groundnuts in various forms; in Nigeria, by contrast, export crops include palm products, cotton, cocoa, rubber, groundnuts and tropical hardwoods. Between 1968 and 1970 the basic structure of the Gambian economy did not alter; however, in the same two years the structure of the Nigerian economy altered dramatically. The contribution of agriculture to the gross national product fell from 54.6 per cent to 44.1 per cent, while the contribution of the mining industry rose from 3.8 per cent to 13.3 per cent, and the contribution of manufacturing industries increased from 8.6 per cent to 12.3 per cent.

The industrial structure of a state will reflect both the nature of basic resources and the level of development attained. The ideal situation for any country would be to have a self-contained industrial structure. This would mean that the state possessed within its boundaries all the basic resources needed to sustain a rising standard of living for its citizens, and the necessary skills to convert these resources to the various manufactured products. In fact no state is self-sufficient, and all engage in the processes of international trade to make up the deficiencies in resources and skills. There are some examples of regional self-sufficiency among primitive communities in the forests of Brazil and Papua New Guinea, but it is predictable that these communities will eventually be brought into the national economic system.

TABLE VII

THE ECONOMIC STRUCTURE OF SELECTED STATES

(All figures are percentages)

Country	Contribution to Gross National Product				Proportion of imports in total trade	Proportion of exports contributed by largest item	Proportion of food imports in total imports
	Agriculture	Mining	Manufacturing	Other			
Gambia	55.6	0.3	2.1	44.0	66.0	95.4	22.4
Nigeria	44.1	13.3	12.3	30.3	45.5	49.7	7.9
Saudi Arabia	4.8	53.6	8.5	33.1	24.6	100.0	26.9
United Kingdom	2.9	1.6	32.4	63.1	53.3	15.9	20.4
United States of America	3.1	6.2	29.7	61.0	51.0	19.8	12.0

SOURCE: *The Europa Year-Book 1973*, 2 vols., London.

Table VII shows a selection of statistics for five countries which represent a range of different industrial structures. Gambia's industrial structure is typical of those countries with limited resources and development. The primary agricultural sector makes the major contribution to gross national product, and yields only a single export crop, which generates nearly all the country's foreign exchange earnings. Gambia is in the unfortunate position of buying from abroad more than it can sell, and nearly a quarter of its imports are various food products. The manufacturing sector of the economy is poorly developed, and consists only of light consumer industries such as bakeries, breweries and clothing factories. There are several other countries with this type of industrial structure. Other countries with restricted development of the manufacturing sector and an over-dependence on a single export commodity include the Sudan, which produces mainly cotton, Sri Lanka, which exports mainly tea, Mauritius and Fiji, which are both dependent on sugar exports, and Zambia, which relies entirely on copper exports. The political and economic problems for such states is that their earning ability is vulnerable to downward movements in commodity prices, either because of over-production around the world, or because of the introduction of substitutes, or because of the more efficient use of these raw materials by the developed countries. Significant variations in foreign exchange earnings from year to year make it very difficult for governments to plan ahead with confidence. Some of these countries are driven into an unwelcome reliance on foreign aid from wealthier states, as their foreign exchange reserves are eroded by a visible trade deficit.

There is one group of countries, which depend on a single commodity, which do not at present face serious economic problems: these are the world's major oil producers. The statistics for Saudi Arabia show the total dependence on petroleum for foreign exchange earnings, and the dominant role of mining in the gross national product. The world's major oil producers began operating in a sellers' market during 1973, when the Organisation of Petroleum Exporting States (OPEC) decided to increase prices and curtail increases in production. The decisive action was taken at the time of the war between Israel and its Arab neighbours in October 1973, but the professed political aim of the Arab oil-producing states was always subordinate to the economic aim of securing higher returns from their oil supplies for a longer period. This policy will succeed so long as the existing patterns of oil production and consumption remain unchanged; however, the development of different sources of power and any return to the condition of over-supply of petroleum, which existed in the mid 1960s, will create fresh problems of industrial imbalance for the Arab oil-producing states.

Nigeria is typical of those countries that possess a rich variety of resources, which are now being harnessed in a manner that promises important and beneficial changes in the country's industrial structure. Such states have a number of mineral and agricultural exports and a sufficiently large population to generate a domestic market for manufactured goods without being so large that it stultifies planning and progress. Brazil, Malaysia, Thailand and perhaps Ivory Coast are other countries in this group.

The United Kingdom and the United States represent those countries which have developed a major industrial sector and a diverse export trade, which in normal circumstances roughly balances with the level of imports. All industrial countries need to import raw materials of some description and it is possible further to subdivide them on this basis. There is an evident distinction between Australia and Canada on one hand and Japan and the United Kingdom on the other. Australia and Canada produce large volumes of primary agricultural and mineral products for export, while possessing a well-developed manufacturing sector. The other two countries have a less important primary sector, but the manufacturing industry is much bigger and more varied in its range of products.

The different industrial structures create differing political and economic problems. The creation of effective defence forces requires either a developed manufacturing industry, such as that of the United States, which can construct war planes, naval vessels and military equipment, or a large trading surplus, on the scale of Iran, which will allow the purchase of these items from abroad. Otherwise states must rely on allies to supply equipment on credit terms, as Egypt relies on the Soviet Union. The forward planning of major capital projects, such as railways and hydro-electric schemes, requires confidence about the levels of the nation's income. Many countries dependent upon agricultural exports have faced long periods of falling prices, when any expansion of production did not produce an equivalent rise in foreign earnings. With rising levels of education around the world and the more efficient production of crops and minerals, there is a demand for employment outside the primary sector. Many governments of developing countries see industrialisation as a partial solution to this difficulty. Finally, if states rely on other countries for strategic imports of minerals and fuels, they may be subject to pressure regarding particular economic and political policies. The pressure exerted by Arab oil-producing countries on Japan during 1973 and 1974 caused that country to change its professed attitude to political issues in the Middle East.

To reduce these problems governments will initiate policies to change the industrial structure to a more favourable form [Prescott, 1968, chapters 3, 5]. One obvious group of policies relates to the reduction of imports in order to improve the visible trading balance. The reduction of food imports is a popular target. The Government of Sierra Leone in common with many other African countries, such as Nigeria, Ghana and Zambia, has launched a scheme to make the country self-sufficient in rice production. During the crop year 1972–3 the area cultivated was increased from 10,125 hectares (25,000 acres) to 22,275 hectares (55,000 acres), and plans exist to develop a further 10,530 hectares (26,000 acres) in the Rhombe swamp. Tractors for ploughing and harrowing are made available to rice farmers at a subsidised charge, and the guaranteed price for rice was raised by fifteen per cent in 1974 to encourage production. The yields in Sierra Leone are still low by Asian standards and help is being sought from Taiwan and the World Bank to raise these yields. The establishment of factories producing such commodities as cement, matches, shoes and cheap cotton clothing is also being undertaken in many developing countries to reduce the cost of imports.

Many governments encourage the growth of industries within their borders in a number of different ways. The provision of a protective tariff wall shields developing industries from the full brunt of overseas competition; and industrial development can also be promoted by restrictions on the export of untreated raw materials. It is believed that the Spanish and Portuguese restrictions on the export of raw cork were designed to force the development of a domestic cork manufacturing industry, and many mineral and agricultural exports are now partly processed in the country of origin.

To raise the revenue derived from primary exports, and to make that revenue more secure, developing states have engaged in a number of policies. Some have tried to diversify their export production, but there is a danger that this may cause over-production of the particular crop and further price instability. Others have secured long-term contracts at guaranteed prices with the consuming countries: this and other multilateral policies are considered in the section on the comparative economic structure of states.

To avoid a dangerous dependence on strategic supplies from one foreign source, some governments try to diversify their sources of supply. There are two other policies which can reduce this danger. The first involves building large stockpiles of the strategic material, and this does not change the industrial structure of the state. During the Korean War the United States constructed enormous stockpiles of such minerals as chrome and copper. It is estimated that South Africa, which has been repeatedly threatened with an oil embargo, has eighteen months supply of this fuel. The second strategy involves searching for deposits of the resources within the state's territory. Since the rise in oil prices in 1973–4, several governments have expedited plans to search for oil in their own territory, including their continental shelves. To meet domestic needs during world shortages the United States has decided to make new areas of the continental shelf available for exploration, to encourage further research into the extraction of oil from oil shales, which exist in vast quantities in Colorado, Wyoming and Utah, and to experiment with new techniques for converting coal to clean gas.

3 Regional Structure

Even the most casual traveller through a state will easily detect regional differences in the levels of economic development and prosperity. Such differences can be traced to a number of underlying causes. Some of the most obvious differences find a ready explanation in the variety of resources regionally available. The contrasts between the Canadian Shield and the St Lawrence Lowlands and between the Paris Basin and the Massif Central illustrate this type of situation. In some cases regional inequalities have developed because of changes in the nature of resources or in patterns of production. The exhaustion of mineral deposits is a common cause of regional depression.

It is in West Durham that the coal-mining industry's problems are most acute. There, seams are generally thin, near the surface, and lacking in continuity; costs of extraction are high, mechanisation is difficult or uneconomic, and the workable reserves of many pits are approaching exhaustion . . . by the end of this century it seems probable that coal-mining will have virtually ceased in the western part of the coalfield. [Bowden 1965]

The increasing salt concentrations in the upper horizons of soils in irrigation districts of the Australian Riverina have caused some local depression. When paper production was based on coal-fired steam engines, rather than water power, during the nineteenth century, there was a decline in the level of production around Maidstone in southeast England, and a corresponding expansion on the Lancashire coalfield. Regional inequalities are encouraged by some government policies designed to create maximum development in the most favourable areas.

For these and other reasons, regional economic inequalities must be accepted as a fact of political life, and normally a government will attempt to reduce these inequalities only when they appear to be creating political dangers. There are two situations which generally give rise to political concern. The first occurs when seriously depressed areas emerge in the national territory, which can be recognised in several ways. First, the income per head of depressed regions falls significantly below the national average. Second, the level of unemployment stands much higher than the national average. Third, there is generally an outflow of young people, seeking work, from the depressed areas, which begin to develop a population structure dominated by middle-aged and old people. Fourth, there is often a much lower rate of new building and capital investment in the depressed area than in more prosperous regions, and the depressed region contains surplus capacity in social institutions such as schools and hospitals. The political risks for governments in such areas is that they will become centres of disaffection and opposition, leading to demands for a measure of self-government, or special economic treatment. The current demands advanced by Welsh and Scottish nationalists have a strong economic basis.

The second situation occurs when one region reaches an exceptional level of development and prosperity compared with the rest of the country. This situation occurred in Katanga in Zaïre and Eastern Region in Nigeria. The remarkable wealth of these areas, based respectively on copper and petroleum, encouraged their political leaders to establish secessionist movements, both of which succeeded for a short time. The civil wars required to retain these two areas retarded the development of both states. A similar situation may develop in Bougainville, now that Papua New Guinea has become independent. This island produces enormous quantities of copper, which generate most of the country's foreign exchange earnings. There have been murmurings in the past about the secession of Bougainville, and it is possible that this may be raised again. Problems of regional economic inequalities become more critical when the distinctive region is also distinguished on ethnic grounds associated with nationality, language or tribe. Hamilton [1968], writing about Yugoslavia, has shown how the distinction on ground of national origin, between the depressed areas of Macedonia, Montenegro and Kosovo-Metohija and the developed areas of Slovenia and Croatia, has made the solution to economic problems more urgent.

When governments begin to detect critical problems associated with an imbalance in the regional structure of the state's economy, they have a wide range of policies which they can use to improve the situation. Koropeckyj [1972] has prepared a valuable account of the attempts of communist governments to reduce the regional imbalance of their countries. This is apparently as much a matter of ideology as practical politics.

First, according to Socialist ideology, this system can be introduced only in a country that is economically well developed. It follows that all regions of such a country must be equally advanced; otherwise it becomes illogical for some more advanced regions to be Socialist while less developed regions are not. Second, one of the main characteristics of socialism is egalitarianism; therefore all citizens, no matter in which region they reside, should be assured equal opportunity for a higher standard of living and for social advancement. Third, the Socialists believe that in a multinational state, in which various nationalities inhabit their own ethnic territories, the economic equality of these regions is a precondition of achieving political, social and cultural equality.

It follows that communist governments are better able to reduce the economic imbalance between regions by direct prescription, than democratic governments, which rely on the persuasion of particular policies. It is, however, possibly true that communist governments are less sensitive to dissatisfaction which may develop in depressed areas. To reduce the economic imbalance between regions, governments must intervene to eliminate the operation of processes causing or perpetuating the disparity: and this intervention can be directed in favour of the depressed area, or to the disadvantage of the developed region.

A number of developing countries, including Brazil and Chile, use multiple exchange rates for foreign currency to help the poorer regions attract investment [Prescott 1968, pp. 170–1].

In South Africa, the Government has developed a policy of decentralisation, which is designed to encourage manufacturers to construct their factories in development zones around the borders of Bantustan homelands, which are planned to become independent states. The policy operates in two ways. First, the Minister for Planning can make it very difficult for those industries, which require a high proportion of African to European labour, to establish themselves, or expand, in industrial centres such as Johannesburg. Second, companies locating new premises in the homeland borders obtain several financial benefits. They obtain subsidised freight rates; allowances are available for training African workers; a proportion of capital investment will rank as tax deductions in many cases; assistance will be given in the construction of factories, and local government authorities will be provided with low interest loans to construct any essential service facilities. This scheme, which began in 1960, had provided 87,000 new jobs during the first decade. Successive British governments have introduced various policies to rejuvenate the economies of areas such as northeast England, Northern Ireland and Cumberland. These policies have included the establishment of major administrative offices in these regions; the construction of trading estates, where light industries employing female labour can be established; and the improvement of communications and local services. Other European governments, especially in Italy and Belgium, have adopted similar measures, and these policies have created difficulties for the European Economic Community. Economic integration, which is a prime aim of the Community, tends to increase the problems experienced by depressed areas because they face further competition from efficient areas outside the state. This realisation has led most of the governments to claim exemption from the operation of the Community's regulations, for preferential policies designed to help their depressed regions. Several governments, including Australia's, have offered economic incentives to industries which establish themselves in rural areas rather than in large cities. Such inducement aims at restricting the congestion of cities while providing employment for young people in farming areas.

In a description of the patterns of regional inequalities, Williamson [1965] demonstrated that they are low when the level of economic development is primitive. As economic development proceeds, regional inequalities begin to develop and grow at a significant pace. It is at this stage that most of the countries of the Third World stand at present, with Brazil probably the classical example of a country with severe problems of regional imbalance in the state's economic structure. According to Williamson [1965], the level of regional disparity is generally reduced as the state reaches higher levels of development: but there are evidently exceptions to this rule, provided by southern Italy and the Borinage of Belgium. It is also possible that Northern Ireland could be included as an example, but the obvious relevance of political factors obscures the pattern there. The illuminating study by Morris [1972] on the regional economic development of Argentina does not support Williamson's model. Morris found that the discrepancy between the developed Pampas and the poorer interior has not diminished. The Pampas region includes Buenos Aires Province, together with large parts of Santa Fe, Cordoba, Entre Rios and La Pampa. The city of Buenos Aires has become the country's major port, its administrative capital, and the centre of the manufacturing industry, which also extends along a corridor near the River Plate. The surrounding rural area is eminently suited to the production of wheat and beef, which provide the country's major exports. The drier climate, which places the interior at a disadvantage from the point of view of agriculture, appears to be offset by the presence of petroleum, copper and iron deposits and the potential for producing hydro-electricity, which are not available in the Pampas. Unfortunately for the economy of the interior, the oil is conducted by pipeline to the industrial zone of the Pampas, and the minerals will probably only be concentrated in the interior: their final manufacture will occur near Buenos Aires.

It is evident from this brief discussion that developing countries will often have to make a critical choice. They can either seek to maximise development of the most favourable regions, at the risk of creating regional imbalances in the economic structure, or they can restrict the rate of development to one which allows all regions to develop at the same pace. Renaud, writing about precisely this problem in Korea, summarised the problem as follows:

The problem is one of defining appropriate policies for depressed regions which will not reward failure, and others for congested areas which will not penalise success and affect economic growth negatively [Renaud 1972, p. 444].

4 Sectional Structure

The wealth ana means of production available in any state are unequally distributed amongst the people. When there is a serious imbalance in the distribution of wealth throughout any society and widespread poverty exists alongside the great wealth of a smaller number, there may be serious political consequences. For example, Malefakis [1970] is one of many authors who judges that one of the prime causes of the Spanish Civil War in 1936 was the failure of the Second Spanish Republic to produce an effective policy of agrarian reform. More recently, in 1974, riots and the first general strike in Ethiopia were caused by rapidly rising food prices, which affected the poor, the great majority of the population, whose depressed condition contrasts with the great wealth of the land-owning Ethiopian aristocracy. Some social geographers, notably Brunn and Wheeler [1971] and Morrill and Wohlenberg [1972], have tried to identify the distribution of poverty in the United States and to suggest policies which will redress this social disease. The causes of poverty in countries such as the United States and Australia are many and complex, and they are a proper subject for analysis by sociologists, economists, economic historians, social geographers and statisticians. It is suggested that the political geographer will be more usefully employed in examining those situations where an unbalanced sectional structure, with possible political consequences, results from the operation of one of two processes. The first process involves the accumulation of people with different origins in a single area, in such a way that the economic divisions within that society coincide with the ethnic differences. Such a situation occurred in East Africa, where Asians, mainly from the Indian subcontinent, controlled most of the region's retail trade; in Northern Ireland, where there is a marked contrast between the levels of rural prosperity of Protestants and Roman Catholics; and in South Africa and Rhodesia. The second process is an historical one, and results in *latifundio* land tenure systems, which concentrate the ownership of land in the hands of a minority, which accumulates great wealth at the expense of a much larger number of tenant farmers [Burke 1970]. Iraq, Bolivia and Spain are only three of the many states which have been beset by problems associated with this process during the present century. Plainly this second process can operate in a society with homogeneous ethnic characteristics. Governments faced with the problems consequent upon these processes will usually try to reduce the level of sectional imbalance in the state's economy, and their policies will often affect the economic and political geography of the state.

The policies adopted by governments of states where the economic and ethnic divisions of the population coincide, will clearly depend on which section of the population controls authority. Thus the policies adopted by the South African and Rhodesian governments, which are controlled by the affluent minority, stand in sharp contrast with the policies of Uganda and Nigeria, where the governments are drawn from the less affluent majority. The aim of the South African and Rhodesian governments is to eliminate the pronounced differences between the standards of living of white and black sections of the community by a gradual raising of the standards of the black population, although the two countries are pursuing different paths to this goal. In South Africa the Government follows a policy called separate development, which should result in the construction of eight independent black states and one independent white state. The policy of the Rhodesian Government is neither so clear nor so consistent. There are regulations which allow a considerable measure of economic integration and others which enforce strict residential separation. Because of the Rhodesian uncertainty, it seems better to concentrate on the example of South Africa.

The foundation of the South African policy of separate development was established in 1913 when Bantu tribal land was declared to be inalienable Bantu territory. A further act in 1936 provided for the expansion and consolidation of Bantu territory. Then, after the Second World War, a succession of acts prepared the way for the various Bantustan homelands to become independent states. There are a number of obvious problems associated with this policy. First there is the fact that most of the homelands consist of scattered parcels of territory of different sizes. Only the Basotho-Quaqua homeland, immediately north of Lesotho, consists of a single block of 114,355 acres. The Kwazulu homeland is the most divided, consisting of twenty-nine blocks of land. The South African Government is producing consolidation schemes for each of the divided homelands, which involve some exchange of territory between Whites and Blacks. The scheme proposed for the Bophuthatswana homeland illustrates this process. This homeland occupies nineteen blocks of land in the western Transvaal, northwestern Cape and the eastern Orange Free State which occupy a total of 3,800,943 hectares (9,385,045 acres). The single area in the Orange Free State is 240 kilometres (150 miles) away from the nearest other section of the homeland.

The preliminary proposals announced in March 1973 would reduce the number of areas to between three and six, as shown in figure 6.1. It is estimated that the various exchanges of land would entail the resettlement of about 120,000 Tzwana people [*Africa Research Bulletin* 1973, p.2857]. Even if the patches of territory could be reduced to three blocks, it would still be an awkward area to administer as a separate state, with two of the parts being enclaves in white South Africa.

The second problem is that none of the three homelands with a coastal location possesses a port. The administration of the Transkei has been demanding Port St Johns at the mouth of the Umzimbuvu River for several years, and there were reports in December 1973 that this small white enclave might be transferred to the Transkei, in accordance with a recommendation from the Department of Bantu Administration. The settlement is a popular holiday resort and a haven for retired persons, and it has a permanent white population of about five hundred. Over the years the port has silted up and investigations in the past suggest that it would be uneconomic to redevelop as a port. A much more important gesture would be the eventual transference of the growing port complex at Richards Bay to the Kwazulu homeland. If the homelands on the coast cannot obtain direct access to a port, they will have to depend on the goodwill of the white South African Government in conducting overseas trade, in the same manner as Swaziland and Lesotho.

The third problem is that there are serious doubts about the ability of the homeland territories to support the rising numbers of Africans. The African leaders in the homelands have no doubts on this matter: they judge the present areas to be too small and they have made strong demands for large additional areas. For example, the Bophuthatswans Legislative Assembly, in April 1973, demanded an additional area twice as big as their existing territory. The South African Government believes that the ability of the homelands to

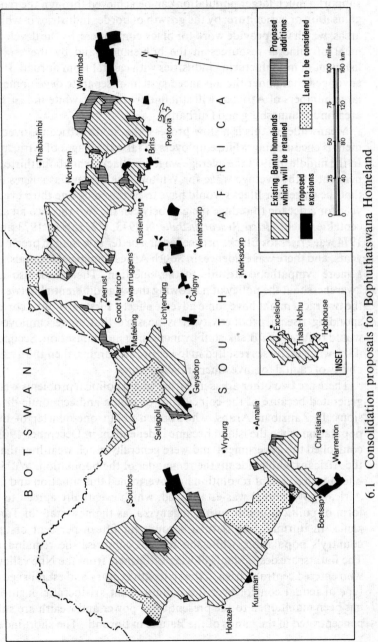

6.1 Consolidation proposals for Bophuthatswana Homeland

support a much larger population can be achieved through the reorganisation of agriculture; by the growth of border industries in white areas, which will provide work for black commuters; by the development of mineral resources in the homelands; and by the establishment of manufacturing industries with capital from abroad. It is envisaged that under the advanced system of separate development large numbers of Africans will still find work in the white industrial areas in Johannesburg and Durban.

Meanwhile, as this is a slow process, the South African Government is encouraging white employers to raise the wages of Africans. In the middle of 1973 the average wage for Blacks was about thirteen per cent of the average wage for Whites. One survey has suggested that the wages for Blacks would have to be raised by one third every year for a decade to reduce the gap between the two races to an acceptable level [*Africa Research Bulletin* 1973, p.2715]. In 1973 and 1974 wage rises for Blacks proceeded at a better rate than in previous years, and there was evidence, in South African financial journals, of a more sympathetic attitude to this question. There was also an awareness that the policy of narrowing the wage differential between the two races might have some adverse effects. First, without a corresponding rise in productivity it is possible that some employers would reduce their Black staff by increasing mechanisation. Second, if the wage increases resulted in lower profit margins, then the availability of capital for investment might decline.

There are two other areas in Africa where political problems were generated because of the coincidence of ethnic and economic divisions. In Zanzibar, Arabs, who formed about one-quarter of the population when the island became independent in December 1963, controlled the government and were generally much wealthier than the Africans who made up the remainder of the population. Within one month a violent revolution had overturned this situation and an African government was established, which eventually agreed to a form of political union with Tanganyika, as the new state of Tanzania. In Burundi, the Batutsi account for fifteen per cent of the country's population, while the Bahutu comprise the remainder. The Batutsi are descendants of warrior farmers from the Nile valley, who entered central Africa in the sixteenth century and established a type of feudal control over the Bahutu. That aristocratic position has been maintained to the present time; power and wealth are still concentrated in the hands of the Batutsi in Burundi. The short independent history of this state is replete with attempted revolutions and fearful massacres. The situation is made particularly unstable because Rwanda, Burundi's northern neighbour, is governed by Bahutu, who form ninety-five per cent of the population.

Countries where the government is drawn from the less affluent majority can adopt more direct policies to change the sectional structure of the state's economy. In many countries of Africa and southeast Asia aliens achieved a dominant position in the retail and financial sections of the economy during the colonial period. The alien groups include Chinese in Sabah and Sarawak; Indians and Pakistanis in Kenya and Uganda; Greeks and Armenians in Ethiopia; and Lebanese in Nigeria and some other west African states. Most of the governments of these states have recently started to pursue policies of 'indigenisation', an awkward word which refers to regulations designed to force the aliens to hand their economic activities to the indigenous population. In Uganda, during the last few months of 1972, General Amin expelled about 60,000 Asians, who held British passports, and nationalised several British commercial and agricultural firms. Less drastic action has been taken by other countries, which simply reserve certain activities for their own citizens, and therefore force aliens either to sell their businesses or to take in indigenous partners, who must play a dominant role. In 1973, the Kenyan, Nigerian and Senegalese governments adopted policies aimed at forcing this type of change. Regulations on licences for persons engaged in the tourist trade in Kenya will restrict this activity to Kenya citizens, while in Senegal only indigenes will be allowed to take part in the country's wholesale trade. In Nigeria a list of twenty-two businesses from which aliens will be barred was published, and the list included all forms of food production and distribution, retail industries, haulage contracting, advertising and publishing. These are all activities where aliens played a dominant role in management. In addition to identifying these attempts to alter the sectional structure of the state, it is important that political and economic geographers should assess the effects of these changes on the economic geography of the state, after an appropriate period.

The *latifundio* land tenure system is characterised by a dichotomy between a few wealthy land-owners, who control very large areas of the state's agricultural land, and the numerous poor tenant farmers and freehold farmers, who control only a small proportion of the agricultural land. This situation was revealed by the 1950 census in Ecuador. Eighty per cent of the smallest agricultural units occupied only one per cent of the state's territory, while six per cent of the largest estates constituted ninety-two per cent of the area. This census also revealed another common characteristic of this system: namely that the land on the small-holdings is much more intensively used than the land on the large estates. On the small farms which made up eighty per cent of productive units, forty-four per cent of the available area was cultivated; on the large estates which made up six per cent of the total, only 0.01 per cent was cultivated. In the countries of South America, the Middle East and Asia where this system still exists, or has existed, there are many variations in its origin and operation. The *zamindari* system of the Indian subcontinent resulted from the imposition of regulations by the British administration in 1793 [Ahmed and Timmons 1971]. These regulations fixed the revenue payable by the landlords in perpetuity. The rising value of production from their estates gave the landlords an increasing surplus after the payment of revenue, and they generally retired to the cities and sublet all or part of their estates to intermediaries. They, in their turn, became wealthy and by the middle of the twentieth century there were sometimes fifteen or twenty middle-men receiving rent between the tenant farmer and the land-owner. In Iraq the opportunity for a landed class to develop occurred in the late nineteenth century, when first the Turkish administrators, and then their British successors, registered tribal lands and fixed the holdings of each group. Previously the amount of land used by any tribe was in direct proportion to its strength. Tribes could no longer expand at the expense of their neighbours when differential growth of population created land shortages: they had to make the best of the land they possessed. Holdings became fragmented and some men were able, either by virtue of inherited wealth or by superior business acumen, to acquire large estates.

The *latifundio* system is generally considered to be bad from the point of view of social justice and economic productivity, and not surprisingly it has been cast in the role of the chief obstacle to a better way of life for the citizens of any state where it flourishes, by reformers of different political persuasions [Fernea 1969, p.358]. Too often it has been easily assumed that the redistribution of land to landless peasants would solve serious economic, social and political questions, not only by providing these people with economic incentives, but also by breaking any political power of the land-owners. In fact, the clear message of all detailed studies of this question, by authors such as Warriner [1969], Burke [1970], Fernea [1969] and Blankstein and Zuvekas [1973], is that land redistribution must be accompanied by comprehensive and continuing agrarian reforms associated with the investment of capital and technology, if they are to be successful.

Warriner and Fernea make the very important point for geographers that the programmes designed to cope with *latifundio* systems will vary with the particular circumstances of the state involved:

> The only sound basis on which it is possible to determine the principles which should guide land reform policy in conditions so diverse is to ascertain what scale and form or organisation can be shown to have increased productivity *in the conditions of the country concerned.* [Warriner 1969, p.41]

It is clearly important that political geographers should be prepared to examine the policies of governments which wish to reduce the sectional inequalities caused by *latifundio* land tenure systems, in order to establish the extent to which they achieve their aim, and the effects they have on the rural landscape and the national economy.

5 The Comparative Economic Structure of States

Because states have different resources and have experienced distinct processes of economic and political development, they each possess an economy with a unique combination of industrial, regional and sectional structures. Since no state is economically self-contained they must all engage in relations with other countries to overcome the deficiencies in their resource base, and to benefit from the commercial advantages created by their unique economic circumstances. These international transactions between states, which involve both co-operation and conflict are a proper matter for consideration by political geographers, who will focus most attention on economic alliances, bilateral and multilateral trade treaties, commodity agreements and foreign aid arrangements.

Since the Second World War various groups of states have tried to forge economic alliances in order to make themselves more prosperous. Some of these alliances have aimed at complete economic integration, seeking the benefits of operations at a larger scale; others have more limited targets, such as the provision of access to the sea for a landlocked state. The most important grouping is the European Economic Community, consisting of France, West Germany, the Netherlands, Belgium, Luxembourg, Italy, the United Kingdom, Ireland and Denmark. In population, production and trade the European Economic Community forms a powerful economic unit, which ranks with the United States and the Soviet Union (see pp. 222–6). Here it seems worthwhile to consider a smaller grouping as an example of economic alliances. The East African Community consists of Kenya, Tanzania and Uganda, and the present organisation was formally created in June 1967. However, the origins of this economic alliance can be traced to the beginning of the century, when Britain governed the colonies of Kenya and Uganda and Germany controlled Tanganyika. The completion of the railway linking Mombasa and the lake port of Kisumu provided an important stimulus for close economic relations between the three states, which were further cemented by the creation of Postal and Customs Unions in 1917. In 1920 Britain acquired control over Tanganyika, and the three British Governors of the adjacent territories formed the Governors' Conference, which met periodically to discuss matters of joint interest and to co-ordinate economic policies. In 1926 a permanent Secretariat was established in Nairobi, which was deliberately developed as the unofficial capital of British East Africa. The secretariat was responsible for administering common services connected with railways, customs, posts, research and commercial law. The High Commission of East Africa was created after the Second World War to provide a constitutional framework within which the integrated services could be administered. All these arrangements could be concluded easily under the uniform British administration, but the ending of colonial rule marked the beginning of economic discords as the various leaders pressed narrower national viewpoints. However, these differences were overcome and the Treaty for East African Co-operation was agreed and signed in June 1967. The intention of the organisation is typical of all economic alliances:

> The primary aim of the Community is to strengthen and regulate the industrial, commercial and other relations of the partner states to the end that there shall be accelerated, harmonious and

balanced development and sustained expansion of economic activities, the benefits whereof shall be equitably shared. [Maina 1974]

After seven years of operation, the Community has made only slight progress towards that aim. Indeed the co-operation established during the colonial period has been reduced. There is no longer a common East African currency; income tax is no longer collected on a common basis; and national universities have been substituted for the associated university colleges in the state capitals.

The basic problem facing the Community is that the three members are not economic equals, and derive unequal advantages from membership. Kenya has a much stronger economy than the other two states, and has apparently grown stronger during the life of the Community. Kenya's favourable trade balance with the other two states has increased, and Kenya has attracted more industrial development than either Uganda or Tanzania. These poorer countries are naturally suspicious of Kenya's increasing economic dominance, and have tried to establish Community policies which will offset Kenya's advantages and redistribute revenue and manufacturing activity in Uganda and Tanzania. This has resulted in voices being raised in Kenya against the Community acting as a brake on Kenya's growth. Kenya provides fifty-five per cent of the Community's budget and, while the East African Development Bank receives an equal contribution from the three members, it is only allowed to invest twenty-two per cent of its funds in Kenya. In addition the comparatively low salaries paid by the Community discourage Kenyans from seeking employment in Community services, which means that they are increasingly being dominated by Ugandans and Tanzanians. This problem of regional disparity bedevils many attempts to form economic unions. It is unquestionably one of the most serious problems facing the European Economic Community, where the relatively depressed areas of southern Italy, Northern Ireland and Eire contrast with the more uniformly prosperous areas of France, West Germany and the Netherlands. So long as the present suspicions remain, it is unlikely that the East African Community will succeed in achieving its primary aim, and it is also unlikely that additional states will be admitted to the Community. Zambia, Burundi, Ethiopia and Somalia lodged applications to join the Community in 1968, but internal difficulties within the Community, including border fighting between Tanzania and Uganda and political problems in Somalia, Ethiopia and Burundi, have prevented the negotiations reaching any conclusion.

Pounds [1972, p.335] correctly noted that economic alliances usually develop slowly, so that the barriers to circulation are lowered at a rate which will allow units of production, such as factories and farms, to adjust to the new circumstances. This gradual development affords an admirable opportunity for geographers to identify and measure the changes which result.

States conclude trade agreements with each other in an effort to create stable conditions which allow forward planning on a reliable basis. The exporting country seeks a guaranteed market and the importing country a guaranteed supply. The trade agreements may refer to specific mechanisms of commerce. Tariffs are one means by which states try to regulate trade and stimulate domestic industry. More than fifty years ago, Culbertson [1924] wrote a classical analysis of tariff policies, in which he distinguished three categories of commodities. The first includes those items on which the state is wholly dependent on foreign supplies. It follows that the consumers in the state who use such items will wish to obtain them as cheaply as possible. Accordingly it can be expected that the government will not impose tariffs unless it wishes to raise revenue, or seeks to reduce consumption of the commodity to improve the balance of visible trade or, if the import is a mineral, it desires to encourage exploration within the state for domestic supplies. The second category consists of items where the state produces enough to satisfy its own needs and where it has a surplus for export. This situation does not allow a firm prediction about tariff policies. If domestic production is cheaper than the production of imported items no tariff protection will be necessary; but if the imports have a price advantage then some level of tariff may be imposed. The third category includes products where the state's domestic output must be supplemented by imports. This again creates a complex situation where differing policies may be appropriate. If domestic production can be increased, then the government may decide to impose a tariff to encourage this expansion. If production cannot be rapidly expanded, then the government must balance the interests of the domestic producers and consumers. Culbertson's analysis led him to the following important conclusion: '. . . import tariffs are not determined according to some general theory of free trade or protection, but by the conditions of each particular case in accordance with the national need' [Culbertson 1924, p.21]. This statement reinforces the point made earlier in this chapter that the individual nature of the structure of states' economies makes them appropriate for geographical analysis.

Export tariffs may also be imposed by states to collect revenue, as in India, in respect of tea and jute, and in Chile, in respect of sodium nitrate [Towle 1956]. Export tariffs may also be designed to promote the processing of a particular raw material in the country of origin.

In their negotiations with other countries, states will usually seek to ensure that no other state is treated more favourably. This concept of the most-favoured-nation status does not apply to very low tariffs, which often operate in respect of persons living in the borderland of two states, or to the tariffs levied between two states that enjoy special relationships, such as a metropolitan power and a colony.

States also seek to regulate commerce by imposing quotas on the volume or value of goods which may be imported in any period. These quotas may be constructed to protect domestic production, as in the case of restrictions on the import of Australian meat into the United States, or to share the opportunities for trade among a number of small developing countries.

Increasingly the developed countries, particularly Japan, are seeking long-term contracts for the supply of raw materials, so that future uncertainties may be avoided. The producing countries see the advantage of such agreements in times of stable or falling prices, but they are less attracted in times of rising prices, or rapid inflation, and these conditions began to operate together in 1972. In the period 1972–4, the rising level of world demand for various raw materials coincided with shortfalls in production, due to drought in the case of agricultural items and to political instability in the case of copper. This period was also marked by lower than average world stocks of several raw materials and the instability of some major currencies. All these factors, operating in a complex fashion, combined to force up the prices for many commodities, making the developed countries more enthusiastic about long-term contracts than the developing countries. However, the present situation may well prove to be unstable. Increased levels of primary production and a reduced level of demand from the developed countries could force prices to drop sharply, and then the developing countries would be seeking long-term contracts.

It is often assumed that the basic pattern of world trade consists of

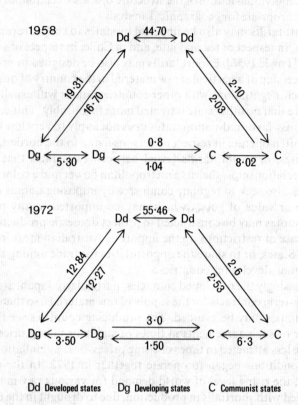

1958

Dd $\xleftarrow{\quad 44\cdot70 \quad}$ Dd

19.31   16.70

2·10   2·03

Dg $\xleftarrow{\quad}$ Dg $\xleftarrow{\quad 0\cdot8 \quad}$ C $\xleftarrow{\quad}$ C
     5·30   1·04   8·02

1972

Dd $\xleftarrow{\quad 55\cdot46 \quad}$ Dd

12.84   12.27

2·6   2·53

Dg $\xleftarrow{\quad}$ Dg $\xleftarrow{\quad 3\cdot0 \quad}$ C $\xleftarrow{\quad}$ C
     3·50   1·50   6·3

Dd Developed states   **Dg** Developing states   **C** Communist states

6.2   Proportions of world trade conducted between and within the world's major trading groups (after Pounds)

the developing countries supplying raw materials to the developed countries in return for manufactured products. Pounds [1972, pp. 304–5] showed the falsity of this picture, and figure 6.2 shows the generalised pattern of trade among three major groups of states: the developed states consisting of Canada, the United States, the countries of Western Europe together with Turkey and Yugoslavia, Australia, New Zealand, Japan and South Africa; the communist states; and developing countries. The diagrams, representing the situation in 1958 and 1972, reveal the following important points. The volume of trade between the developed countries exceeds the total of all other trade, and this sector of the world's trade is tending to contribute a larger proportion. Trade between the developed and developing groups of states accounts for the second largest proportion of world trade, but this percentage showed a relative decline in the period 1958–71. Although the developing group of states is the most numerous, trade among its members is lower than trade within the other two groups, and it is tending to decline in relative importance. Because the figures in any one year may be exceptional it would be unwise to be dogmatic about their interpretation; for example, increased petroleum prices will tilt the trade figures in favour of the developing countries in 1974. However, it seems fair to note that the opportunities for trade within the developing group are restricted, because nearly all rely on the export of primary products, and some compete with each other. If trade is to be a major means of redistributing the world's wealth, then the trade connections between the developing and developed countries will be the most important avenue.

The third means by which states conduct their international commercial transactions is through commodity agreements. Once again the purpose of these agreements is to avoid the severe fluctuations in price of raw materials, which can cause economic dislocation for states which supply and consume them. According to Hudson, three types of commodity agreements may be concluded between producing and consuming countries.

Out of more than thirty years' study of commodity problems and the subsequent application of international commodity agreements, three distinct types of agreements have emerged. These are the 'export quota' type adopted as the basis of the Sugar Agreement, the 'buffer stock' type used in the Tin Agreement, and the 'multilateral contract' type which is employed in the Wheat Agreement. [Hudson 1961, p.510]

The Sugar Agreement of 1958 specified the basic export levels of each exporting member, defined how the alteration of quotas could occur, and stipulated the amounts of sugar that importing countries were allowed to produce or import from states not party to the Agreement. This Agreement lapsed in 1973 when there was a marked difference between the price demanded, by countries such as Australia and Cuba, and offered, by countries such as Canada and Japan. However, 1973 did witness the reconstruction of the International Cocoa Agreement, which fixed a floor and ceiling price for that commodity. This represents a buffer stock arrangement. When the cocoa price falls below the floor price the international commission will buy cocoa, and it will sell when the price exceeds the ceiling price. The Cocoa Agreement also set quotas for the nine major cocoa producers. Multilateral contracts fix a price range for the particular commodity, but in this case the exporting countries guarantee to supply a fixed proportion of the item below the maximum price and the importing states guarantee to purchase a fixed proportion above the minimum price. Courtenay [1961], Ojala [1967] and Gwyer [1972] have written very interesting studies on international commodity agreements.

In 1973 a new form of commodity agreement emerged, and this was one which involved only the producing countries. The twelve members of the Organisation of Petroleum Exporting Countries agreed to double the price of crude petroleum, and at the same time the Arab members of the Organisation decided to reduce the output from their wells, in an effort to induce developed countries to adopt a pro-Arab attitude towards the Palestinian question. The unilateral raising of prices succeeded in this case for two reasons. First, the production for export is concentrated in the hands of a few countries; and second, the commodity is vital to the economies of the developed countries, which possess no immediate substitutes for petroleum. It is likely that as soon as the dangers for the developed countries were perceived, policies were put in train which would reduce this level of dependence on foreign fuel supplies. Measures have been introduced to conserve supplies, to search for new oil fields, and to develop alternative supplies of fuel, which become economically feasible through the increased price of petroleum. It seems probable that in the foreseeable future the ability of the oil exporting states to dictate price levels will be eroded. Warman [1972] and Odell [1973] present contrasting pictures of the future supplies of crude petroleum, with the latter author reaching more optimistic conclusions.

When the dimensions of the oil shortage were first recognised, it was not generally realised that the developing states would be among the hardest hit. While they do not use such large amounts of petroleum as the developed states, the increased cost of imports affects them much more severely. The developing countries are also likely to find that the oil shortages will cause corresponding shortages in oil-based fertilisers produced by the developed countries, and such supplies as are available will be more costly. Finally, if the oil shortages cause even a mild economic recession among the developed states, this will result in reduced imports of the raw materials on which the economies of many developing countries rely.

Foreign aid represents the final form of international commercial transaction. This aid is generally given to the developing states by the developed states of the communist and non-communist groups. It is very hard to measure the exact volume of aid provided by any country, because some of it is provided in material, technology and training facilities in the donor country. There have not been many studies by geographers of this subject, and those by Black [1963], Scheel [1963] and Symons [1967] are the most important. Aid is probably given for a variety of reasons, which include the desire to avoid criticism, the hope that political influence will be increased, the expectation that trade agreements may follow, and the wish to alleviate human suffering after the occurrence of some natural disaster. It will always be easier to identify the geographical consequences of aid programmes than to determine the motive of the donor state. The construction of the Aswan High Dam in Egypt, with Soviet aid, and of the railway from Dar es Salaam to the Zambian Copper Belt with Chinese aid, are examples of developments which will have important consequences for the landscapes of the regions involved.

Conclusion

There are four reasons why political geographers study the structure of a state's economy. First, the strength of that economic structure makes an obvious contribution to the power of the state. Even though it is not possible to measure that contribution exactly, marked differences in economic strength provide rough guides to differences in state power.

Second, most national governments are now deeply involved in the economic life of the state; laissez faire economic policies are now a subject for historians. Although the geography of a state will not determine the economic policies of the government, it is likely to impose limitations on the choices available. The relationship between geography and the formation of economic policy is an important part of political geography.

Third, geographers must also be aware that the application of economic policies may produce changes in the regional, industrial and sectional structure of the state's economy, and may produce important alterations in the landscape.

Finally, the economic relations between states are among the most important and numerous of international relations, and they offer many opportunities for co-operation and conflict. The geographer is interested in such relations because they will be conditioned by the economic structure of the states concerned, and by such other factors as proximity and access to ocean routes.

7 The Territorial Structure of the State's Administration

> The form and structure of local government throughout the world today are the products of a history that covers many centuries . . . while there are many variations, there are no accidents; each and every beam or column has a meaning of its own . . . they tell about how things once were, or about what people thought should be, or perhaps what might be in the future if all went well.
>
> [Alderfer 1964, p. 17]

> Many scholars have tended to overlook the importance and significance of internal administrative changes in the development of nations.
>
> [McColl 1963]

With the exception of some tiny states, such as Andorra and the Vatican, governments delegate certain powers to subordinate authorities, which exercise them in a defined area of the state's territory. The counties of the United States, the county boroughs of England, the *départements* of France, the *amter* of Denmark and the *ken* of Japan provide examples of these local authorities. These bodies are all responsible for a variety of subjects, which include the repair of roads, the collection of refuse and the supervision of building standards. Frequently governments will also create subordinate boards responsible for a single activity, such as the provision of household electricity. In each case the government makes these arrangements to provide efficient administration and to promote the development of the state.

Political geographers have a threefold interest in the territorial structure of the state's administration. First, the territorial patterns of power form part of the state's political landscape, and therefore political geographers are obliged to describe them. The variety, number and location of the internal administrative units are among the basic facts which must be provided in any account of the political geography of a country. The territorial divisions of power can be very complex, and it is always easier to explain them when they exist, than in periods long after they have been replaced. The second interest is based on the fact that the territorial division of administrative power may have important geographical consequences. The policies of local governments may influence the location of factories and the rate at which rural land is subdivided for residential purposes. In many ways the differential exercise of local power may be a more relevant factor in determining the development of a particular area than factors of slope, soil and accessibility. Local government in certain circumstances may be an important element in the growth of regional consciousness among the population. Finally, friction between adjacent local authorities, or authorities at different levels may create boundary disputes. The third interest arises because political geographers can make a contribution when changes in the territorial structure of the state appear to be necessary. Fawcett was convinced that if changes had to be made in the administrative structure, then 'the way to achieve them was to create provinces which were meaningful geographically' [Fawcett 1961, p. 13].

Pounds [1972, p. 208] describes a dual approach to the study of administrative areas.

> The study of politically organised areas can be approached from at least two points of view. The first and more geographical is that of the shape and size of these administrative units and the ways in which those of the lower levels of responsibility nest within the boundaries of those higher in the scale. The second is the division of responsibility between the several levels of local government and the State itself.

In his study Pounds proceeds to place much greater emphasis on the first approach, which really corresponds to the first interest noted above, namely the concern with description. This is an important activity, but one of its chief values is that it lays the groundwork for analysis. The political geographer's analysis should concentrate on four aspects. First, the origin of the administrative boundaries must be established and their subsequent changes must be recorded and explained as far as possible. Second, the variety of administrative boundaries should be examined so that their degree of correspondence with each other, and with patterns of physical geography, economic activity and human settlement, can be measured. Third, the impact of the local administrations on the development of the landscape must be assessed. And finally, the emergence of problems and disputes associated with the local authorities should be monitored.

Fesler [1949] has correctly stressed that there are two main types of subordinate administrative areas. Governmental areas are those which have a measure of functional and fiscal autonomy and which serve many purposes, such as the municipal councils of England. Field service areas, in contrast, are constructed to serve the purpose of a single government department or service agency, such as the gas board or the electoral office. The following account is based on this prime division, together with a final section which examines a current trend towards regional planning and regional government.

1 Governmental Areas

The states within a federation are the most important governmental areas, and they generally have a number of characteristics which distinguish them from all others. In federations there is a division of powers between the central and regional authorities, so that each has exclusive responsibility for separate administrative matters. The agreement of the regional authority is necessary to vary that division. In the case of other governmental areas the central authority always has overriding authority, which allows it to subtract certain matters from the competence of local administrations. The component states of federations have usually either had a separate political existence before federation, as in the case of the Australian colonies, or they were formed when the territory was added to the federation, as in the case of the United States and Canada. Federal boundaries have a greater similarity with international boundaries than with other internal boundaries. They are usually agreed between two administrations; they are carefully defined in schedules, and often demarcated; and they are usually very hard to alter. For example, in the United States, apart from the creation of Washington D.C., only two states have yielded territory to new jurisdictions: part of Massachusetts was transferred to Maine, and Virginia was divided to create the two states of Virginia and West Virginia. In Canada the areas of states could not be diminished once they had been established, and Nicholson [1954] has shown that the underlying principle in creating new units was to produce new states or provinces with approximately equal areas. This attitude explained the extensions of Alberta and Saskatchewan in 1905, and the additions to Manitoba, Ontario and Quebec in 1912.

The federal boundaries of Australia evolved between 1826 and 1862 as the boundaries of separate British colonies, and they were drawn in a fairly arbitrary fashion to enclose coastal concentrations of settlement at Perth, Sydney, Brisbane, Melbourne and Adelaide. The Australian constitution makes provision for the alteration of these boundaries, but the agreement of the state that will lose territory must always be obtained, and no alterations have been made. By contrast with the cases just described, the federal boundaries of the Soviet Union have been changed frequently to conform with significant changes in population and industrial development [Shabad 1956].

It should not be thought, however, that there are never major territorial changes within federations. The Indian Government has created several new states in order to satisfy demands for local autonomy. The hill areas of Assam, in the cul de sac north of Bangladesh, have proved to be troublesome regions for the central government [Schweinfurth 1968]. Riots and rebellion by Naga and Mizo tribes created security problems in a zone which was too close to the Chinese border for comfort. The area of Nagaland was the first to win a measure of autonomy, and then in January 1972 the Indian Government created three new states within the federation – Meghalaya, Manipur and Tripura – and two new Union Territories – Mizoram, in the extreme south of the cul de sac, and Arunachal Pradesh, in the north along the Chinese border. Federations may also split up into separate states, as Malaysia did when Singapore seceded in 1965, or simply be transformed into a unitary state. This last situation occurred in November 1962 when the Ethiopian Government dissolved the federal status of Eritrea, which had existed since September 1952, and made it part of the unitary state. The Eritrean liberation movement began the following year and has persisted ever since. Nicholson [1968] has written a very interesting account of the problems associated with the further partition of Canada's Northwest Territories. He notes that while trappers, hunters and fishermen, who lead a nomadic existence, prefer boundaries which coincide with linear features of the physical landscape, miners and foresters prefer straight lines which enable them to know in which jurisdiction they lie when they plot their position precisely by accurate survey methods.

Consideration of the study of boundary correspondence will be left to the section dealing with the governmental boundaries of unitary states.

Ullman, Rose and Logan have examined the influence of federal boundaries on the development of the landscape in the United States and Australia. Ullman [1939] examined the eastern Rhode Island –Massachusetts boundary and discovered that it did influence the establishment of factories south of the Fall River. The industries were located in Rhode Island to gain tax concessions, but the tenements for workers were located in Massachusetts so that they could continue to enjoy the superior social and cultural amenities offered by that state. Rose [1955] studied the coastal section of the boundary between New South Wales and Queensland, and encountered some landscape differences which had arisen since the boundary had been delimited and which could not be explained by environmental differences. In one area there was intensive orchard development on the Tableland in Queensland, whereas in the adjoining area of New South Wales ranching remained the staple industry. Apparently the orchards developed because the Queensland Government had a deliberate policy of closer settlement for soldiers returning from the First World War. The fruit industry was further encouraged by the provision of efficient marketing and transport facilities.

Before 1901 Victoria and South Australia were individual colonies and the boundary between them was similar in many respects to an international boundary. However, Logan [1968] found that policies enacted on either side of the boundary had little effect upon the border landscape or the circulation of people and goods. This was explained by the fact that the two colonies had similar origins and administrations, and similar patterns of production and deficiencies. The Victorian Government's policy of protection for domestic industries was much less significant along this border than it was along the border with New South Wales. People moved freely across the boundary; during the Victorian gold rushes in the mid-nineteenth century, many people came from South Australia; and the Victorian Wimmera, a wheat growing area in the northwest, was partly settled by farmers from South Australia. During the economic depressions in Victoria at the end of the nineteenth century many citizens of Melbourne migrated westwards into regions which included rural South

Australia. After 1901 when the Australian federation was formed, there was theoretically less scope for differential policies to influence the landscape, but some changes did occur. Owing to an original surveying error, Victoria gained a narrow strip of territory which should have been located in South Australia. In order to justify their case for retaining the zone, in the face of South Australian protests, the Victorian Government used some of the land for soldier settlement after the First World War, and this landscape contrasts with the pastoral areas and forest reserves in South Australia. Part of the boundary is marked by the abrupt transition from the softwood plantations of South Australia, planted to reduce the state's shortage of timber, to the eucalyptus woodlands of Victoria.

The disputes, with a geographical basis, which arise between states in a federation, and between the regional and central authorities of a federation, are generally of a more serious and enduring nature than equivalent disputes in a unitary state. These disputes involve questions connected with the location of boundaries and economic policies. For example, the boundaries of Texas have provided several interesting disputes which have been studied mainly by historians. Bowman [1923], Carpenter [1925] and Billington [1959] have examined the boundary dispute between Oklahoma and Texas, along the Red River. This dispute arose because the northern boundary of Texas was defined as the south bank of the river, while the southern boundary of Oklahoma was put along the middle of the main channel. In any case Oklahoma had no rights over the bed of the river, because it was not navigable when Oklahoma was admitted to the Union: these rights belong to the federal government. For a time the non-coincidence of the boundaries was only an academic matter, but this situation altered when oil was discovered on the south bank of the river. Immediately there was a flood of prospectors, and licences were granted by Texas, Oklahoma and the federal government. The dispute was further complicated by recent accretionary changes in the course of the Red River, and the presence of an Indian Reservation in the Oklahoma border.

Before the Nigerian Civil War, which lasted from 1967–70, the states of the federation – called regions – had engaged in a number of boundary disputes, which arose because the federal boundaries divided some tribes. The boundaries had been drawn by British officers during the colonial period, and since they had not interfered with the circulation of people and goods, and since almost identical policies were applied on both sides of the boundary, they did not cause any significant problems. With the approach of independence tribal loyalties were transferred to political parties, and these parties began to demand boundary revision, so that tribes could be re-united within a single state. The most serious problems occurred along the boundary between Western and Northern Regions, near Ilorin, and between Eastern and Western Regions, where the Niger formed the boundary. The boundary south of Ilorin divided two sections of the Yoruba tribe, itself a confederation. When British officers drew this boundary in 1894, they had in fact marked a ceasefire line between two warring Yoruba factions. Ilorin marked the southernmost advance of the Moslem invasion from Sokoto and Gando, and the surrounding district was organised in the same manner as the northern emirates.

The river Niger was selected as the boundary because it seemed an obvious dividing line in 1939, when it was decided to separate the Eastern and Western Regions because of the different administrative problems they presented in connection with the collection of taxes. The well-organised tribal structure of the Yoruba confederation and the Benin kingdom simplified the collection of taxes, which was difficult among the Ibo and Ijaw tribes because they had no political structures above the family or clan level. The use of the Niger River placed Ibo on the west bank of the river in Western Region, and the incorporation of this area in Eastern Region was sought by the political party which represented Ibos [Prescott 1959]. Because of sharp disagreements about what should be done, no alterations were made in the boundary locations, and since the Civil War the central authority has assumed overriding powers, and the states which now make up Nigeria are more like the major administrative divisions of unitary states.

In Australia disputes over boundaries between states are now a matter of history [Prescott 1968, pp. 106; 176–7], and problems of relations between the state and central governments are more important. One dispute concerns sovereignty over the continental shelf between the low-water mark and the outer limit of territorial waters. This issue has become crucial for states such as Victoria and Western Australia, in view of the petroleum and natural gas fields discovered in Bass Strait and the northwest shelf respectively. O'Connell [1968; 1970] has published detailed accounts of the issues involved in this dispute. There have been similar problems in the federations of

Canada, West Germany, Malaysia and the United States of America. For example, in 1969, the Government of Canada established certain 'mineral resource administration lines' over the continental shelves, and allocated the areas landward of them to the coastal provinces, which control mining operations and acquire all the resulting revenue. Beyond these lines the Canadian Government administers the continental shelf, and it has undertaken to allot half of the resulting revenue to a common fund, which will be available for all the provinces.

The Queensland Government has recently had two disputes with the Australian Government. First, the Queensland Government objected to federal policies connected with coal exports. New open-cut coal mines in Queensland give the companies involved a price advantage over the older shaft mines of New South Wales. The Australian Labor Government, elected in 1972, is anxious that importers should take a proportion of the more expensive New South Wales coal, and this would naturally reduce the opportunities for coal exports from Queensland. Second, the federal government wishes to redraw the boundary between Australia and Papua New Guinea, so that the islands in Torres Strait, which are very close to the Papuan coast, are ceded to the new country. Queensland was allowed to acquire these islands in 1884, for security and commercial reasons, by the British Government which had no desire to declare a protectorate over the Papuan coast. However, almost immediately the British Government changed its mind and annexed Papua to forestall German occupation of the eastern half of New Guinea. Proposals to shift the boundary south into Torres Strait failed to be passed by the Queensland Parliament before the Australian federation was formed, and the issue became a matter for the federal government. Nothing was done and the matter lapsed until the late 1960s, when independence for Papua New Guinea began to be discussed. Now the government of the new state wants the boundary shifted south, and the Labor Government of Australia agrees that this should be done. Unfortunately for the Australian Government it seems to be hamstrung by the constitution, because the alteration of a state's boundaries requires the approval of the state concerned and the Queensland Parliament has indicated that this approval will not be forthcoming.

It is now necessary to turn to the other governmental areas which will be found within unitary states and within the component states of a federation. These governmental areas usually form a hierarchy, and during the progression from larger to smaller areas there is a

TABLE VIII

FRENCH GOVERNMENTAL AREAS IN 1968

Name	Number	Average area (sq km)
Département	95	5804.7
Arrondissement	322	1712.5
Canton	3209	171.9
Commune	37,708	14.5

SOURCE: *The Statesman's Year-Book 1973–4*, Macmillan, London.

diminution in the range of responsibilities and powers. Pounds [1972, pp. 208–17] describes the hierarchy of local government areas in the United States, England and Wales, France and West Germany. For example, France possesses five levels of local administration, and some of their characteristics are shown in table VIII.

It is common to find considerable variation in the area and population of units at the same level: for example in France, in 1968, there were 33,305 communes with populations smaller than 1500 and 334 with populations in excess of 20,000. Sharpe [1971, p. 152] records that the largest county borough in England had a population of 1,074,900 in 1969, compared with the smallest, which had a population of 32,790.

Tracing the origin of governmental areas can require extensive historical research in countries where there is a long period of indigenous government, such as Japan and France. Yonekura [1956] traced the evolution of the forty-six *ken* of modern Japan. He noted that they bear a close relationship with the sixty-eight *kuni* of the seventh century. These were administrative divisions with populations varying from 50,000–100,000, which were bounded by physical features such as rivers and watersheds. The *kuni* boundaries survived the establishment of feudal provinces, which existed from the eighth to the mid-eighteenth centuries, within boundaries which were superimposed upon the *kuni* pattern. Yonekura's general conclusion that the politico-administrative divisions of a country may form a 'regional provincial system' or a 'departmental system' having their origins in the feudal Middle Ages and ancient civilisations respectively, needs further substantiation by examples from states other than Japan. Lipman [1949] provides an interesting account of the way in which the division of France into *départements* was accomplished. The Commission of 1789 was influenced by four main considerations. First, there was the egalitarian spirit of the day which demanded equality in area. Second, there were d'Argenson's views that the divisions should be as large as possible to secure efficiency without endangering the authority of the state. Third, there was the scheme of Condorcet that each division should not exceed a maximum radius, which was determined by ease of transport and community of culture, customs and habit. And fourth, there was a map prepared by Robert de Hesseln that divided France into eighty-one areas measuring eighteen league square. The report of Thouret to the Assembly explained how the final decision to create eighty *départements* was implemented: the basic geometric pattern was distorted to take account of the cultural and physical features of the landscape, including the existence of former historical boundaries. Fenelon [1956] explores the correspondence between the boundaries established and the former diocesan and county limits and linear features of the physical landscape.

In tracing the origins of governmental areas political geographers will find it useful to reconstruct the human and social geography of the area concerned, because, as Alderfer's quotation at the head of this chapter indicates, the explanation of present administrative arrangements will often be found in geographical patterns which have ceased to exist. Because the political, geographical, economic and social characteristics of a state change, it is often found necessary to alter the administrative structure in one of two ways. In the first case all that is necessary is the definition of new boundaries; in the second case a complete reorganisation of the administrative hierarchy is essential.

There are several reasons why states may decide to redraw the boundaries of governmental areas. The prime reason concerns changes in the distribution of population. There has traditionally been a division into large urban areas and other parts of the state, reflected in the rural and urban districts of England and Wales. During the twentieth century, and especially since the Second World War, there has been a marked growth in towns and cities, which have generally spilled beyond their original boundaries. This has created serious administrative problems connected with the provision of services. The urban growth has been matched by rural decline in some areas, which has severely reduced their ratable revenue and made it difficult for them to carry out all their responsibilities. The use of motor cars and fast trains for commuters enables many people to live in semi-rural settings and work in the cities, and some administrators agree with Sharpe [1971, p. 154] that 'there is ceasing to be town and country in the socio-economic sense'. This development makes a rural–urban division unnecessary and perhaps unsuitable.

Changes in the boundaries of governmental areas may be desired in order to reduce the threat provided by a rising level of regional consciousness. In Zambia, Zaïre and Uganda, regions where secessionist movements have arisen have been subdivided, and evocative names such as Katanga, Barotseland and Buganda have been replaced. Figure 7.1 shows the subdivision of Buganda into four parts after the unsuccessful attempt of the population to secede from Uganda in 1966. One of the reasons for the dissatisfaction of Buganda with the central government was the detachment of Buyaga and Bugangadzi counties from Buganda, and their inclusion in Bunyoro in 1964. Some governments, instead of trying to crush the threat posed by a rising level of regional consciousness by subdividing the area, may seek to satisfy the regional demands by granting a measure of local autonomy. Reference has already been made to the use of this tactic by the Indian Government in Assam's hill districts; successive Iraqi governments have offered various forms of limited autonomy to Kurds living along the border with Iran. Helin [1967] in his admirable account of the changing administrative map of Rumania notes that the seven regions, constructed by the National-Peasant Government in 1928–30, were intended to give expression to the different cultures and aspirations of people in different parts of the state.

Administrative areas may also be altered during periods of conquest and development. As Northern Nigeria was acquired by British authorities, new provinces were created to assign areas of responsibility in which the authorities would contact and pacify the indigenous population. This process resulted in the multiplication of provinces until the entire area was covered. Rather later, the need for economies in administrative costs resulted in several boundary changes and amalgamations, and other changes were made in order to make the work of administering areas easier for

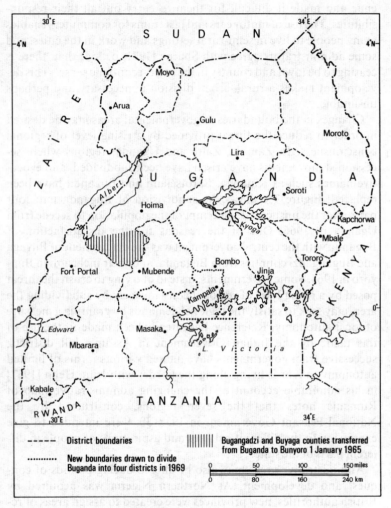

7.1 Boundary changes in Buganda

the officers concerned. The important point to recognise is that some of the provincial boundaries, drawn in haste during the programme of pacification, still survive today as the boundaries of states within the Nigerian Federation [Prescott 1968, pp. 158–71]. As figure 7.2 shows, the economic development of French Guiana made the original division of the territory into a coastal and interior zone unsatisfactory, and new administrative areas were laid out during the late 1960s.

Changes in the administrative structure of governmental areas will occur less frequently than alterations in the boundaries of such areas, because structural changes require an admission that the existing system is unsatisfactory, and because administrative authorities have a vested interest in preserving the old system. According to Despicht [1971, p. 65], such changes will only occur when the central authorities have no easier alternative.

> I am too old a bureaucrat to believe that the existence of unavoidable problems is in itself sufficient to inspire public authorities to take positive action. Disaster is usually an essential addition. And so I would suggest to you that, traditionally, it has not been 'regional problems' that have occupied the attention of public authorities but rather 'problem-regions', i.e. those areas in which purely regional problems have generated poverty, injustice, or squalor on a scale that cannot be ignored with impunity.

In England and Wales the drive to change the structure of governmental areas stemmed from the need for larger units so that they could deal efficiently and economically with the expanded range of functions that had been given to local authorities since their establishment, and so that the planning of harmonious social and economic development could be effective.

When investigating the origin and stability of administrative boundaries, geographers will find it useful to construct maps showing the degree of boundary permanence. Day [1949] pointed to the value of this technique when he discussed the boundaries of India during the Hindu and Mughul Empires, and Spate [1957] used it to construct a useful map of boundary permanence in the Indian subcontinent. In making such a map [Prescott 1968, p. 130], the age of a particular boundary in one location is indicated by the thickness of the line. Since boundaries vary in their importance it is wise to con-

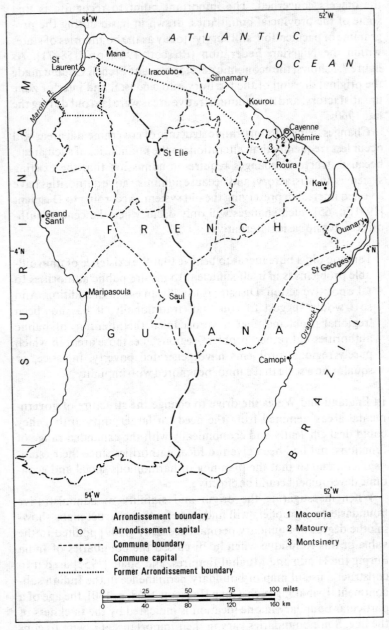

7.2 Boundary changes in French Guiana

struct a separate map for each administrative level, and if necessary these can be superimposed on each other for comparison.

Cartographic analysis is also the most convenient way to establish the degree of correspondence between governmental boundaries and other dividing lines or zones in the landscape. The coincidence of boundaries with linear physical features such as a hill crest or a river can be easily established. It is harder to relate the boundary to the distribution of population characteristics, such as race, nationality and tribe, or occupation, density and political persuasion. Part of this difficulty arises from the fact that the statistics on which such patterns can be constructed are collected within the existing governmental areas. But the effort to make this comparison is worthwhile, because it will serve to show when there are serious discrepancies which may be causing administrative problems. This problem does not exist in South Africa, South West Africa and Rhodesia, where there is an almost complete correspondence between racial groups and administrative areas. The task of comparing current boundaries with earlier patterns of occupance is even more difficult, but again, this may be a necessary undertaking to explain the alignment of particular boundaries.

Douglas [1964] suggested that political geographers should try to measure the effectiveness of administration, which was defined as the degree to which the central government has adapted the administrative pattern to take account of different cultural regions within the state. The method outlined by Douglas involves three stages. First, the geographer should make a detailed regional study to gain the essential understanding of geographical conditions. Second, the most important attitude-forming circulation fields must be identified. Douglas believes that the important circulation fields concern journeys to work, school, shops and recreational areas. He drew part of his inspiration from Gilbert [1948, p. 198], who wrote as follows: 'Whatever is done or not done, it is vital that the administrative map of England and Wales should be drawn so that it accords with the social geography of the country.'

More recently, Sharpe [1971, p. 153] diagnosed a serious weakness in the existing British system of local government to be 'the lack of correspondence between popular living patterns and local authority areas'. The third stage of Douglas's plan involves the comparison of the circulation fields and the administrative pattern. A close correspondence shows an effective system, while major discrepancies indicate the need for change. This is an interesting idea and it is regrettable that it has not been pursued by geographers.

Nelson [1952] examined the boundaries of a governmental area in California, to assess their contribution to an understanding 'of the areal distribution and functioning association' of various elements of the landscape. He plotted the distribution of residential, commercial, public, industrial and transport land-use and found that the boundaries of Vernon coincided with significant landscape differences. There was a remarkable concentration of land devoted to industry and transport within Vernon, almost to the complete exclusion of the other three categories. It also emerged that the other boundaries in the Vernon area did not coincide with similar distinctions in land-use, and it was possible to proceed to show how the authorities responsible for the Vernon area had contributed to this position. Logan [1963] found that the boundaries of governmental areas in southwest Victoria had little effect on the development of the cultural landscape. A motel and a drive-in cinema were located on the outskirts of Hamilton, in the Shire of Dundas, in order to take advantage of the shire's lower rates. This location was close to the people who would use the facilities and the electricity and water services provided by Hamilton. Another case was discovered where different building regulations of the Shire of Portland allowed the clustering of holiday homes just outside the town of Portland, which had more rigorous regulations. Since 1957 the shire has adopted the same building regulations as the town.

Fielding [1964, p. 10] quotes an interesting case of the policies of a local authority creating landscape changes at its boundary. During the spread of population in southern California after the Second World War, dairy farmers were regularly forced to vacate land zoned residential. Major improvements to their properties were obstructed by law and it was difficult to maintain satisfactory health standards with old equipment and barns. Complaints by neighbours about flies, odours and unseemly sights, together with increasing rates made it very difficult for dairy farmers to remain. Since, in California, any area with more than 500 persons can be constituted into a city, three neighbouring dairy areas formed three adjacent cities. They occupy 46.6 square kilometres (eighteen square miles) and have a population of 6000 people and 75,000 cows. They have established their own zoning laws and property taxes, and can ensure that the area is preserved for dairying.

Some of the most obvious effects of local authorities upon the landscape are found in Matabeleland in Rhodesia, where African and European farmland adjoin. The much higher population and stock densities in the African areas result in the deterioration of grazing and woodland, and provide sharp contrasts with the well-managed European areas [Prescott 1972]. The Rhodesian authorities are trying to persuade Africans to make better use of their land by culling weak, useless stock, and aiming at quality in their herds instead of quantity. They are also assisting the Africans to plan their use of the area to allow a proper rotation of grazing and cultivation.

2 Field Service Areas

These areas are drawn to serve a single function of government and they have no fiscal autonomy. Gilbert [1948] in a pioneer paper, still the best in this field, distinguished three kinds of government functions, which we can apply to field service areas. They are administration, data collection and defence. Apart from defence, which today is primarily concerned with civil defence in wartime and disaster-planning regions in peacetime, the other two categories contain a large number of individual areas. For example, in most democratic states the field service areas connected with administration would include some dealing with public works, mining, health and education standards, forests, national parks, police, justice, elections and fire brigades. The data collection areas will cover a multitude of subjects including weather, employment, agriculture and people. It should be noted at this stage that some of these field service areas are comprehensive in the sense that they cover the state. For example, there is no area of England or the United States that does not form part of a parliamentary or congressional electorate, nor is there any part of Belgium that does not fall into one of the country's police districts. However, there are some field service areas which occupy only part of the state's territory. These include national parks, irrigation areas and forest reserves.

The field service areas vary very widely in the method of construction and the ease with which the boundaries may be altered. In many cases the boundaries are selected by the head of the particular department, who probably begins by picking a number of centres at which the subordinate headquarters will be established, and then drawing boundaries around them to suit the convenience of the governed and the governors as far as possible. Lipman [1949, pp. 50–2] shows that this was the system by which sanitary districts were fixed in Britain in the period before 1870, and it is certainly the way in which some field service areas are fixed in Australia today. In the case of national parks and forest reserves the limits are often described in great detail in government gazettes, so that there can be no doubt about which areas are affected. It is comparatively difficult to change such areas because this involves the acquisition of adjoining land, which may be privately owned. Electoral boundaries in democracies are usually determined by an independent tribunal, which has to construct them according to fairly precise instructions. For example, electoral commissioners will be told how many electorates they are to construct, and the variation in numbers of electors permitted between the largest and smallest. They may also be told that when drawing the boundaries they must take into account previous boundaries, community of interest, the likelihood of changes in population distribution and growth, ease of communication, and physical features such as rivers. It can be very difficult to change electoral boundaries since the approval of parliament is always required, and sometimes different parties control the upper and lower houses. The need to change electorates arises because of the redistribution of population which takes place through two processes common in many societies. First, there is the drift from rural to urban areas, which makes the rural electorates too small and some urban electorates too large. Second, there is intra-urban migration from the city centre towards the peripheral suburbs, where some of the inner seats have numbers of voters well below the quota, while suburban seats have numbers well above. This trend is often reinforced by the younger age structure of suburbs, which have a higher birthrate and a greater number of young people becoming eligible to vote than in the city centre.

When geographers examine the correspondence of field service boundaries they are concerned with two sets of relationships. First, there is the correspondence of the various boundaries with each other, and second, there is the correspondence of individual boundaries with patterns of the cultural and physical landscape. If all the field service boundaries of any state are plotted on a map, there will be some sections where several correspond closely, and others where there is no apparent correspondence whatsoever. In some cases it is obviously a matter of unimportance that field service areas fail to correspond. For example, there is no compelling reason why the areas within which employment statistics are collected should match zones within which fire brigades operate. However, there are a number of cases where close correspondence seems sensible. A single set of statistical divisions will be much more useful than separate areas for each set of information; identical districts for police operations and the administration of justice would also seem to be advantageous; and correspondence between areas of weather forecasting and agricultural advisory services would be helpful.

The extent to which the field service boundaries should correspond with divisions in the physical and cultural landscapes will obviously vary. Statistical divisions should preferably contain uniform conditions, especially those divisions connected with the collection of economic information, otherwise their interpretation becomes more difficult. Field service areas concerned with irrigation works and water supply should surely correspond with river catchments. It is a very difficult question to decide whether electoral districts should be drawn to comprehend uniform groups of voters, or whether a conscious effort should be made to ensure that each seat contains a balanced number of the supporters of the main parties. The answer adopted will influence the election results.

When we consider the effects which the pattern of field service areas may have on the landscape, it is immediately evident that in some cases there will be no effect whatsoever. Statistical divisions, and areas dealing with the provision of services such as gas and electricity cannot be expected to influence the development of a landscape in a way which will be evident at the boundary with an adjoining zone. There are some districts, such as those dealing with irrigation, forestry and national parks, where there will be abrupt changes in the rural landscape at their borders. It should also be mentioned that the way in which electoral boundaries are constructed may have a determining influence on which political party forms the government. There are two ways in which the manipulation of electoral boundaries can determine the result. The first method is known as weighting. This involves having significantly different numbers of electors in different constituencies. For example, in Australia, South Africa, New Zealand and parts of Canada, it is traditional for rural electorates to have smaller numbers of voters than urban electorates. This arrangement was justified in earlier periods by the much greater areas occupied by rural electorates, because of their lower population density. But clearly this arrangement gives greater weight to a single rural vote than to an urban vote, and this arrangement in Australia has allowed the Country Party to win more seats than its proportion of the vote would justify. In view of the significant improvements in communication today, this traditional view is challenged in many countries, especially by parties which draw their support from urban areas. There was a suggestion by the Australian Labor Party that the electorates should be drawn to include equal numbers of people, rather than equal numbers of voters. This would give the Labor Party an advantage, since some of its urban seats have a higher proportion of non-voting migrants and children, than the urban seats of its opponents.

The second method is known as a gerrymander. This system produces seats with equal numbers of voters but draws the boundaries in such a way that one party consistently wins seats by a narrow majority, while other parties win their seats with enormous majorities. In short this is simply a device by which a party in power uses its votes most efficiently. Pounds [1972, pp. 231–3] records some cases of gerrymandering in the United States. Such electorates can always be recognised by their irregular and curious shapes, compared with the compact shapes of other electorates.

Field service boundaries do not usually give rise to disputes, for the simple reason that there is an overriding authority over any two adjoining areas. Thus if difficulties begin to arise over a boundary connected with the provision of gas, then the gas board concerned can quite easily alter the boundary, or make such departmental reorganisations as are necessary. Problems may arise along the borders between forest reserves and farm land because of vermin sheltering in the forest, or the risk of fire danger from either side. One very real problem, rather than dispute, may concern difficulties associated with regional planning because of the lack of correspondence between field service boundaries. Steiner [1965] has referred to the situation where there are overlapping boundaries as 'the muddle of functions', and he has shown how such a situation in Japan has created difficulties. Gilbert [1948] and Lipman [1949] are other authors who have pointed to this general problem. Efforts to overcome this through regional planning are the subject of the next section.

3 Regional Planning Areas

Kalk [1971], in a most useful study, has shown that there is an increasing tendency for national planning to be organised within regional units, in both communist and non-communist developed states. There are two prime reasons for this development. First, several central authorities deem it desirable to break down national plans so that they can be based on realistic regional estimates and adapted to distinct local and regional conditions. Second, it has become apparent that the growing number of functions performed by local authorities cannot be carried out efficiently at the local level, but should be carried out by aggregates of local authorities forming regions. For example, Maes [1971] has shown that in Belgium the administration by communes, created in 1836, is now unsatisfactory. Twenty-one per cent of the communes have populations smaller than 500, and eight per cent have populations exceeding 10,000. The small communes cannot measure up to their tasks connected with roads, sewerage, public lighting, ambulance and fire-fighting services, cultural development and economic expansion. Some of the large communes lack a hinterland necessary for their proper development, and some of the aggregates of communes in the cities have common problems which would be more susceptible to solution by larger authorities. Legislation exists which allows communes to develop voluntary associations, but the 2586 communes had developed only 205 such associations in the forty-seven years ending in 1969.

Kalk shows that it is useful to consider the emerging regional bodies at two levels. The local regional units occupy the level immediately above local authorities and are formed by the amalgamation of such bodies. The new units are based on the requirement for the increasing activities of local authorities to be conducted on a larger scale, and the local authorities are usually strongly represented in the new structure. Examples of the new local regional authorities are provided by *communautés urbaines*, which were created in the French cities of Lyon, Strasbourg, Bordeaux, Dunkirk and Lille-Roubaix-Tourcoing. Central regional authorities occupy a position immediately below the central government, and they generally emerge because of the desire to decentralise the government's activities and responsibilities. These units are few in number. In the United Kingdom, for example, Wales, Scotland and Northern Ireland each form a single planning region, and England is divided into eight.

While the local regional units may serve both planning and other functions, the central regional authorities are invariably connected with economic planning.

It will be interesting in the future to see whether this trend equally applies to developing countries, and whether, in either category of states, the emergence of regional planning units leads to regional government.

Conclusion

The previous sections have shown that geography may play an important role in the origin and detailed delimitation of the administrative structure of the state, in the reasons why changes in that system or its boundaries become necessary, and in the problems which may arise between authorities at the same or different levels in the hierarchy. It has also been demonstrated that the operation of distinct local authorities in different parts of the state may contribute to the development of landscape differences.

The recent trends towards regional planning in developed countries should be welcomed by geographers who, more than any other group of scholars, have contributed to a body of regional theory and to the practical techniques by which regions can be recognised. Fawcett [1961], Gilbert [1948] and Taylor [1942] offered sound advice on the construction of local government boundaries, and a more recent generation of geographers has experimented with useful statistical techniques to supplement that advice. The geographer's main contribution lies in accumulating information, based on detailed case studies, about the evolution of existing boundaries; their effect on the landscape and the attitudes of populations; and the economic, social and historic threads that give particular regions their degree of cohesion. Without this kind of information there can be no guarantee that the new boundaries and administrative structures will be more successful than their predecessors.

8 The Political Geography of the Sea

Are we witnessing a gradual closure of the seas?

[Fawcett 1973]

There can be no doubt that the I.L.C. (International Law Commission) *as a body* recognised that the legal Continental Shelf might extend beyond the geologic continental shelf.

[Brown 1971]

The states of the world are crowded on its land area, which makes up only twenty-nine per cent of its surface, but this in no sense implies that they are uninterested in the remaining seventy-one per cent which is made up of the oceans and their contained seas. There is, in fact, only one ocean, since the separately named parts are interconnected and much the greater part of this is water subject to tidal influences and to movements at different levels resulting from differential temperatures, winds and varying inflow from rivers and glacier meltwaters. The ocean's waters are broadly rich in their biological and mineral content and they vary in depth, salinity and temperature. Beneath the waters of the oceans and seas the sea-bed varies greatly in its relief, superficial cover and contained minerals. In a wide variety of ways the oceans and seas have lured man as a valuable and essential part of his habitat and, as his power over his environment has greatly increased with his control of mechanical energy and technological advances, interest in, and use of the ocean have taken on ever more visible prominence. The political interests which attach to the oceans and seas include surface and underwater transport, fish and whales, the riches beneath the sea-bed, international waterways, marine boundaries, strategy and defence, and the special problems of access to the seas faced by land-locked states.

1 International Law and the Seas

If only for the evident reason that the seas, unlike the land, are incapable, except marginally, of permanent appropriation, they have come to generate their own body of international law. For many centuries the Roman legal maxim that the seas were *res communés* (i.e. available for all to use) was challenged in practice by states that commanded a measure of naval power and claimed and exercised political control of maritime sectors. The grandest of these claims were made by Spain and Portugal, who regarded the Pacific Ocean and the Indian Ocean respectively as their own by right of discovery. Lesser claims were made, for example, by the Venetian Republic which claimed control of the Adriatic Sea, and by England, which claimed dominion over the waters around the British Isles to outer limits at Cape Finisterre in Spain and in northern Norway. Inflated as such claims may appear, it should be recognised that, without the naval policing that these claimants partially provided, the seas, open to all, were subject to the flourishing trade of piracy.

The formulation of doctrines of what came to be known as international law in the seventeenth century attempted to reduce the lawlessness of those modern absolutist states of Europe which recognised no earthly superior and even applied the principles of Machiavelli's *The Prince* with its belief that moral behaviour has no place in political and military affairs. Grotius argued that the seas should be free of territorial sovereignty and from this view evolved the concept of the high seas to which all have free and equal access. Inevitably, however, as responses to the hard facts of geography, it was necessary to establish rules relating to seas marginal to the land, including straits and gulfs. The idea of *mare clausum*, a semi-enclosed sea or stretch of sea, to which a single state asserted and enforced its own control, long persisted. We may recall that the Black Sea, to which marine access is confined to the narrow waterways of the Dardanelles, the Sea of Marmara and the Bosporus, was for several centuries surrounded by European and Asiatic territories of the Ottoman Turkish Empire. This exercised an exclusive dominion over the Black Sea until the year 1774 and onwards when, by unilateral concessions, it began to permit entry to vessels of foreign powers. And even today, in accordance with the Convention of Montreux of 1936, the Turkish Republic, successor and residual state of the Turkish Empire, enjoys the legal right to control passage through the

Dardanelles and Bosporus in time of war. Similarly Denmark, alleging that the Sound – the principal water route into and from the Baltic – was only a wide waterway lying within its territory, levied tolls on the shipping which used it until their repeal in 1858. The Behring Sea has had the doctrine of *mare clausum* applied to it – by Russia in 1821–5 and in 1887 by the United States, then intent on preserving its seal-hunting there. An arbitral decision in 1893 disposed of the American claim as illegal but specified a code to be observed by seal-hunters in this sea. In more recent times, although the doctrine of the free use of the high seas is accepted, great powers have been at pains to secure their own military control of narrow waterways conceived to be of strategic importance to them. Thus the United Kingdom, at first by its control of Egypt and in the 1930s, by its control solely of the Suez Canal Zone, sought to ensure that it could not be denied use of this waterway. In a similar way the United States, which constructed the Panama Canal and is clearly its chief beneficiary, negotiated with the Panama Republic for the control of the Panama Canal Zone which it still holds.

While navigation on the so-called high seas is free for all and subject only to restrictions imposed by belligerents on neutral states in times of war, it has long been recognised that states should possess special rights over their coastal waters. These, together with the seabed and the overlying airspace, are held to fall within the jurisdiction of the neighbouring state as part of its territory. The 'territorial waters or sea', through which 'innocent passage' is allowed to foreign shipping, is properly regarded as a protective insulation to a state's lands and a medium for coastwise transport. At first, and most commonly, international law recognised a three-mile limit to territorial seas, and this breadth had its origin in either the maritime league, a convenient if double-edged yardstick*, or, as is more usually believed, in the maximum range of guns, which until the end of the eighteenth century did not reach three nautical miles. Within its territorial seas, a state naturally claimed a monopoly in fishing as well as naval control for defence, police, immigration, customs and sanitation purposes. Clearly the cannon-shot rule defining a breadth of three nautical miles has long ceased to be meaningful and the use of aircraft has still more reduced the degree of protection that territorial

* While in southern and western Europe the maritime league was a twentieth part of one degree, or three nautical miles, in Scandinavia it was one-fifteenth part of a degree, that is four nautical miles. This is the breadth of the territorial sea still claimed by Finland, Norway, Sweden and Iceland.

seas can offer to a state navally prepared. As a result, and in pursuit of ever wider fish reserves easily accessible to their coasts, states have claimed ever wider stretches of territorial seas: indeed many claims to waters in excess of the three-nautical mile breadth were made several centuries ago. Denmark, for example, claimed in the 1590s eight nautical miles of territorial waters around Iceland, the Faroes and Norway, and in 1650 enlarged this to twenty-four miles. In 1958, forty-eight out of seventy-three maritime countries adhered to the three-nautical mile limit for their territorial seas. However, in this year the Territorial Sea Convention set a limit of twelve nautical miles to the contiguous zone and this came to be taken to permit a twelve-nautical mile breadth of territorial sea with no contiguous zone beyond. Since international law differs from municipal law in that it can seek only to establish agreement between states that it cannot enforce, it is not surprising that by 1973 more than half of the states with coasts claim territorial seas of twelve nautical miles or more in breadth. Of 111 states listed by the Geographer of the United States in March 1973, 50.5 per cent claimed territorial sea limits of twelve nautical miles, 9 per cent those of six nautical miles, 22.5 per cent those of three nautical miles, but no less than 7.2 per cent set their limits 200 nautical miles from their shores. Indeed there is a wide variety here with claims from three to two hundred nautical miles by various states, and Turkey claims twelve nautical miles on its Black Sea coast and six nautical miles on its Mediterranean shores. Some states, including Lebanon and Nicaragua, give no specific figure.

Fifty states claim exactly the same width for both fishing and territorial sea – that is, they are coincident. Twenty-seven states make no official claim to exclusive fishing zones, and therefore it might be presumed that they also claim only their territorial waters. Thirty-three states claim wider exclusive fishing zones than their territorial sea. This includes several European states. Eight of these states claim more than twelve nautical miles for their exclusive fishing zone; only the United Kingdom in this group claims less than twelve nautical miles. Six states appear to claim narrower exclusive fishing zones than territorial waters, but this is probably because they have not amended the regulations and, since territorial waters give exclusive fishing rights, they should be added to the fifty states mentioned first. Finally three states, Argentina, Brazil and Uruguay, license other nationals to fish in the outer areas of their territorial waters – Brazil between 100–200 nautical miles; the other two from 12–200 nautical miles. Unfortunately the attempt to establish as a principle of international law that exclusive fishing zones should extend for twelve nautical miles narrowly failed to obtain a sufficient majority at the United Nations Conferences on the laws of the sea at Geneva in 1958 and 1960. And when states apply a policy of extending their fishery zones unilaterally, thus attempting to deny to others rights to fish in waters of the high seas, it is not surprising that disputes have arisen.

Some countries exercise jurisdiction over a zone of water stretching beyond their territorial sea for a similar breadth. This is known as the 'contiguous zone' and is recognised by international law for such purposes as controlling immigration, preventing smuggling and controlling sanitation and pollution. While the coastal state can operate as if this zone is part of its territory, it is nevertheless held to be part of the high seas for the purpose of navigation, as also for fishing unless it falls within claimed fishing limits.

2 Maritime Boundaries

Since states have rights and responsibilities of a legal kind over their territorial seas and sea-bed, it is necessary to know with some degree of precision over what area of waters these apply; hence the need to record on charts maritime boundaries, the lines which mark the outer limits of territorial seas. This task raises a variety of difficulties owing to the often irregular configuration of coasts, which may be broken by river estuaries, bays, inlets or lagoons, and include projecting headlands and off-shore islands. A baseline beyond which the zone of the territorial sea can be measured has first to be determined and a simple illustration will show what problems are encountered and how they have been overcome.

Norway had drawn straight baselines as early as 1869 as we learn from a judgment of the International Court of Justice of 18 December 1951 and, given the physical geography of Norway's coast, such a baseline is clearly appropriate. However, the language of the clause in the convention allowing states to establish straight baselines rather than using the normal low-water mark is vague.

> In localities where the coastline is deeply indented and cut into, or if there is a fringe of islands in its immediate vicinity, the method of straight baselines . . . may be employed. [Department of External Affairs 1958]

There can be no valid objection to the use of straight baselines along parts of the coast of Norway, Sweden, Denmark, West Germany and Yugoslavia, where there are model conditions for drawing straight baselines. But there is no justification for the very extensive systems of straight baselines drawn by Ecuador and Burma, to name only the two most flagrant cases. In fact it is possible to assert that on the precedent of straight baselines already in existence, it would be possible to draw straight baselines along any coast!

Indonesia's straight baselines measure 8167.6 nautical miles and enclose 666,000 square nautical miles of what was previously high seas. The Philippines baseline is seven nautical miles longer but the enclosed sea is only 148,921.5 square nautical miles in extent. By the middle of 1974 twelve archipelagos, controlled by ten states, were surrounded by baselines. The largest have already been mentioned; the Galapagos Islands represent the medium range and the Faroes the small size. There are other archipelago states, such as Japan, New Zealand and Papua New Guinea, which could make similar claims if this concept secured legal respectability. There is an obvious risk that further areas of the high seas will be eroded by claims to straight baselines.

3 The Sea-Bed and Its Resources

Shallow seas, known as 'continental shelves' and 'insular shelves' which are conventionally rather than actually reckoned to be those with less than 100 fathoms, or 200 metres or 600 feet of water, account for more than ten per cent of the oceans and seas. These areas may have been or might become dry land, representing as they do the fluctuating zone of transition between land and deep sea, and they are subject to a variety of physical forces such as changes in ocean level, tides and isostatic adjustments, so that they contract or expand marginally even during relatively short phases of time. As their names indicate these shelves border the continents and islands and are of varying breadth, lying at depths which in places well exceed 200 metres: they are taken to end where the sea floor plunges sharply beneath deeper water. Biologically these shelves tend to be rich, since additional nutrient salts brought down by rivers, shallow water through which energising light can penetrate and, in many areas, the effects of surface-water currents all tend to encourage plant plankton growth. It is well known that such conditions sustain the productive fishing grounds on the shelves off western Europe, Iceland and Newfoundland as also those of the Caspian Sea and the seas of Okhotsk and Japan. Lying near to their mainlands, the shelves enjoy ease of access and, as exploration, prospecting and technological means ever improve, their resource content, exploitable either now or in the years ahead, becomes better known. While interest centres chiefly on natural gas and petroleum resources beneath the shelves – in the Persian Gulf, the Gulf of Mexico, the Caspian Sea, off southern California and, more recently discovered, off Angola and in the North Sea – other mineral resources on the seabed and beneath it will doubtless be sought and found as the scarcity of minerals won from the lands and the rising costs of their recovery turn attention to off-shore resources, as also to those on and below the deep sea-bed.

It has become clear during the last ten years or so that the mineral deposits, in the form of polymetallic nodules lying on the floor of the shelves and of the deep sea, constitute enormous potential reserves which very greatly exceed those known and accessible on the land. Large nodules, primarily of manganese but containing copper, nickel, cobalt, titanium and other metals, have been found to occur widely, and already from parts of continental shelves phosphorites, tin and diamonds are being won. A report given in *The Times* of 11 May 1972 tells of concentrations of metals, including gold, silver and copper, in sediments beneath the floor of the Red Sea. The technological problems of deep-sea mining, notably by the United States, are being researched at considerable cost, so that increasingly some of the mineral wealth of the seas and oceans will be acquired by the technologically advanced and richer nations. These new developments appear to foreshadow an ultimate share-out of the ocean, a pointer to which was given by the peaceful sharing and appropriation of the North and Irish Seas (both by nature continental shelves although largely high seas) by the bordering countries, intent on the now proved resources of petroleum and natural gas. The international problems and dangers inherent in this attempt to acquire sea-bed resources are clearly great, the more so since the law of the sea is as yet so unclear. At the U.N. conference on the law of the sea in 1958 an approach was made to clarify national rights of sovereignty over the sea-beds of continental shelves outwards from the shore to a depth of 200 metres. However, the door was left wide open for further extensions of sovereignty 'beyond that limit, to where the depth of the super-adjacent waters admits of the exploitation of the natural resources of the said areas'. Indeed, international law lags far behind political action and already in 1945, by a simple proclamation, President Truman appropriated to the United States the subsoil development and fishery rights of the continental shelves off its coasts, adding very considerably at a stroke to the estate of his country. Admittedly this proclamation affirmed that conservation zones for fish would be established and that fishing and drilling there would be regulated.

It should be added that the phrase 'admits of the exploitation of the natural resource' is too vague to be very useful. Clearly this is an invitation to the stronger and technologically advanced countries to extend their enterprises seawards, but it leaves unclear whether these have to be profitable or alternatively can be subsidised by the state.

4 Land-Locked States

Territorial seas and direct access through them to the oceans are normal attributes of independent states, but, even so, an increasing number lack coasts of their own. In 1959 there were fourteen land-locked states, distributed between three continents – Europe, Asia and South America; another such (Ethiopia) existed until 1952 when, following a United Nations decision, it incorporated the former Italian colony of Eritrea with its Red Sea port of Massawa. By 1973, however, the total had increased to twenty-seven by the addition of new African states which won independence in and after 1960 as a result of decolonisation. Thus land-locked states then accounted for eighteen per cent of independent states, compared with only about fifteen per cent in 1959 [East 1960].

Table IX identifies and locates the land-locked states in 1959 and gives some particulars about them.

To this list of land-locked states, most of which are of long standing, must be added thirteen in Africa which emerged in the 1960s (see table X). This figure does not include Rhodesia which has only *de facto* and not legally recognised independence.

These twenty-seven states make up an ill-assorted list and have little or nothing in common except their detachment from the sea. They include many with vast territories, most notably in Africa, but

TABLE IX

THE LAND-LOCKED SOVEREIGN STATES AS NOW AND BEFORE 1960

Name	Political organisation	Area (sq km)	Population 1972 (millions)	Density (per sq km)
Europe				
Czechoslovakia	People's Republic	127,870	14.5	113
Hungary	People's Republic	93,030	10.4	112
Austria	Republic	83,849	7.4	88
Switzerland	Federal Republic	41,288	6.3	153
Luxembourg	Grand Duchy	2586	0.35	135
Liechtenstein	Principality	160	0.017	279
San Marino	Republic	61	0.018	113
Vatican City	Holy See	0.44	0.001	2380
Asia				
Afghanistan	Kingdom	657,500	17.5	27
Nepal	Kingdom	141,400	11.3	80
Mongolia	People's Republic	1,565,000	1.3	1
Laos	Kingdom	235,700	3.1	13
South America				
Bolivia	Republic	1,098,580	5.2	5
Paraguay	Republic	406,752	2.5	6

SOURCE: *The Statesman's Year-Book 1972–3 and 1973–4*, Macmillan, London.

TABLE X

THE INDEPENDENT LAND-LOCKED STATES OF AFRICA IN 1973

Name	Date of independence	Area (sq km)	Population 1973 (millions)	Density (per sq km)
Former French Dependencies				
Central African Republic	1960	624,930	1.6	2.6
Chad Republic	1960	1,284,400	3.8	3.0
Mali Republic	1960	1,204,021	5.3	4.4
Niger Republic	1960	1,187,000	4.2	3.5
Upper Volta Republic	1960	274,122	5.5	20.0
Former Belgian U.N. Trust Territories				
Burundi Republic	1962	27,834	3.6	129.3
Rwanda Republic	1962	26,330	3.8	144.3
Former British Dependencies				
Botswana Republic	1966	575,000	0.67	1.2
Lesotho Kingdom	1966	30,340	0.97	32.0
Malawi Republic	1964	94,084	4.7	50.0
Swaziland (Kingdom)	1968	17,400	0.42	24.1
Uganda Republic	1962	193,600	10.5	54.2
Zambia Republic	1964	752,262	4.5	6.0

NB. Area figures exclude water areas, in some cases large.

SOURCE: *The Statesman's Year-Book 1972–3 and 1973–4*, Macmillan, London.

at the other end of the scale are three microstates, of which one, the Vatican City State, has only 43 hectares (106 acres). They contrast, too, in their capacity to support population. The European group are relatively populous, but most of the others have low or extremely low population densities which reflect both stern geographical limitations arising from mountainous systems and hot desert or tropical climates and their economic underdevelopment.

To explain fully how these states came to be land-locked would involve a study of their case histories, each uniquely different. Yet a few generalisations may be ventured which may throw some light on all of them. When the scale and shapes of continental areas are considered, it might be expected that the odds are against the sharing of coasts among *all* the states which have emerged. A simple model is provided in ancient Greece (figure 8.1), when the city-state of Arcadia in the Peloponnesos found itself islanded by five neighbours, each with its stretch of coast on the Aegean Sea, the Ionian Sea or the Gulf of Corinth. Arcadia, which was described as a land of bears and of woods, and of shepherds and huntsmen, was established in highland country within a ring of mountains where many rivers had their sources. It was reckoned a country of little account in its cultural and economic life, well-rated for hospitality but not for intelligence, well-known for its export of asses and mercenaries and for providing the sites for many battles. It was clearly a backward state, giving credence to the long-held idea that contact with the sea brings strength and stimulus to political life. Given the limited means of transport in ancient Greece and the physical geography of the Peloponnesos, the existence of the land-locked state of Arcadia, useful as a buffer or shock-absorber between its more active maritime neighbours, appears unsurprising if not actually inevitable.

But clearly this has no application in the present century when means of transport and communication are both speedy and efficient. As a striking illustration of modern improvements in surface transport, Kirk noted that, by new road works, the People's Republic of China reduced the journey from Pekin to Lhasa, Tibet's capital, from three months to three days [East, Spate and Fisher 1971]. The great breadth of Africa and South America south of the equator might well suggest how difficult it has been to devise states there, each with a share of the coasts; yet to sheer extent must be added, as the main challenges to political organisation, climate, mountainous terrain, vegetation cover and stage of

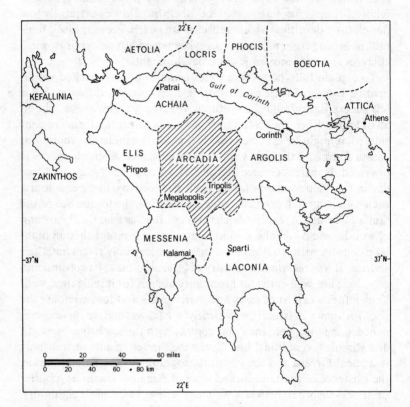

8.1 Arcadia

economic development. However, for all its vast scale, North America is organised into only two states and for no brief time Spain in South America and Britain and France in Africa controlled as dependencies territories now independent and land-locked and provided for them access to seaports although at some distance away. Surprisingly, at least on geographical ground, it is Europe that has the largest number of land-locked states proportionately to its area – no less than eight – and these are found in its peninsular western part.

Clearly the obvious reason for so many land-locked states is found in the process of decolonisation, which went hand in hand with the break-up of empires. This explanation accounts for all the African and South American inland states, most of those in Europe and half of those in Asia. It is notable, too, that many of the older states without coasts had, more evidently in the past than today, the function of 'buffer states': they were interposed between two powerful countries and, by their presence, served to prevent border friction and more serious conflict between them. Thus Switzerland and Luxembourg, both with territories carrying routes between France and Germany, were conceived as useful buffers by the great powers of Europe which gave them guaranteed neutral status in 1815 and 1867 respectively. Both Bolivia and Paraguay may be also regarded as buffer states, the former set between Argentina, Chile and Brazil, and the latter between Argentina and Brazil. Mongolia, formerly one of the outer territories of the Chinese Empire and occupying a vast territory bordering both the Soviet Union and the People's Republic of China, has become closely allied to and dependent on the Soviet Union, although clearly, as for a time before its independence, it could serve as a separating zone, largely empty and but little developed as yet, between these two powerful states. Afghanistan, an old, semi-feudal, land-locked state, long attracted international interest because of its buffer character, being placed between the Russian Empire in Central Asia and British imperial and protected territories in India and around the Persian Gulf. Laos too, which once formed part of French Indo-China and thus enjoyed access to the sea, was set up in 1954 by the Geneva Conference as a virtually neutralised inland state: it was certainly conceived as a buffer state that might help to preserve peace. 'It is in everybody's interest', wrote *The Times* Bangkok correspondent on 21 June 1958, 'to keep Laos as a buffer state.' Yet in 1974 it was still engulfed by military conflict despite the ceasefire that has brought one sort of end to the Vietnam war. And the Himalayan kingdom of Nepal appeared to be a buffer between China and India, although the reassertion by China of control over Tibet and its efforts in 1962 to rectify its boundaries with India indicated that this buffer function was lessening. In Africa, too, a few land-locked states had buffer characteristics, notably Botswana, Lesotho and Swaziland. These were used by the British in the last two decades of the nineteenth century to insulate the independent Boer Republic from contact with German South West Africa to the west and from access to the sea to the east.

Decolonisation leaves unexplained a number of the land-locked states. In earlier times, although Afghanistan was part of the Persian Empire as also part of those of Alexander the Great and the Caliphate, it escaped absorption into the British and Russian Empires and remained semi-independent since the mid-eighteenth century. Nepal, too, escaped the expansionism of both the British and Chinese Empires. The independence of Afghanistan and Nepal thus appears to result from their usefulness as buffers and the fact that better means than conquest and annexation could be used by their powerful neighbours to exercise sufficient control over them. Lastly, as for Liechtenstein, San Marino and the Vatican City State, they are vestiges of the past in a continent which has lived through much history.

(i) Access to the Sea

It is axiomatic that all states, though in different degrees related to the stages of their economic development, have the need of access to the seaways of transport along which world trade is carried. It is no less obvious that for inland states there always exists one or more land routes to seaboard ports: typically such ports lie only a few hundred or more kilometres away and exceptionally 1609 kilometres (one thousand miles) or more away, as for Mongolia. No special difficulties would seem to arise other than high freight costs if it were generally accepted, as some international lawyers believe, that the right of passage to the sea is an inescapable obligation on states seaward of land-locked ones. However, more international lawyers believe that right of access to the sea through a neighbour's territory can be acquired only by inter-state agreements. Certainly, already by 1921 progress in this regard was made by the Convention and Statute on Freedom of Transit at the Barcelona Conference, when the states represented there recognised the right of land-locked countries to transit through surrounding countries with equality of treatment and specified the means of settling any disputes that arose therefrom. Also a solemn declaration, made at this Conference, agreed to recognition of the flag of vessels of such countries provided they were registered at a specified place within their territories: use of this right is made by some, at least, of the land-locked states, notably by Switzerland, Austria, Hungary and Paraguay. Even so, it is clear that, in the absence of neighbourly good-will, land-locked states could at times be seriously disadvantaged, the more so since, being mostly weak states, their bargaining power is impaired. Their special position and difficulties were publicised in 1958 when, in advance of the United Nations conference on the law of the sea, Switzerland, as host country, invited twelve other land-locked countries to discuss their common problems at Geneva. Those who were invited and attended included Byelorussia, a U.N. member but not an independent state, and San Marino, independent but not a U.N. member. Liechtenstein and Mongolia, neither then a U.N. member, were not invited.

The discussions at the conference showed that, chiefly by means of bilateral agreements with neighbours, the land-locked states of that time had largely managed to overcome their disability by securing access by surface routes to the high seas. This was usually achieved by their obtaining transit rights across neighbouring territory and by concessions to use there a 'free zone' in one or more specified seaports. This fractional area of territory remains under the sovereignty of the state in which it lies but outside its customs regime. Improvements in surface transport certainly helped land-locked states and in some cases, too, their access was much improved by the availability of a navigable waterway, such as the Rhine for Switzerland and the Parana River for Paraguay, which enjoyed the legal status of an 'international river' and was thus available to them by right. It became clear at this Geneva conference that, whereas some land-locked states took a very serious and indeed emotive view of their geographical limitation, others were little concerned about it. On the one hand, there were sturdy complaints from the representatives of Afghanistan, Bolivia and Paraguay, but, on the other, Switzerland emphasised that transit is a two-way traffic and that reciprocal relations between countries with and without coasts could be settled sensibly around the conference table. Whereas some states, notably Afghanistan, Nepal, Czechoslovakia and Bolivia desired that access to the sea should be written into international law and guaranteed, others, notably Switzerland and Austria, were content with the *status quo* and did not want to form a bloc of land-locked states.

It is evident that when a land-locked state suffers the ill-will or, worse still, the enmity of its neighbours, its situation can become difficult or even painful, as a few illustrations show. Afghanistan enjoys transit rights in the Soviet Union and in Pakistan where it can use the port of Karachi, yet in 1958, according to the Pakistan newspaper *Dawn*, it gave the impression that Pakistan was 'strangling a poor land-locked country like Afghanistan'. But this was at a time when the Afghan Government had been pursuing a 'Pakhtunistan' policy which sought to win from Pakistan some two million Pathans living there! Bolivia, however, had more cause for complaint, because it had lost to Chile its originally held Pacific seaboard in the War of the Pacific (1879–83). It has formal agreements with both Chile and Peru which give it free transit by rail for its mineral exports and for its imports and thus it enjoys sea access as well as the use of 'free ports' in four Pacific ports – Arica and Antafagasta in Chile and Mollendo and Matarani in Peru. Even so, 'the one platform on which all Bolivians are politically united is their demand for an outlet on the sea and the lack of a seaboard is the country's most vociferous grievance' [Osborne 1954]. And Paraguay's representative to the 1958 U.N. conference stated and her attitude remains unchanged) that 'the country's most serious problem, from its earliest days as an independent nation, has been that it is land-locked.'

For most of the new African states within or south of the Sahara which lack coasts, this deficiency adds to an already long list of difficulties. Including Rhodesia, which despite U.N. sanctions is effectively viable, these account for twenty-two per cent of the continent's area but only twenty per cent of its population. With a few exceptions, notably Zambia and Rhodesia, industrial development has made little headway and agriculture remains economically basic. However, this involves, as well as subsistence farming, the production of cash crops, such as cotton, coffee, groundnuts and tobacco, for which access to the sea and world markets is needed. Low population densities, long distances, inadequate roads and few railways, given the existing levels of material culture and technology, all tend to slow down economic development. Even Rwanda and Burundi, which are among the most populous countries of Africa, have only rudimentary industrial development: set within equatorial plateaux and mountains, many hundreds of miles from seaports, they practise subsistence agriculture and have little except coffee to move to the world market. Yet, as Dale [1968] remarks, the African land-locked states, situated as they are, have the more need to get along well with some, at least, of their neighbours, the average number of which reaches 4.5. In general, these countries have practicable access to seaports thanks to bilateral agreements. Thus, for example, Rhodesia, Botswana, Lesotho and Swaziland use routes, as they did before independence, through the South African Republic, and the first and last can use ports also in Portuguese Mozambique. The former French dependencies without coasts can similarly use old established routes. These have formed customs unions as a means of overcoming the difficulty of sea access, as Uganda has done by its customs union with Tanzania and Zanzibar. But when political relations with a neighbour are strained, as between Zambia and Rhodesia in 1973, the difficulties of a land-locked state are pinpointed. Owing to their common history as British colonies and as members of the short-lived Central African Federation, Zambia and Rhodesia have developed a considerable degree of interdependence. Thus, when Rhodesia closed its border with Zambia because of the danger from terrorists, Zambia, needing to export its copper and to import machinery and transport equipment, was faced with serious transport problems and rising freight costs, for its best route is by railway across Rhodesia to Beira. Incidentally, Zambia's need of imported petroleum has been met since 1968 by the use of a pipeline from Dar-es-Salaam (in Tanzania) to Ndola in its copper belt. Clearly the continuance of bad relations with Rhodesia fully justifies Zambia's foresight in respect of the 1100-mile Tan-Zan railway which will be completed in 1975 and will provide another means of shipment – to Dar-es-Salaam.

5 International Waterways

The configuration of the continents is such that navigation is sharply confined at a number of straits where the legal distinction between territorial and high seas becomes blurred and may give rise to international disputes and require the formulation of agreed regulations. Treaties between states and international decisions have been necessary to clarify user rights of the international canals of Suez and Panama, built to shorten shipping routes. Similar co-operation has made it possible to establish an international regime for a number of navigable rivers which flow indifferently through the territories of several or more states.

(i) Straits

It was noted above that Denmark and Turkey long ago regarded the narrow seas respectively of the Danish and Turkish Straits as internal waters yet came to recognise, in accordance with treaty agreements, that they were open for all to use.

In recent years a new situation has arisen in respect of the Straits of Malacca and of Singapore as a result of the claims of two neighbouring coastal states to wider territorial seas. The Strait of Malacca (figure 8.2) separates the Indonesian island of Sumatra from the Malay peninsula and the island of Singapore. For centuries it has been navigated as the shortest route from the Indian Ocean to the South China Sea, gateway to the East Indies and the Far East, and later to Australia and New Zealand. Through this strait pass yearly 40,000 ships, for the most part cargo ships and tankers (other than those of 200,000 cwt or more) carrying oil to Japan from the Persian Gulf; through it, too, pass warships, as notably in 1971, during the Indo-Pakistan war, those of the United States and the Soviet Union. Avoidance of the Strait of Malacca by a more southerly course adds distance except to and from Australia and New Zealand, and its use is greatly preferred because it leads to the great entrepôt of Singapore and all the facilities for shipping which it provides. The strait is of ample breadth and depth, but narrows to a minimum of 8.4 nautical miles. If Malaysia and Indonesia were content with territorial seas of a three-nautical mile breadth, then the strait would allow the freedom of navigation through high seas for transit. This freedom for the maritime countries appeared threatened, however, when in 1960 Indonesia claimed a twelve-nautical mile width, as did Malaysia in 1969. Moreover, by a treaty of 1970 the two states agreed not only to delimit their territorial seas in this way, but also to share between them the sea-bed of the strait. This treaty acknowledged the right of innocent passage through the strait, but innocent passage falls somewhat short of freedom of the seas [Leifer and Nelson 1973]. While

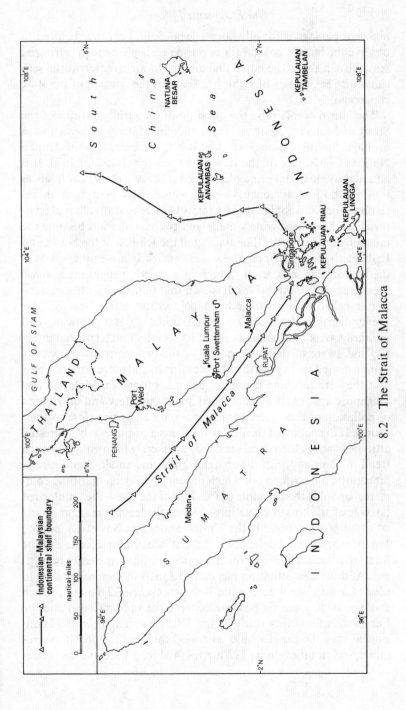

8.2 The Strait of Malacca

innocent passage is for all states a legal right, they are required to observe the laws of coastal states during passage through territorial seas. Also, it should be noted that air navigation over territorial seas cannot be enjoyed as of right, but requires the consent of the state concerned.

The above events raise the question of the juridical status of the Strait of Malacca, as of all straits in general; they present, too, a problem for discussion and, if possible, settlement at the United Nations Conference on the Law of the Sea scheduled for 1974. It is abundantly clear that principles agreed at the two earlier conferences (in 1958 and 1960 at Geneva) were so worded as to permit variant interpretations and applications. Claims to increased stretches of territorial sea have been widely made and twelve miles has become the most favoured breadth. The sharing of the sea-bed of the North and Irish seas between their coastal states has clearly pre-empted parts of the bed of high seas, even though in a strictly geographical sense these are continental shelves. It is clear that Indonesia, with an extensive so-called 'mid-ocean archipelago' territory and a large, yet unevenly distributed population (of 120 millions), is a politically and militarily weak state anxious about its security and territorial integrity and aware of the naval power of the two superpowers, visibly demonstrated as they use the Malacca Strait, and more ominous now that they are reaching a state of accord. Indonesia, Malaysia and Singapore are genuinely concerned about the safety and prevention of pollution of this arterial trade route, which passes close to their shores. If the action of the first two affirms a positive, self-interested attitude towards their local seas, they are merely following a modern trend in company with other states great and small. Significantly, Singapore, the economy of which depends vitally on maritime commerce, upholds the principle of freedom of the seas – the unimpeded passage of all ships of all nations – which the leading maritime and/ or naval powers, notably the United States, the Soviet Union and Japan, proclaim and defend: for the first two, unimpaired use of the Strait of Malacca *inter alia* for strategical purposes is clearly important. And the new situation has turned Japan to reconsider the old idea of a ship canal across the Kra peninsula of Thailand, which could provide a shorter passage between the Indian Ocean and the Far East. A feasibility study by the Thai Government in 1972 considered that the canal would cost $450 million, be 156 kilometres (ninety-seven miles) long, 122 metres (400 feet) wide and 18 metres

(60 feet) deep. The largest tankers able to pass through would have a displacement of 100,000 cwt, which is small by comparison with the very large crude carriers of 500,000 cwt. However, such vessels would be suitable for tankers carrying products, and it is possible that Japan will assist at least one Persian Gulf state to build its own refinery. According to Japanese estimates made in 1963, a canal across the Kra isthmus would save only one day's sailing compared with the Malacca route. Levine [1937] gives a very interesting account of earlier plans to construct this canal.

Not long ago, as a result of the Arab–Israeli war which started in 1948, the Gulf of Akaba became an area of tension and international concern. This gulf at the northern end of the Red Sea is some twenty miles or less in breadth, accessible by sea only through the narrow Strait of Tiran where Egypt at Sharm el Sheik in Egyptian Sinai can control entry. The Gulf washes the coasts of Egypt, Israel, Jordan and Saudi Arabia, providing at Akaba Jordan's only seaport and at Eilat an Israeli seaport which is the more useful to Israel when, as during this war, ships destined for her Mediterranean ports were denied passage through the Suez Canal, and when now (Spring 1974), this canal has not yet been cleared. The legal position was and is clear, namely, that 'all gulfs and bays enclosed by the land of more than one littoral State, however narrow their entrance may be, are non-territorial' (i.e. the Gulf of Akaba is part of the high seas) [Oppenheim 1955]. However, the Strait of Tiran provides part of the territorial waters of Egypt and Saudi Arabia through which ships must pass to enter the Gulf, so that, in time of war against Israel, Egypt can properly exercise rights to blockade. When the United Nations Security Council was required in 1951 to consider Israeli protests against Egypt's restrictions on the access of shipping to its ports, those two countries, while still at war in the legal sense, had concluded an armistice. The Security Council resolution nevertheless found no justification for the continuance of these restrictions and called upon Egypt not to interfere with shipping seeking to pass through the Tiran Strait and the Suez Canal. During 1974 it seemed that the port of Sharm el Sheik was one of the areas of Arab territory which Israel would insist on retaining. The new road built from Eilat to the port after the 1967 war gives some evidence of long-term aims. Significantly, during the 1973 fighting, the Bab al Mandab strait, at the southern entrance to the Red Sea was closed to Israeli shipping by Egyptian and Yemeni vessels.

(ii) Canals and Canalised Routes

Another group of international waterways that are either wholly or in part engineered routes, consists of the canals of Suez, Panama, the St Lawrence Seaway, and on a lesser scale those of Kiel and Corinth, this last-named having been cut by the Emperor Trajan in the second century AD. Features common to the canals are limitations on the draught of ships admitted and the payment of dues, which affect the economics of using shorter routes. Suez Canal, opened in 1869, with permissible draught limits raised to 10.5–11.58 metres (34.4–38 feet) during 1958–67, has scarcely lasted a century despite the high hopes centred on it and its availability to the ships of all the world in peace and in war as agreed by the Turkish Empire in the Convention of Constantinople of 1888. The achievement of French enterprise, it became of first importance to the United Kingdom, being conceived for many years as a jugular vein since, both strategically and commercially, it greatly shortened the route from Britain to India, Malaya, Singapore and East Africa. Its existence served to keep Egypt in political dependence on the United Kingdom, to which it offered not only the convenience of the canal but also a military base with the advantage of accessibility from two oceans. Egypt closed the canal in 1956–7 and again in 1967, and only in 1974 is it being cleared for re-opening. By 1966 its chief importance was for the transport of oil from the Persian Gulf to Western users and oil then made up seventy per cent of all cargoes carried. However, technological changes, notably the building of giant tankers of 200,000–300,000 tons cwt, which effect great manpower economies and thus lower freight costs, radically reduced the importance of the Suez Canal to world shipping. Indeed, when account was taken of the dues payable, it ceased to be profitable as it was incapable, too, of admitting ships of deep draught.

The Panama Canal, an American achievement opened in 1914, has proved mainly important to the United States, which provides the bulk of the traffic between its Atlantic and Pacific coasts and from its east coast to the Far East and western ports of South America. The canal has the disadvantage of a flight of locks to and from Lake Gatun which stands at 26.2 metres (eighty-six feet) above sea level. Also shipping must be adapted to the canal's permitted maximum depth of 12.19 metres (forty feet) which may fall to 10.67 metres (thirty-five feet) during the January to April period. Like Suez it is 'free and open to vessels of commerce and war, of all nations, in peace or war, on terms of equality'. The United States, by a treaty in 1903 with the Republic of Panama, in return for a guarantee of Panama's independence and a money payment, was granted a 16.09 kilometre (ten-mile) wide zone astride the canal and the right, by fortifications within this zone, strongly to protect the canal. However, resort to containerisation (containers being moved by surface transport across the Panama isthmus) somewhat reduces the value of the canal which is unsuitable for the bigger ships of today. Accordingly the United States contemplates the building of another canal about 16.09 kilometres (ten miles) from the present one capable of admitting ships of up to 150,000 cwt [Couper 1972].

Kiel Canal, built by the German Empire and opened in 1903, was conceived to have strategical importance since it shortened by 402 kilometres (250 miles) the water route between Kiel and the estuary of the Elbe, i.e. between the Baltic and the North Sea. Although open to all on payment of dues and admitting ships up to a maximum draught of 9.45 metres (thirty-one feet), it is used mainly for small ships and barges by Germany and other local countries, and carries in fact a considerable bulk of cargo.

The St Lawrence Seaway, a joint United States/Canadian enterprise, resulted from the engineering improvements effected on the 290-kilometre (180-mile) stretch of the St Lawrence upstream from Montreal to the eastern entrance of Lake Ontario, part of which marks the international boundary [Hills 1959]. Here new channels, locks and canals substituted a water depth of 8.1 metres (twenty-seven feet) for the pre-existing 4.2 metres (fourteen feet). Opened in April 1959 it thus provided a route for oceanic shipping carrying up to 9144 tonnes of cargo, to and from the deep interior of North America, to and from the great lakeside cities of Montreal, Toronto, Cleveland, Chicago, Milwaukee and Duluth; and at its extreme western end it serves also the lakehead grain terminals of Canada at Fort William and Port Arthur. It was conceived primarily as a commercial outlet to the ocean rather than as a deepwater route for overseas shipping, and since United States defence interests were involved, notably at the sensitive area of the American Sault Ste Marie locks which link Lakes Huron and Superior, Sino-Soviet ships were precluded from use of these locks (*The Times*, 22 April 1959). The legal status of the St Lawrence Seaway differs somewhat from that of the international canals. Apart from tolls, pilotage is required of foreign vessels and, owing to the winter freeze, use of the Seaway is limited to the open season between varying dates starting in April and ending in December.

6 Fishing and Pollution Problems

Fishing has an important place in the economy of both lightly settled states where other economic opportunities are restricted, such as Norway and Iceland, as also of highly developed and well-settled states, such as the United Kingdom, the Soviet Union and Japan, which have large markets for fish and fish products. The world's catch more than doubled between 1958 and 1970 – from thirty-three million to sixty-eight million tonnes. Population growth has steadily increased the demand for fish while technical efficiency in detecting shoals and in fishing have underlined the importance of conservation. Some nations have attempted to prescribe conservation zones where fishing is to be avoided and a number of measures have been enacted that seek to prevent over-fishing and the catching of immature fish. Related to fishing grounds, although of wider relevance, is the well-appreciated need to check pollution which, we are told, may, for example, turn the Mediterranean into a gigantic cesspool. The Oil in Navigable Waters Act of 1967, to which thirty-six nations subscribed, laid it down that persistent oil should not be discharged, as from the washing of tanks, in certain zones of the sea. Perhaps even more serious are the dangers which follow from the discharge into the sea of pesticides and highly concentrated radioactive materials, which, though dumped in containers, may be ultimately released. Clearly more stringent measures than at present apply towards better conservation and the avoidance of pollution await international agreement and implementation.

Prolonged fishery disputes have for long been common – since about 1700 in the northern seas between Norway, Faroes, Iceland and Greenland [Alexander 1963], as also elsewhere, as for example, between the Russians and the Japanese over the Sea of Okhotsk fishery in the Far East. The continual extension of exclusive fishery zones has been one marked feature of international rivalry, and imprecise and unenforceable international regulations leave the way open to national declarations of spacious fishery zones. In 1970, by the Montevideo Declaration, all the Latin American countries with coasts (Venezuela excepted) claimed the right to as much sea (and sea-bed) beyond their coasts as was thought necessary [Fawcett 1973, p.20]. In the same year Canada, by Act of Parliament, defined zones occupying over 259,000 square kilometres (100,000 square miles) beyond its coasts as fishing zones exclusive to itself. In 1972–3 world attention turned to Iceland's so-called 'Cod War', a dispute with other European countries, but especially with the United Kingdom, which arose out of Iceland's unilateral claim to control exclusively fishing within a zone fifty nautical miles outwards from the baselines drawn between headlands along its coasts. Already in 1958 Iceland extended its exclusive fishing limit from four to twelve nautical miles, arguing that it had a special need of fish as a basis of its economy and also that it could thus apply conservation measures. This meant that Iceland appropriated areas in excess of 200 metres (656 feet) in depth where others, notably British and Germans, had customarily fished. It followed up this policy in 1972 by claiming a zone fifty nautical miles wide, to which Britain stoutly objected and in which its trawlers continued to fish, despite harassment and at times with naval protection. Iceland refused to take its claim to the International Court, a majority decision of which accepted the British case. Certainly fishing is of great importance to Iceland as a basis of industries and of exports and it is of very considerable scale: measured in terms of population per head, Iceland's catch is 190 times that of the United Kingdom. 'We do not deny,' the Icelandic Foreign Minister is reported to have said (*The Times*, 17 March 1972), 'that our ultimate aim is that all, or nearly all, the fish taken in Icelandic waters (sic) should be taken by Icelandic ships. . . . If you like this has an element of selfishness.' Certainly unilateral action of such kind, which is by no means rare and thus far has always succeeded, disfigures international relations and emphasises the need for further international discussions and agreements.

7 Military Uses of the Sea

The seas have always been one milieu for the exercise of political power by means of warships operating from defended bases, and for centuries freedom to navigate the seas and oceans has depended on the backing of naval power to secure routes against enemies and pirates. The political strength often lightly attributed to insular countries is found only when, as in Britain and Japan, they have developed their seafaring skills and naval forces. The American

Captain Mahan [1890] long ago showed clearly in his books some
of the major effects on history which followed from command of the
sea, and for a few centuries the growth, strength and viability of the
British Empire as a mercantile, financial and political structure bore
witness to the efficiency of British foreign policy which sought peaceful stability and survival by means of alliances and the maintenance
of strong naval power. Technological innovations, notably of the
submarine and of aircraft, introduced new dimensions to the strategy
of defence as of war. German submarine warfare in the Second
World War, directed against ships carrying essential cargoes of food
and war material, only narrowly failed in its purpose. Land-based
aircraft, too, challenged the effectiveness of surface fleets in narrow
seas even though the aircraft carrier reinforced the defensive and
offensive strength of surface fleets. Nor has naval power been ren-
dered either unnecessary or useless by the development of nuclear
ballistic missiles which can be launched at long range. Indeed, the
nuclear submarine has achieved, for a time at least, a certain primacy
as the most powerful and forbidding weapon of defence and thus has
served in the maintenance of peace: cruising at depth and capable of
long sessions away from base, it makes sonar detection difficult.
Indeed for submarines generally, of which the Soviet Union and the
United States (in that order) hold the greatest numbers, the future is
still bright. Control of the deep waters might appear to be the key to
the command of the surface sea for the safe passage of commercial
and military cargoes.

For the purposes of defence and war the leading maritime powers
turn with increasing interest to the opportunities offered by the sea
floor, and not only that of their own continental shelves. Submarine
detection and tracking stations can be established on the sea floor.
Already for some years the United States has maintained electronic
listening devices in watertight plastic containers on the Atlantic floor
off the eastern coast, as doubtless elsewhere at selected points off the
Pacific and Mediterranean coasts. Thus from undersea stations a
watch can be kept on enemy submarines intent on attacking merchant ships and from these, too, offensive action against surface
ships can be taken. Further, missiles and anti-missiles could be
launched from fixed stations set on high ridges of the sea-bed and
thus nearer to their targets. Clearly the oceans, and perhaps the
Arctic especially, offer new military possibilities and it is disturbing
to recall that international law is far from clear about national rights

to the sea-bed [Luard 1968]. Certainly it is the advanced technological nations that are already able, and still become increasingly
prepared, to take advantage of them. In 1969 the Russian delegate at
the seventeen-nation disarmament conference at Geneva tabled a
draft treaty, the purpose of which was to deny the use of the sea-bed
outside territorial waters for military purposes but rather to retain it
as a sphere for man's peaceful activities [*The Times*, 19 March 1969;
Butler 1971]. The United States at this time wished only to prohibit
'the emplacement or fixing of nuclear weapons of mass destruction
on the sea-bed' (i.e. it did not want a complete demilitarisation of the
sea-bed).

Conclusion

Now that the world's land area has been shared between states we
witness an unmistakable trend towards the appropriation of the
larger resources which the oceans and seas present. Either individually or in associated groups, states have been nibbling at the
margins of the high seas where they approach their coasts as they
have been substituting in their enlarged territorial seas the right of
innocent passage for the fuller right to freedom of the seas. Considerable progress has been made in this century in the acceptance by
states of agreed principles – inscribed in treaties and conventions and
in decisions of the International Court – which make for fair dealing,
reasonable exploitation of marine and submarine resources, and the
easement of maritime transport. Thus ships make their way – in time
of peace at least – with little let or hindrance and needed resources,
especially of natural gas and petroleum, are won from beneath the
sea-bed by those technologically able and geographically well-
placed. Yet it is clear that the quarrels of, and friction between states
extend increasingly to the seas and that the practice of unilateral or
group declarations by states conflicts with the rights and interests of
others. Further, the practice of states refusing to put a case to the International Court when one has been made against them, or of refusing to accept Court decisions when made, introduces an anarchical
element into international relations. At another level difficulties on
which wide agreement is needed arise as, for example, over nuclear
explosions, marine pollution, the military use of the sea-bed, conservation and the compulsory routing of ships in waters hazardous
through wrecks, such as the North Sea and the English Channel. This

doubtless indicates that problems abound for consideration and decision at United Nations Conferences on the Law of the Sea – not that one should expect then any final solution of such problems.

It was believed that the conference at Caracas in the summer of 1974 would find it harder to reach agreement on important questions than did the conferences at the Hague in 1930 and at Geneva in 1958 and 1960 [Luard 1974]. Indeed, no less than 148 states sent their representatives, among them the People's Republic of China, which was interested to champion the cause of the Third World against the 'imperial hegemony' of the sea held by the Soviet Union and the United States. Another difficulty facing this conference was that a number of states had already, by unilateral action, made decisions about historic bays, straight baselines, archipelagos and fishing zones.

The Caracas conference gave vent to narrow nationalist interests and, although it lasted ten weeks, reached no agreement on specific principles that could be codified into law. It exposed the divergence of views between the developed nations, including the major maritime powers, and the developing nations. Whereas the former wanted to preserve their rights to sea-bed exploitation and to naval passage on unrestricted high seas, the latter wanted to apply a strong international regime to waters outside territorial jurisdiction (*The Times*, 30 August 1974). At least the conference agreed to meet again at Geneva in the spring of 1975 and succeeded in isolating the main issues and in reducing the number of possible solutions on which agreement might be eventually found. Wide support too was forthcoming for a twelve-mile broad territorial sea, although this would bring about a hundred straits within the territorial waters of adjoining states (Luard, *The Sunday Times*, 1 September 1974). There was wide interest also in agreement on a 200-mile offshore economic zone in which a state would control all economic resources. In short, the importance of the problems raised by the seas, as mankind's ultimate treasure store of food and raw materials, is now recognised, but there seems little prospect that this will be shared in any equitable way for the benefit of the international community.

9 The Grouping of States

I object to stray little states lying in the way of great powers.

(Bernard Shaw)*

I blush to say it, but independence is the sole good we have gained at the expense of everything else.

(Simón Bolívar 1830)†

It is paradoxical that in recent decades the successful launching of new independent states has been matched by persistent efforts to create new groupings or associations of states for a variety of purposes. As political attitudes changed and opportunities presented themselves to national and other groups, wishful to escape from imperialist restraints and to govern themselves in their own ways, the world political map has come to assume an increasingly fragmented pattern. That political independence has been achieved often by peaceful negotiation rather than by military struggle is doubtless a matter for legitimate rejoicing, but independence merely transfers to new rulers all the problems and difficulties involved in the making of decisions about their own internal and external affairs. In most cases, but with glaring exceptions such as the Belgian Congo, the transfer of power to new rulers, backed by governmental institutions, police and armed forces, made provision for a fair start for the voyage into uncharted seas. Independence did not eliminate dependence: rather it highlighted the financial and economic dependence of new states on the strong, creating situations for which the word 'neocolonialism' was coined [Nkrumah 1965]. Clearly difficulties arose and adaptations had to be made before workable and appropriate

---

* A surprising view from a Fabian socialist, this was expressed in support of the imperialism of Lord Rosebery. See Lawrence, D. H., ed. [1972]: *Bernard Shaw: Collected Letters*, vol. II (1898–1910), London, p. 14.

† Cited by R.A. Humphreys, *The Times*, 22 May 1972.

systems of government were found. In many cases, as with some former British colonies, the democratic system, modelled on that of the United Kingdom, proved too mature and too difficult to apply successfully and was replaced by variant systems involving a personal leader who was often, as in Nigeria, Uganda and Niger, a soldier. At the worst, as in the former Belgian colonies of Congo, Rwanda and Burundi, there has been inter-tribal warfare and much bloodshed, suggesting that in these cases decolonisation was an unprepared and over-hasty process: indeed such cases show the stupidity and wrongheadedness of applying with insufficient thought the United Nations policy of rapidly emancipating colonial peoples. But in the main the new states have grappled with their internal problems and many, notably in Africa, whose viability was gravely doubted at their birth, have by their survival confounded the prophets of doom.

States, like individuals, cannot live alone and apart; rather they form units in a world of states which, as Mackinder [1919] emphasised, is a 'Going Concern', a delicate, interlocking mechanism, susceptible to jarring at any point. These many former colonies which emerged as independent states, their independence acclaimed and formally recognised by membership of the United Nations, entered a world where wealth, power and decision-making had long been the prerogative of the leading powers and where, accordingly, their independence from external pressures and coercion, as also their territorial integrity, appeared to be at risk. This seemed to be likely in the light of history, contemporary as well as past, since, given the sharp inequalities in the scale, wealth and power of states, their relationships have involved continual armed conflict. Yet, although war has been a recurrent feature of international relations since the end of the Second World War, and notably in Korea, Vietnam and the Middle East, it is no less clear that this is only one of the ways, though the most dramatic, in which states behave. Many of the ways in which states conduct their external relationships are at once so necessary, habitual and mundane as to escape the attention they deserve. While so much publicity is given by the press, radio and television to international disputes and wars, a great deal of effective and peaceful co-operation sustains the world as a 'Going Concern' and provides the means of civilised living. Consider the work done by the fourteen agencies set up and operated by the United Nations, which deal successfully with matters fundamental to the well-being of all as, for example, by the World Health Organisation, the Food and Agriculture Organisation, the World Postal Organisation, and by others dealing with labour relations, cultural matters (UNESCO), and the problems arising from trafficking in drugs. There are grounds here for an optimistic view of human progress, as diseases such as malaria are widely eliminated, as pests, such as locust swarms, are controlled if not wholly effaced, as letters and parcels make their ways between the ends of the earth, as UNESCO tries to promote the understanding and association of contrasting cultures and as the Council of Europe, at a lower level, has tried to improve the national textbooks of history and geography in Europe.

One might deduce from the above that, where a common interest is widely shared, virtually world-wide co-operation can be successfully achieved. Unfortunately the rulers of states, and often too their citizens, are actuated by fears, aspirations and commercial, territorial and other forms of self-interest which, expressed and applied in their foreign policies, exert a divisive effect in that they create groupings of states for specific purposes not always appreciated by other states. Yet this tendency towards the grouping of states is not just divisive, for it also points the way to larger, composite political associations and may mark a stage in the slow progression from a fragmented to a unified world.

1 The Trend Towards International Groupings

Persistent efforts to form groupings of states of several different kinds took place in a world where political and military power was polarised between the United States and the Soviet Union and where industrial and commercial corporations grew vastly in scale as they expanded their operations across international frontiers and, backed by financial and economic strength, like the feudal barons of medieval times, wielded considerable political power both at home and abroad. However, they took place also at a time when, for a variety of reasons, the brute strength of the leading states could no longer be freely exercised at the expense of the weak. Colonialism or imperialism – it is the same phenomenon – no longer appeared feasible or profitable: it is now widely held that small states should be free to make their way and be helped by stronger states so to do; the General Assembly of the United Nations provides a forum where all member nations can air their views; and the so-called nuclear stalemate between the two super powers has ensured a certain global security from major war despite many localised military operations. Actually the weaker states, including those newly launched, had a fairer start than might have been expected: by grouping together they could win publicity at the United Nations for policies that irked their stronger fellow members; by exploiting the rivalry of the superpowers, countries like Afghanistan, Egypt and Cuba were able to win financial aid and political support; and even in the wider context of world politics rather than of national and self-interested policy, small states have had the power to act: witness a tribute paid by Dr Waldheim (*The Times*, 6 November 1973) to the contribution of the eight non-permanent members of the United Nations Security Council for their initiative in ensuring that the United Nations emergency force sent to separate the combatants and to police the ceasefire in the Middle East should not include troops of the five permanent members of this Council. Even so, given that states are arranged in hierarchical order because of their differences in manpower, level of economic and technological development, command of resources and many other respects, and given also the interdependence of the World Community, the need for association with others, the better to guarantee security and to promote national interests, has come to characterise the policies of both weak and strong states.

Fully ten per cent of all independent states, and among these some of the most populous, are federally organised, thus testifying that federalism can provide a valid state-idea. But the widespread application of the federal principle faces severe limitations: blue-prints, easily and hopefully drawn, have often failed miserably (see pp. 123–4). While it is still true that some states, such as the Soviet Union and the South African Republic administer under constraint a wide range of peoples, for the most part wider political unities have to be based on genuine common interest to be successful. The difficulties that accordingly arise point to the need for associations less ambitious and complete than federations and to those limited to specific objectives about which common interest is sufficiently strong. Such developments, growing from grass roots, offer more promise and may contain the seeds of political growth. Certainly the marked trend towards wider political association which has manifested itself since 1945, while repeating much which smacks of the past, expresses, too, fresh efforts of progressive thinking.

What Hartshorne [1954] referred to as 'political organisations at higher ranks' may be more briefly called 'blocs' or, more accurately, 'international blocs'. Their nature is aptly defined in Webster's *International Dictionary* (1937) as 'a combination of persons, interests, usually inharmonious, but temporarily drawn together by a common cause'. The international blocs of today, for the greater part freely negotiated, are broadly regional in pattern and variously functional in purpose, the purposes ranging from defence, economic production and trade, to the cultural and political spheres.* The objective of really close association might seem implicit in the use for some of these of terms such as 'community' and 'integration'. A pragmatic realism largely explains the creation of these blocs yet, in some instances at least, the goals set involve an element of idealism. The European Economic Community (E.E.C.) from its inception envisaged an ultimate goal of political integration, thus looking forward towards the effacement of the concept, as some would think outworn, of national sovereignty. Here, indeed, a revolutionary note is struck in favour of a large, well-ordered, multi-national society.

2 The United Nations

In their breadth of purpose, cohesion, inclusiveness and selectivity, as well as in their effectiveness, existing international blocs invite attention as a potent means of both dividing and uniting nations. By achieving a high degree of universality the United Nations (U.N.) stands first. It was wisely initiated in 1945 before the Second World War had ended while the western allies and co-belligerents still shared the common purpose of winning the war. It was able to profit from the failure of the League of Nations, which was lame from the start because the United States had refused to join. In its provision for an assembly where all member states had an equal voice and vote, it created a forum for well-publicised discussions and the chance for inner groups to form and to co-operate in policy-making. Yet it realistically recognised the inequalities in the world of states by naming the five major allies who won the war – the United States, the Soviet Union, the United Kingdom, France and China – as permanent

* For more information about international organisations than can be given here, the reader is referred to *The Statesman's Yearbook 1973–1974* [1973]: Macmillan, London, pp. 3–53.

members, with a right of veto, of the Security Council. Events in mainland China, where communist forces, led by General Mao Tse-Tung, gained control in 1949 and from which Marshal Chang Kai Chek fled to the island of Formosa (Taiwan), introduced the anomaly that Taiwan held China's permanent seat on the Security Council. The siting of the U.N. headquarters in New York may arguably have been unwise, but again testifies to the primacy of wealth and military power held by the United States which, until 1948, was the sole owner of the atomic bomb. However, the European office of the United Nations at Geneva is being so expanded as to provide more capacity than its New York headquarters.

At its start the U.N. numbered only forty-five members, more than half of the total of independent states. However, its membership grew fast – to 82 in 1957, 113 in 1964 and 126 in 1973 – thus keeping pace with the emergence of new states mainly in Asia and Africa, but also in Central America and in Europe. Thus the U.N. approaches universality, the more so when account is taken of the fact that non-members include states which are neutral and others too small to play an effective part. These include Switzerland, which does not wish to impair its neutrality by joining, partitioned states like Korea and Vietnam, and microstates like Monaco that are too small to share its major responsibilities. Such non-member states, however, often share in U.N. activities. The admission of the People's Republic of China in 1972 and of the two German republics in 1973 has remedied some of these difficulties and the only state that briefly withdrew – Indonesia – resumed its membership.

Although the U.N. increasingly approximates to universality, its institutions in no sense monopolise international politics, much of which is conducted outside its orbit, as formerly by De Gaulle and more recently by President Nixon and Mr Brezhnev. The U.N. has not failed to register some successes. In the absence of the Soviet representative, the Security Council was able to sponsor resistance to North Korean forces in Korea, by the use of its peace-keeping forces to avert further civil war in the Belgian Congo (now Zaïre) and in Cyprus, and to provide similar help in the Middle East in the attempt to secure peace between Israel and the Arab states. A great deal of quietly effective work, as we have already noted, is carried out by its agencies. Moreover, the General Assembly provides a forum for the public expression of every range of political view and gives weak states the chance at least to be heard. As Dean Rusk noted [Wainhouse 1964], in theory a two-thirds majority of the General Assembly could be got by nations with only ten per cent of the world's population and who contribute only five per cent of its assessed budget. In theory again, the Afro-Asian bloc can appear very strong, at least numerically. Even if the venting of national views achieves little in the short run, it may lessen tensions and contribute to changing political attitudes and policies. Certainly the U.N. bids fair to endure, although rather than uniting the world it exposes its disunity. It demonstrates, too, the need for regional blocs.

3 The Commonwealth

This successor to, or as some may well think, ghost of the British Empire, dates from the Statute of Westminster of 1931, which accorded political independence to the former self-governing dominions of Canada, Newfoundland, South Africa, Australia and New Zealand [Jennings 1954]. In step with the largely peaceful process by which Britain handed over power to most of its dependencies, these, including India, Pakistan and Ceylon in 1947, as sovereign states, joined the Commonwealth, which numbered twenty-two members in 1965 and had increased to thirty-six by Christmas 1973. The Republic of Ireland and Burma did not choose to join and the South African Republic, Rhodesia and Pakistan have withdrawn. A measure of community of interest is provided by the wide use of the English language and, in varying degrees, that of English law and institutions, membership (except for Canada) of the sterling bloc, and common experience of British rule.

The zaniest of planners could never have conceived, still less have drawn, the blue-print of an international bloc such as the Commonwealth. Some observers regard it as a myth rather than a political reality, or at best as a club. Around an inner core of countries, the populations of which are to a large but lessening extent the descendants of immigrants from the British Isles – Canada, Australia and New Zealand – are grouped numerous others whose populations are neither British nor indeed Christian. The geographical extent and distribution of the Commonwealth is certainly striking, as is also its weight of population which accounts for twenty to twenty-five per cent of mankind. What strength and reality the Commonwealth possesses rests on the fact that it is a free association of countries, drawn from every continent, which find some advantage and convenience by staying together and by the meetings of presidents and prime ministers in full conference to exchange ideas and information. It implies some degree of friendliness and mutual support, rather than formal obligations, between members, and shares confidential information which is distributed by its secretariat set up in 1965. It assembles kingdoms and republics of remarkably different scale and living standards, all of which acknowledge the British monarch as its Head. It has not been able to exert enough influence to settle either the Kashmir dispute which has long divided India and Pakistan, or the racialist problem posed by Rhodesia's unilateral declaration of independence in 1965. But it brought enough pressure to secure the withdrawal of South Africa in 1961, and it was not disrupted by the entry of the United Kingdom into the European Economic Community in 1972.

The Commonwealth is neither a political nor a military bloc, since it has no common foreign policy or common defence policy. Some of its members are associated together, as are the United Kingdom and Canada in NATO and Australia and New Zealand in ANZUS. Some members may at times adopt a neutralist position in world politics or, like India, are at pains to establish good relations with the Soviet Union. At least this widest and loosest of blocs brings together a medley of nations, races and creeds, the rich and the poor, the technologically advanced and the developing countries, the representatives of which can periodically review basic world issues, not least of which is racialism, above all in Africa, from which a third of its membership is drawn.

4 Regional Blocs: Defensive

The need for defensive regional blocs sprang from the need, if states were to preserve their independence, of alliances to secure a balance of power. The Second World War had demonstrated to continents old and new alike the dangers of the armed might of Germany and Japan. Its end brought the collapse of the powers that had sought to achieve world mastery, but at the same time created an entirely new balance of power, the major control of which fell to the United States, which alone until 1949 commanded atomic weapons, and the Soviet Union, which maintained the most powerful army in Europe.

In Europe and Asia the Red Army appeared formidable and the Soviet Union recovered not only those territories which Hitler's

9.1   The Soviet Union's satellites in Europe

armies had occupied and devastated, but also the so-called 'western territories' which had been formerly held by Russia but lost to the new Soviet regime [East 1951]. Further, in the wake of its advancing army, it was able to set up along its western border a tier of allied and satellite states (figure 9.1) under communist, one-party regimes. Defeated Germany, which had made itself for a time the power centre of Europe, was, as official language described it, both truncated and partitioned. On its eastern flank it lost territory mainly to Poland but also (in East Prussia) to the Soviet Union, while to allay Stalin's fear of a renewal of German militarism and aggression, it was divided into two parts, the eastern of which, stretching westwards astride the Elbe River, as the German Democratic Republic, was occupied by Soviet troops and organised as a communist dictatorship. In a sharply visible way emerged the so-called Iron Curtain, a rigid, fortified boundary, marking the western limits of the communist states where they impinged upon the democratic systems of the nations of northern, western and southern Europe.

'Who can believe that there will be permanent peace in Europe, or in the whole world, while the frontiers of Asia rest on the Elbe?' asked Sir Winston Churchill (*The Times*, 24 January 1948), in reference to this westward territorial expansion of the Soviet Union that appeared to threaten the security of the remaining countries of the continent. These occupied its relatively restricted western, insular and peninsular extremities between the Atlantic Ocean and the Mediterranean Sea. And it was in reaction to this external danger and to the Soviet Union's implacable attitude of non-co-operation that, as a measure of communal defence, the North Atlantic Treaty Organisation was formed in 1949 under the leadership of the United States, itself aware that its own safety depended upon European allies.

(i) The North Atlantic Treaty Organisation

At its inception by the North Atlantic Treaty of April 1949, NATO associated in collective defence the United States, Canada and ten countries of western Europe – the United Kingdom, Iceland, France, Norway, Denmark, Belgium, the Netherlands, Luxembourg, Italy and Portugal. In 1952 Greece and Turkey joined, and in 1955 the Federal Republic of Germany (figure 9.2). An armed attack on one or more of the members, it was agreed, was an attack on all, and integrated military forces, together with similarly organised naval forces, were set up. Special features of this alliance are that Iceland provides the American base at Reykjavik and neither Norway nor Denmark permits nuclear weapons on its territory. It is noteworthy that this treaty bridged the North Atlantic in a mutual defensive system and that this was extended to include the Mediterranean Sea, where the American sixth fleet held control and where NATO was afforded a valuable right flank stretching 3218 kilometres (2000 miles) [East 1953]. The defection of France in 1966 from NATO's integrated military command and the invasion of Czechoslovakia in 1968 by communist forces to prevent the liberalising changes sought by the Dubcek government, underlined for NATO the strategic importance of the so-called 'grey areas' of central Europe [Gasteyger 1974]. These were the countries outside the military blocs, whether neutral like Sweden, Switzerland and Austria, or communist but unaligned like Yugoslavia, which separated NATO's northern and southern (Mediterranean) members. In particular, Yugoslavia gives access from central Europe to Italy, Greece and the Mediterranean via the Adriatic Sea. When Czechoslovakia was invaded, NATO and the American Secretary of State issued statements making clear their views of the importance of the continuing independence of these countries, as also that of Rumania, to the stability and security of Europe. It should be noted that Ireland and Spain also lie outside the major defence blocs and that Finland, with military forces suitable only for home security, is bound to the Soviet Union by a treaty of friendship of 1948.

NATO has its headquarters in Brussels and to regard it as a grouping of wholly democratic nations is inaccurate, since Portugal, Greece and Turkey have or have long had authoritarian regimes. A long-term aim of the original creators of NATO that there might develop a North Atlantic community has in no sense been achieved, yet for twenty-five years or so it has fulfilled its chief purpose – the preservation of peace in Europe and North America. Although the Soviet press has described NATO as 'a military colossus', it is generally believed that it is opposed in central Europe by overwhelmingly stronger forces (*The Times*, 5 April 1974). In some respects NATO's defensive system has weakened as a result of the Soviet Union's assertion of power over Czechoslovakia and of the considerable naval forces that it has built up in the Mediterranean, although it does not have the use there of either Yugoslav or Albanian ports or

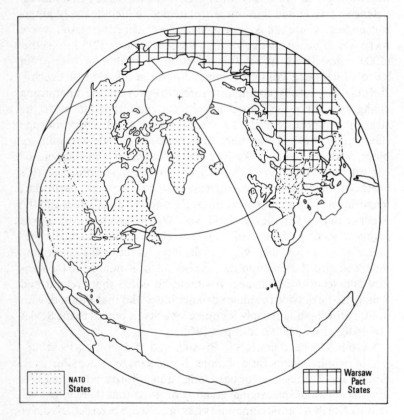

9.2   NATO and Warsaw Pact states

of local bases for air surveillance. The re-opening of the Suez Canal, which appears likely in 1975, should add to the strategical value of this sea, in which access is controlled from the Atlantic by American air forces based in Spain and from the Black Sea by Turkey, which controls the Bosporus, the Sea of Marmara and the Dardanelles.

(ii) The Warsaw Treaty Organisation (W.T.O.)

The Soviet response to NATO was this similarly defensive bloc, which it organised in 1955 by associating for defence under its control its allies – the German Democratic Republic, Poland, Czechoslovakia, Hungary, Rumania, Bulgaria and Albania. Albania left the alliance in 1962, having opted to follow Chairman Mao's leadership, and Yugoslavia preferred to adopt an uncommitted attitude towards the rival blocs. Clearly the Soviet Union holds control over W.T.O. It maintains Red Army forces in the territories of most of its allies and its military intervention in East Germany, Poland and Hungary in 1956, followed by a similar operation mounted by W.T.O. against Czechoslovakia in 1968, illustrates what is meant by the so-called Brezhnev doctrine of limited sovereignty, namely that members of the Warsaw Pact are not at liberty to weaken its collective strength. This alliance of socialist countries is reinforced by the economic and commercial grouping called COMECON, to which we shall refer, and by the fact that the Soviet Union supplies petroleum to Czechoslovakia, Poland, East Germany and Hungary by the friendship pipeline from the distant Volga-Ural field.

(iii) Other Defensive Groupings

Other regional defensive systems are the Central Treaty Organisation (CENTO) and that forged between the United States, Australia and New Zealand (ANZUS). CENTO is an attempt to preserve peace and foster economic development in southwest Asia where the Soviet Union makes territorial contact with Turkey and Iran and on which the United States and western Europe are dependent for supplies of oil. Turkey and Iran, and formerly Iraq, are joined in a mutual defence pact with Great Britain, and the United States, although not formally a member, associates itself with the work of committees of the CENTO Council. This alliance can be regarded as affording support to NATO and a precaution against Soviet expansion such as might threaten to deny oil supplies and achieve an overland link with the Persian Gulf, which Arab states now call the 'Arabian Gulf'. The American sixth fleet, with use of Turkish ports, brings American power close to this theatre of international concern and danger. Similarly, the South-East Asia Collective Defence Treaty of 1954 was organised by the United States, together with Australia, France, New Zealand, Pakistan, the Philippines, Thailand and the United Kingdom, to provide a collective defence system in an area where Chinese communist pressure and expansion were feared; with it, too, were associated efforts to strengthen democratic institutions and to effect economic and technical co-operation. Lastly, ANZUS, a defensive alliance among the United States, Australia and New Zealand, gave recognition to the importance of Australia, revealed during the Second World War, as a major base for the defence of both southeast Asia and the Pacific. While all these regional defence systems fitted into the framework of the U.N., they were responses to the polarity of power held by the two opposed superstates and to the dichotomy of the world in which two irreconcilable ideologies sturdily asserted their claims. The defensive systems, it will be noted, were located both around the inner and outer rims of communist power, represented by the Soviet Union and the People's Republic of China and their allies in Europe and Asia.

5 Regional Blocs: Economic

(i) The European Economic Community (E.E.C.)

Loosely referred to as the Common Market or Little Europe, this marked the culmination of the efforts of west European countries to reorient and restore their economies after the destruction of the Second World War. In this aim they were aided by the stimulus provided by American financial aid, imaginatively conceived and applied under the Marshall Plan, which gave promise that they would be able once again to utilise effectively their pool of highly skilled labour and other resources as also their financial, technological and commercial abilities. Among a number of co-operative associations which prepared the way for the European Economic Community, both BENELUX and the European Coal and Steel Community

(E.C.S.C.) are of special interest. BENELUX registered the success of three small countries – Belgium, the Netherlands and Luxembourg – in creating and operating a common market, showing that even on this small scale such an objective could not be easily and rapidly attained. E.C.S.C., launched in 1952, resulted from the bold initiative in one major field of production of six countries – France, the Federal Republic of Germany, Italy and the three BENELUX countries. Their iron and steel industries with their need for coal, ore and scrap were clearly interdependent and hindered by the effect of international boundaries: if organised as a whole there were much better chances of rationalisation, of economies of scale, and of the free flow of fuel, ore and finished products within an enlarged single market. Thus in a dramatic way E.C.S.C. united France and West Germany, intermittently enemies since 1870, in a promising and, as it proved, successful venture. Later the same six countries entered into a solemn and far-reaching agreement, which in its historic import has been likened to the United States Constitution [Nystrom and Malof 1962]. This was the Treaty of Rome of 1957 in which they undertook to work by stages, by abolishing tariffs on trade between themselves, to create a single large-scale market with a common external tariff, and to seek continuous and balanced economic expansion, raised living standards, increased stability and, as an ultimate purpose, political union.

To effect its high objectives this treaty prescribed institutions, as it also laid down a time-table for action: a Court of Justice (sitting at Luxembourg) served not only the E.E.C. but also the E.C.S.C. and EURATOM (which had already been launched to explore the peaceful uses of atomic energy), a High Assembly, a Council of Ministers and the Common Market Commission. The Assembly which sits at Strasbourg is not directly elected and has, as yet, rather limited powers: initially it comprised 142 members appointed by and from the national parliaments. The Council, normally attended by Foreign Ministers, employs a system of weighted voting: France, Germany and Italy have four votes each, Belgium and the Netherlands have two each, and Luxembourg has one. This is the prime decision-making body and it is assisted by an Economic and Social Committee. Of special interest, as the executive hub of the E.E.C. is its Commission, which is located in Brussels. Responsible to the Community as a whole, this originally had nine full-time members, not more than two of which could be nationals of one member country and which were chosen by common agreement on the basis of their professional ability. Its functions include supervision of the operation of the Treaty and of day-to-day operations, and the making of policy recommendations.

On the one hand, the E.E.C. marked a turning point in history away from narrow divisive nationalisms and offered to the world a model for regional co-operation. On the other, with its emphasis on free and fair competition and its scale of operations, it appears a powerful capitalist structure which, because of its external tariffs and quotas, challenges other trading groups and might appear to divide both Europe and the world. Similarly, while it was inward-looking and seemingly exclusive – a rich man's club – it provided from the start the means of its own enlargement by the admission of other like-minded European nations and also the means, by the offer of associate membership, of helping developing countries, primarily those which had formerly been colonies of The Six, mainly in Africa: the number of associates is large, including Greece and Turkey in Europe and more than twenty outside it. Certainly the E.E.C. commands, in addition to its high tradition of industrial production and commercial activity, great resources of labour, foodstuffs and fuel, above all in the Ruhr coalfield, the natural gas of the Netherlands, and the hydro-electricity of Italy and France. Its early years showed its capacity to develop into a major unit of world industry and trade, comparable in scale with the United States and the Soviet Union. Its need for additional labour was usefully met, until the building in 1961 of the Berlin Wall, by migrant Germans from Eastern Europe and, in particular, from East Germany. And it has drawn heavily on workers from southern Italy, southern Europe, Africa, and even Asia – from Spain, Portugal, Yugoslavia, Greece, Turkey, Algeria, Morocco, Tunisia and Indonesia. Thus in France, for example, thirty per cent of workers in building and public works and twenty-two per cent of those in Renault factories were foreign, and in the whole of the E.E.C. an estimated fifteen per cent of the workforce was made up of migrant labour (*The Times*, 23 May 1973). Although all six countries had suffered the destruction and dislocation of the Second World War, they presented sharp differences of every kind in language, social, economic and legal systems, resources, the balance between agriculture and industry, living standards and much else. Within each country, too, there were difficult regional problems, such, for example, as those presented by the poverty of the over-populated south of Italy and the internal conflict in Belgium between Walloons and Flemings. Yet the centripetal forces have so far proved strong enough to preserve the cohesion of the community: these were an attachment to the democratic system of government and the will to pull together in a common purpose. Despite periodical crises, which discussion has overcome, it would seem that the E.E.C. has reached the point of no return. Indeed, it was able to enlarge itself in 1973 to nine countries by the inclusion of Britain, Ireland and Denmark.

The E.E.C. set itself such an ambitious programme that it was hardly to be expected that all could be achieved within a few decades. It has brought a degree of unity, prosperity and stability to western Europe: it has accorded economic help to a large and increasing number of developing countries and, by extending to them its generalised preference system, stimulated their exports. By its regional policy, too, it is helping also those areas within its own borders that are falling behind through lack of capital investment, unemployment and insufficient industrial growth. So, too, the Community has created institutions which work smoothly and which can be expected to effect further advances. Over thirty outside countries have diplomatic representatives accredited to it at Brussels, thus testifying to its important position in the world. At times it has seemed that France in particular has tried to apply brakes to the E.E.C.'s momentum: the Commission's initiative has been curtailed and the Council of Ministers which meets four times a year has, since 1966, required unanimity, where formerly much could be decided by majority vote; nor has the Assembly yet become a popularly elected body with real teeth, such as it might have if it controlled the Community budget. The E.E.C. has no policy for environmental protection from the evils of pollution, as of the Rhine and the Italian seas. Nor has it developed a common foreign policy: witness its disarray when the Arab oil producers imposed a boycott on the Netherlands in 1973. Indeed, the prime failure of the E.E.C. has been over its major political objective of union, without which common policy, notably on monetary standards, faces almost insuperable difficulties. Here the chief obstacles are presented by nationalist attitudes, especially of France and the United Kingdom: to create even a loose federal structure – a *union de patries* – requires, as the Treaty of Rome envisaged, conceding a measure of national sovereignty. Complete economic and monetary union and political unity were agreed to be goals for 1980 at the Paris Summit of Heads of Government in 1972 (*The Times*, 24 October 1972), but these, together with the assumption of democratic control by the Assembly, would appear by no means certainly attainable.

(ii) The Council for Mutual Economic Assistance (COMECON)

Sensitive to the success of the co-operative efforts of western Europe, the Soviet Union set up this Council in 1949. With itself it associated as founding members Albania, Czechoslovakia, Hungary, Poland, Rumania and Bulgaria, while in 1950 the German Democratic Republic, destined to become the strongest industrial unit of the Soviet Union's allies, also joined. Albania left the group in 1961; Yugoslavia accepted only associate status; but COMECON broadened its European base by admitting Cuba and Mongolia in 1962.

COMECON's original purpose was to facilitate trade, including barter, within the bloc but specially with, and to the advantage of the Soviet Union. From the mid-1950s onwards more ambitious policies were conceived and have to some extent been applied. These sought co-operation so as to ensure the most rational use of natural resources and the acceleration of the development of productive forces. Attempts were made to secure specialisation and co-ordination of labour and production in the several countries in ways that made sense on economic ground but aroused some resistance, as in Rumania, on national ground. An international bank, using transferable roubles, was set up in 1964 to facilitate inter-bloc trading and an international investment bank in 1971. COMECON members, which had before the Second World War traded widely with western Europe, found their chief market was the Soviet Union which, however, gave reality to the organisation by supplying raw cotton, petroleum, electric power [Kish 1968], and to a modest extent other goods and help when needed. But since the late 1960s the Soviet Union's partners have been told that they must seek additional oil from elsewhere, since available supplies from Siberia (of both gas and oil) may be offered to Japan, the Federal Republic of Germany and the United States.

Although well over half of the trade of COMECON countries is inter-bloc, the rethinking of commercial policy in relation to the decentralisation of industrial management and the faster growth of E.E.C. inter-bloc trade has been taking place and bearing fruit [Shonfield

1968]. Indeed, a new phase of COMECON's activities began in 1972 when the Soviet Union, compromising its political ideology because of its need for credits and technological help, made agreements with both West Germany and the United States on trade and economic co-operation, and West Germany made a similar agreement with Czechoslovakia. As a new departure, COMECON now turns its attention to the problems of financing trade between its members and countries of the enlarged E.E.C. A breakthrough was reported (Michael Kaser, *The Times*, 6 June 1973) when Rumania was accorded the benefit of the E.E.C.'s generalised preference system, which meant that it could export goods at low or zero tariffs subject to quantitative ceilings. Meanwhile, the members of COMECON prepare to reach agreement with each other by 1975 as a basis for co-ordinated production plans for 1976–80.

(iii) European Free Trade Association (EFTA)

This association was formed by Britain's initiative in 1960 when, conscious of its obligations to the Commonwealth and wary of the political implications of the Treaty of Rome, it refused to become a founding member of the E.E.C. It created EFTA, also known at first as the 'Outer Seven', by a series of trading agreements which associated with itself Austria, Denmark, Norway, Portugal, Switzerland and Sweden, with the modest aim of reducing and later eliminating tariffs on the importation of industrial goods. This trading group operated successfully; Iceland joined it in 1970 and Finland became earlier an associate. With the entry of Britain and Denmark into the E.E.C., the remaining six members of EFTA, who did not want to join the Community, began negotiations to link themselves with the E.E.C. by bilateral agreements which will reduce its tariffs on their imports. While certain difficulties doubtless remain, it might seem that the union of these two trading blocs may eventually be achieved by the entry of EFTA countries into the Common Market which would then acquire an increasingly European character.

(iv) Latin American Economic Groupings

The Latin American Free Trade Association (LAFTA), with its headquarters at Montevideo, brought together in 1960 the ten major countries of South America. For a variety of reasons – deficiencies in transportation and telecommunications, governmental instability, the sharp economic inequality between the partners, their very diverse levels of development, and the fact that their trade was almost all with non-LAFTA markets – this organisation failed [*Focus* 1973]. Rather more success has so far attended the Andean Common Market (ANCOM), which the eastern countries of South America – Bolivia, Chile, Colombia, Peru and Ecuador – formed in 1969, and which Venezuela joined in 1973. ANCOM also is an ambitious venture, involving a population of about seventy millions, which occupies distended territories in area about two-thirds that of the United States. It controls considerable mineral resources including coal and has great potential hydro-electricity. Its objectives appear modelled on those set by the Treaty of Rome, notably the removal of tariffs within the bloc and a common tariff on imports from outside. The obstacles are formidable: deficiencies of infrastructure, notably in respect of means of transportation, little complementarity in agricultural produce, and nationalist attitudes which invite confrontation with the United States, the chief market and source of investment capital for bloc members.

(v) The Caribbean Free Trade Area (CARIFTA)

Yet another grouping designed to stimulate economic co-operation was created in 1968 when eleven British Commonwealth nations and territories became associated. It now brings together mainland Guyana and Belize together with the insular countries of Jamaica, Trinidad and Tobago, Antigua, the Bahamas, Barbados, Dominica, Grenada, St Kitts-Nevis-Anguilla, St Lucia, Monserrat and St Vincent. This is a widely distributed group, extending at its extreme limits through over twenty degrees of latitude (from Trinidad to British Honduras) and through a similar range of longitude from the Bahamas to Guyana. It may be regarded as an attempt to co-operate economically where a more integrative federal union had proved unsuccessful (see p. 124).

(vi) Association of Southeast Asian Nations (ASEAN)

This grouping emerged in 1967 when, after a period of political confrontation with Malaysia, Indonesia associated with this country, the Philippines, Thailand and Singapore, in an effort to secure regional peace and stability and to accelerate their economic growth and social progress. This is in population a group of 202 millions (1970), with a growth rate of 5.2 per cent. But it lacks a secretariat, has not yet held a meeting of finance ministers, and the objective to create a common market is not yet in prospect (*The Times*, 8 May 1972).

6 Regional Blocs: Political

Blocs are not easily categorised since, although one purpose such as defence or trade may be dominant, they share a variety of purposes. The three to which we now turn are distinguished by their enormous geographical scale in that they bring together members from one or more continents, and their objectives are primarily political.

(i) The Organisation of American States (o.a.s.)

The beginnings of this association which go back to 1890, sprang from the United States' policy of rejecting European imperialism and of taking measures to prevent its recurrence in the western hemisphere. The Charter of O.A.S. of 1948, and as subsequently amended, seeks formally to preserve peace, order and justice, to stimulate collaboration for economic and social betterment, and to secure the defence, sovereignty and territorial integrity of member states. These now number twenty-four and embrace besides the United States nearly all the independent states of Central and South America. For much the most part members are republics, although this has not prevented Jamaica and Trinidad, formally kingdoms, from joining, although it is one reason why Canada, anxious to preserve some independence of Washington, stands aloof. This organisation is distinguished by having one member in a clearly hegemonic position and certainly at times the United States has tried to dominate it. It compares with the Commonwealth in the range of countries that it comprises – rich and poor, developed and underdeveloped, culturally diverse, politically mature and immature, as appear many of the South American states. It has a permanent secretariat at Washington, D.C. and a number of councils and commissions to carry out its set tasks: much is done to improve education, provide advisory services, and formulate programmes for economic and social development. Clearly, given its superior financial and military strength, the

United States assumes the major responsibility for the defence. The Organisation of American States, however, maintains a voting equality and, through political coups and by nationalisation, South American states have certainly challenged American overlordship. The organisation showed a certain solidarity in ejecting Cuba after the U.S.S.R.–U.S.A. confrontation in 1962, but it has been re-admitted.

(ii) The Organisation of African Unity (o.a.u.)

This was set up in 1963 when heads of state or of government of thirty countries met at Addis Ababa, capital of Africa's most ancient empire, to sign a charter, the objectives of which were the preservation of the independence and territorial integrity of the member states, the furtherance of African unity and solidarity, the elimination of colonialism in Africa and the co-ordination of policies. It created organs by means of which these important and widely ranging aims might be pursued: a secretariat-general, arrangements for holding summit conferences, a council of foreign ministers and a commission of mediation, conciliation and arbitration. The territorial expansion of Israel has engaged the prime interest of some members, notably Egypt and Libya, but for most the largely ineffective liberation movements directed against Portugal, Rhodesia and South Africa have been of the greatest concern. At the tenth birthday meeting of the O.A.U. in May 1973, the Council of Foreign Ministers were faced by the hard problem whether it should seek 'an evolutionary accommodation with white power in the next decade, or . . . drift . . . into a clash which might introduce non-African influences and weaken rather than strengthen African control over African destinies' (*The Times*, 22 May 1973).

(iii) The Arab League

This has as its basis 'Arabism', attempting to bring together for common action peoples who, for much the greater part, share a common culture. They share the Arabic language and a common history and the religion of Islam which prescribes, too, a common pattern of social behaviour. Although the idea of forming such a grouping goes back to the time when the Ottoman Turkish Empire held sway over most of the Arab countries, the Arab League came into being only in

1945, when nearly all of them had won their independence. They occupy an enormous area spread east–westwards from the Arabian peninsula to the Atlantic coast of Morocco and north–southwards from Syria and Tunisia to the Bay of Aden and the Persian Gulf. The different nations of this League stand at low but rising living standards as they confront the problems of economic development and social betterment; they have been subjected for periods to alien rule – by British, French and Italians – and total over this vast area only about 120 millions. They have found a unifying element in their common hostility to Israel, and come to control considerable though impermanent resources through the discovery of petroleum deposits, not only within the Arabian peninsula but also in Algeria, Libya and Egypt. The League has a permanent secretariat, a council and specialised committees: it allows an equal vote to all thirteen members, despite their evident inequalities both in wealth and population, but council members have the right of veto. In 1965 the United Arab Republic (Egypt), Iraq, Syria and Jordan agreed to create a common market which other League members may join. To its objectives of collective security and the economic and cultural advancement of its peoples, the Arab League adds co-operation with countries outside the Arabian peninsula and northern Africa. Egypt, the most populous and industrially developed member, has provided leadership, yet pan-Arabism, which the League was formed to promote, has not generated much unity of policy and action. The intrusion into these countries of the European territorial concept of nationalism, dependence on outside countries for armaments and the products of modern industry but not for investment capital, and serious domestic problems, all have served as centrifugal and divisive forces.

Conclusion

The attempts to form international associations to carry out specific functions is doubtless a commentary on the shortcomings of the independent state, so many of which are literally small, alike in area, population and resources, and, in addition, narrowly nationalistic in their attitudes. Certainly a number of relatively small states are outstanding for their cultural and other achievements and provide satisfying frameworks for modern living. Of Einstein, who had been speaking of the countries he had lived in, it is recorded [Snow 1967] that 'he preferred them in inverse relation to their size'. Yet in many respects the independent nation state is too small a unit within which to conduct large-scale production and trade and to develop and apply modern science and technology. So also in a world where military, economic and financial power is highly concentrated in a few states or groups of states of considerable scale, the progress and survival of small ones are by no means easy. The bloc-forming activities of recent decades, experimental though they would appear, exhibit a promising movement towards international co-operation and understanding on the basis of known and agreed purposes. The various names applied to the blocs which we have reviewed briefly above (organisation, league, association, commonwealth and community) indicate the range and degrees of unity sought – from the looseness of the league to the more integrative goal implied by 'community'. There is encouragement here that in these many regional pacts, based on a common will and growing from grass roots, new forces are operative to check political fragmentation, even though the new blocs that they produce inject new and divisive elements into the international scene.

10 Compass of the World

We deal with rapidly developing and diverse human societies in relation to an earth of which we have an ever-expanding knowledge.

[Isaiah Bowman 1944, p. 51]

The concern for man and his destiny must always be the chief interest of all technical effort. Never forget it among your diagrams and equations.

[Einstein, cited by Snow 1967]

It is the whole world that the geographer undertakes to study and explain and it is not surprising, in view of the complexities which this presents, that he shies away, seeking refuge in simpler, more specific and specialised tasks. Yet the political geographer can, and should attempt to girdle the earth. This is not to suggest that he can settle major problems of the day or formulate ready-made and guaranteed political programmes. He can, however, by careful and objective analysis, as we have indicated in this book, draw attention to those basic historical and geographical realities which enter into the making of policy and, also, he may contribute to the better understanding of a world which has, most evidently in this age of jet transport and telecommunications, become a single system.

1 'Geopolitik' and Geopolitics

These should be, and were long ago sharply distinguished, the one bogus and dangerous, the other legitimate and useful (Ancel 1936; East 1937; Bowman 1944). *Geopolitik* drew some support from Ratzel's conception of states as organisms which, if strong, must grow territorially at the expense of the weak, or risk disintegration and decay. The inventor of the term *Geopolitik*, however, was Rudolf Kjellen, a Swedish political scientist of the 1920s and his book

Grossmächte, translated into German by Karl Haushofer in 1930, provided in Germany a basis, suited to the political mood of a nation smarting from defeat in the First World War, for the rapid development of this pseudo-science. Publications there in the field of *Geopolitik*, based on material derived from geography and many other disciplines, provided propaganda and specious arguments for Nazi political pretensions and a foreign policy of territorial expansion. For the French geographer Demangeon [1932], *Geopolitik* was 'a national enterprise of propaganda and instruction', while America's leading political geographer, Bowman, disposed of it succinctly when he wrote: 'as disclosed in German writers and policy, it is also illusion, mummery, an apology for theft' [Bowman 1944, p. 52]. *Geopolitik* as such need not detain us; it should be noted, however, that the term 'geopolitics' can be, and is used conveniently to refer to the external geographical relationships of states and, more specifically, to the geographical aspect of those which affect the whole world.

Probably the best illustration that can be offered of geopolitics as a useful and illuminating study for statesmen is provided by Sir Halford Mackinder's work, developed in two publications: a paper published in 1904 entitled 'The Geographical Pivot of History' and his book *Democratic Ideals and Reality* which appeared in 1919. The student of political geography will still find reward in attentively reading these thoughtful essays which distil conclusions reached from a close study, in combination, of both geography and history. Mackinder gave meaning to the claims that history is geography set in motion and that 'the cost of geographical ignorance is immeasurable'. In a world which had become a closely interrelated 'Going Concern', only at their peril would statesmen ignore what he called 'geographical realities' – facts of location, of sheer territorial space, of differences of terrain and of the means of mobility as these exist differentially and change with time. Nor among these realities were to be ignored the character and historical past of nations, notably the Germans and the Russians, the fighting qualities and expansionist tendencies of which had been abundantly demonstrated. Much has been written about Mackinder's key theory of the Heartland, and of his conception of the World-Island (Europe, Asia and Africa), and of the Outer Crescent beyond its bordering oceans. Here we can note only that his warning of the dangers to peace that might result from the proximity of Germans and Russians did not prevent their clash in the Second World War and also have had relevance for many decades to the search for international understanding and peace.

2 Geopolitical Patterns After the Two World Wars

'All is in flux, nor stays, but changes on': Walter de la Mare's line well applies to those restless forces that operate on the international stage of a dynamic world and reflect the incessant changes of the attitudes and material resources of human societies and of the policies of the states that provide their frameworks. Any geographical analysis of the world and its problems at a given time soon becomes historical background to an age faced by new situations and new problems. Bowman's classic *The New World: Problems of Political Geography*, which he published in 1922, presented, with a wealth of significant maps and statistics, the states system and the problems confronting the generation of statesmen at the helm at the end of the First World War. *The Changing World: Studies in Political Geography* [East and Moodie 1956] attempted, as a team effort, a similar analysis of the changed world that had survived the Second World War. No less the mid-1970s present a markedly different international scene, to which we can here only briefly turn attention.

In the world that Bowman reviewed, the League of Nations, but without United States membership, had been born, many new states had emerged out of territories of fallen empires in continental Europe, the United States stood firm as a fortress of democracy, and the old oceanic empires functioned intact. But pointers, as it proved, to future problems of a geopolitical order were the extraordinarily rapid growth of the trade and power of Japan and the triumph in Russia of Bolshevism, a revolutionary and international movement, which for Lenin 'created a new world of hope' but to Bowman appeared 'a step backward toward the barbarism of earlier times'. There were still a number of great powers, virtually all in Europe; Britain controlled Egypt and the Suez Canal, then of great commercial and strategical value, as it controlled also the Indian Ocean from naval bases disposed in Aden, India, Ceylon and East and South Africa. And, thanks to the Panama Canal, which had been constructed with difficulty, the United States was about to extend its power and influence into the Pacific arena on the western margin of which it held the Philippines.

After the Second World War it was necessary to redraw maps of the world on projections suited to an age which had mastered air navigation of the Arctic; no longer was the Mercator projection adequate which had served Mackinder's earlier thinking about the World-Island linked to the Outer Crescent (mainly the Americas and Australasia) by the seaways and submarine cables. In 1945 the United States, with its industries expanded and its territory unscarred by war, had clearly attained superpower status. When a few years later the Soviet Union, too, was arming itself with atomic weapons and thus also acquiring superpower status, an uneasy situation characterised the international scene since the two were fundamentally opposed in their political ideology. The many nations of Europe, despite the considerable degree of common culture which they shared, appeared more divided than ever, although for the most part they came together in defensive and economic blocs, in the west and east, respectively under the protection and leadership of the United States and the Soviet Union. During the ensuing years of the so-called Cold War, the United States, conscious of the wide responsibilities that attached to its dominant power and mindful no less of the need to defend itself at long range from its shores, organised alliances in the Americas, Europe and Asia and created a system of outlying military bases. The prime danger was seen to lie in the bordering lands of the Soviet Union, notably in Europe and the Middle East, into which it might further project its power and extend its territorial hold. When in 1950 the Soviet Union and the People's Republic of China signed a treaty of friendship and alliance, the division of the world into two opposed and irreconcilable parts assumed a pattern of a kind such as Mackinder had envisaged in his thinking. On the one hand appeared a vast continental region of military and revolutionary power stretching from central Europe to the northern borders of the Middle East and to the Pacific coasts of the Soviet Far East and China; on the other hand was the United States, holding superior naval power with fleets operating in the Mediterranean and in the China Seas and supported by allies in Europe and Asia, organised in the alliances discussed in chapter 9.

3 Geopolitical Patterns of the Mid-1970s

A different international scene now presents itself. The United Nations has survived and proved itself by no means ineffective, even though it offers no simple means of exorcising or settling contentious issues. An event of some importance, because of the results that have accrued from it, is the Sino-Soviet quarrel which, since it began about 1960, has shattered any hope they might have shared of a monolithic bloc combining one-third of humanity within a continuous territory from central Europe to the outer borders of China. After rather less than ten years of co-operation, during which the Soviet Union helped China to start its plans for industrialisation by providing equipment and technologists, the two countries fell apart, differing sharply on their interpretations and applications of communist policy and engaging in minor military action over contested boundaries. These, however, were merely the symptoms of an historic Russo-Chinese antipathy. Mutual suspicion of each other's intentions and policy sprang from a basic fact, a geographical reality, namely that the Soviet Union's vast Asiatic territories, despite remarkable industrial and urban development in specific parts, are thinly populated whereas China, with its settled peasantry, has a greater population than any other country. Moreover, China has been fortunate in its leadership which has preserved its unity and stability and asserted control to the outer borders of its territory. The Soviet Union's major base of population and of industry lies still in and west of the Ural Mountains – in Europe, not in Asia – so that it has had to maintain fully equipped military bases at selected points behind the long Sino-Soviet frontier. The Soviet Union has further strengthened its defensive (and offensive) position by its alliance with Mongolia; in air power, too, as in the possession of a superior nuclear arsenal, it has clear advantages over China.

Defence of its Asiatic lands is important to the Soviet Union since, apart from their cotton and surplus grain, they are its long-term storehouse of minerals and energy, the latter including abundant coal, natural gas, petroleum and hydro-electric power. The possibility of becoming involved in widely spread and protracted border warfare in Asia has doubtless induced some modifications of the Soviet Union's policy in Europe and the Middle East, that is to say in two other neighbouring regions of high geopolitical interest. In Europe Stalin earlier had tried but failed to bring pressure on Turkey in respect of the Turkish Straits, and to drive the western allies from Berlin where they shared with him rights of military occupation. His successors have maintained their hold over their European allies by means of the Warsaw Pact, the stationing of troops, and even by

armed intervention, but they have tempered provocation with a care
to avoid major war. More recently the Soviet Union has sought with
some success a political accommodation and trade with both West
Germany and the United States. So also in the Middle East, while it
has sought to win and to hold as allies, not without difficulties, Syria,
Iraq and Egypt, it has recognised that the dependence of Western
countries on Middle East oil and the fate of Israel make this a
dangerous region where, without caution, major conflict could
begin. Farther away, while it has been at pains to break through the
defensive ring within which the United States has tried to contain it,
the Soviet Union has been careful to limit its involvement and has
not subscribed to the view that (for itself) war is the continuation of
foreign policy. Thus it backed down from the confrontation with the
United States over Cuba and has limited itself to supplying arms to
those fighting wars of which it approved or approves, as in Vietnam
and Portuguese African territories. It has entered into treaty relations with India and has built a powerful navy, maintaining forces
in both the Mediterranean and the Indian Ocean, which before the
Second World War was considered to be a British lake. Further,
since it has made considerable strides in developing its economy and
raising the living standards of its peoples, it has much to defend that
modern war could obliterate and has on a number of occasions acted
in a peace-making role, as for example in ending the war in 1962 between India and Pakistan and as, currently, together with the United
States, after the 1973–4 war between Israel and the Arab states.

The policy of the United States, too, has shown marked changes,
and here the background causes would seem to lie in the ever-
continued growth of the Soviet Union's military might, the Sino-
Soviet quarrel, and the lessons learnt from the prolonged and indeci-
sive Vietnam war. The Truman Doctrine of 1947 marked a major
turning point in American history [Acheson 1970]. At a time when
both Greece and Turkey were under severe communist pressure,
President Truman announced that 'it must be the policy of the
United States to support free peoples who are resisting attempted
subjugation by armed minorities or by outside pressures'. As a result
the United States found itself involved in military operations of considerable scale in Korea and in Vietnam, both significantly located
on the margins of Asia, where continental communist power of the
Soviet Union and China made contact with the oceans where it held
aero-naval control. By its military occupation and security treaty

with Japan, its close relations with the Philippines and with Taiwan, to which General Chang kai Chek had retreated from the mainland, and by the retention of some Pacific island bases, the United States became, and has remained, the dominant power in the Far East – yet another area of geopolitical significance. However, the heavy burden of supporting national movements against communist aggression and the indecisiveness of the two Asian wars which left both Korea and Vietnam politically partitioned, have helped to induce a shift in American foreign policy designed sharply to reduce commitments. President Nixon succeeded in achieving détentes with both the Soviet Union and China in the effort to open up better prospects for international trade, peace and stability. This approach towards a situation in which the two superpowers might appear to be making themselves arbiters of world affairs, has had inevitable repercussions. Japan, economically strong yet militarily weak and dependent on the United States, has been seeking to reorient its trade by improving its relations with the Soviet Union and with nearby China. The European Economic Community which, if effectively united, could become a major region of influence and power in the world, has been trying to secure more unity of external policy so that it could speak with one voice.

It is enough to reiterate here that there are certain regions of the world that justify the description 'geopolitical', if only because vital interests of the superpowers and middle powers focus there. These are Central Europe, the Far East and the Middle East. To this last we now turn briefly to illustrate the political geography of one geopolitical region.

4 The Middle East

Any political geographer studying the Middle East in the present century would find a richer variety of subjects than exists in any comparable area. The evolution there of various independent unitary and federal states has involved the collapse of the Ottoman Empire and the termination of British and French protectorates and mandates. During their creation a multitude of boundary disputes of all kinds has occurred, between Israel and its neighbours, and between Saudi Arabia and Oman, Iraq and Kuwait, Iraq and Iran, and Iran and Oman. The construction of continental shelf boundaries in the Persian Gulf has provided a wealth of information about the technical and geographical problems involved. The question of innocent passage through international straits is highlighted by the existence of the straits of Bab al Mandab and Hormuz at the entrances to the Red Sea and Persian Gulf respectively. The location of the Suez Canal and the world's largest reserves of petroleum assured the Middle East of prime strategic importance for major powers in two world wars, and their interest persists. The states of the area have pursued economic and strategic policies which are clearly related to their geography and which, in turn, produced changes in the distribution of people, the extension of agriculture and the patterns of international trade in petroleum. Finally, the Kurdish secessionist movement in Iraq has been amongst the most persistent of this century.

The Middle East, in popular imagery, consists of the Arabian peninsula and Egypt. The political, military and economic crises associated with this area in recent years have given an impression of uniformity that is more apparent than real. The fourteen kingdoms and republics which make up the region show considerable variation in their areas, in the number and ethnic composition of their people, and in the resources available for development. They also face different economic, political and social problems, and are involved to different extents in the international questions associated with the Middle East. The international questions which attract attention from countries outside the region concern the future of Israel and Palestinian refugees, use of the Suez Canal and the production and distribution of petroleum from the Persian Gulf States.

Looking first at the states within the Middle East, it seems logical to begin with Israel and its Arab neighbours, Egypt, Jordan, Syria and Lebanon. Israel was born during a war in 1949, and has been involved in three subsequent wars with some of its neighbours in 1956, 1967 and 1973. The two antagonists have quite different views of these struggles: Israel regards them as wars for survival, while the Arab states believe them to be wars waged for justice for Palestinian refugees and the recapture of lost Arab lands. The clear results of the war in terms of political geography stand in sharp contrast to the inconclusive debates about the origins and justification of the conflicts. The main result has been a marked increase in the area controlled by Israel. The original shape of Israel, which looked like a dagger with the handle near Jerusalem and the point at Eilat, has been broadened to an axehead with the cutting edge along the Gulf of Suez (figure 10.1). The 1967 war left Israel in control of territory four times larger than it originally had and this additional territory was acquired from Syria, Jordan and Egypt.

Syria forfeited about 777 square kilometres (300 square miles) of the Golan Heights in 1967, and a further, small area including Mount Hermon in 1973. This area is of prime strategic importance for both sides since it commands all land within artillery and rocket range to the east, west and south. It is economically important to Syria because it lies in the narrow, western part of the country, where rainfall is adequate for grain cultivation. There is plenty of evidence that Israel intends to keep the Golan Heights. By October 1973, fifteen Jewish settlements had been established in the occupied territory and the army has announced plans for integrating the villages into a defence system, which will mean that they do not have to be evacuated in any future conflict. The Israeli Government lays great emphasis on the need for an urban centre in the Golan occupied area, and plans have already been made for an initial settlement of 8000 people, which will grow to 20,000 by 1988. A target population of 50,000 settlers has been set for this occupied area [*Arab Report and Record* 1973].

In 1967, 5507 square kilometres (2165 square miles) of Jordan, west of the river Jordan, was occupied by Israel, and an Arab population of about one million remained under Israel's administration. The West Bank was an important agricultural region of Jordan, which thus suffered a serious blow. First, the area contained eighty per cent of the country's orchards, forty-five per cent of the vegetable-growing area, and twenty-five per cent of the land under cereals. Second, about a quarter of a million refugees fled into Jordan, swelling the numbers of Palestinian refugees displaced during earlier wars. Economic, political and strategic problems associated with the refugees resulted in political instability and recurring crises in Jordan in 1970–1. Once again there is ample evidence, including the acquisition of land, the redrawing of municipal boundaries and the construction of strategic roads, that Israel intends to keep at least part of the West Bank.

Egypt lost 62,250 square kilometres (24,035 square miles) in the 1967 war, consisting of the arid Sinai peninsula and the Gaza strip. The Arab population of the Gaza strip in 1967 was about365,000, while northern Sinai contained about 33,000 Arabs. This area was of limited economic significance to Egypt. Oilfields in Sinai produced about 4.5 million tonnes of petroleum yearly, which then represented

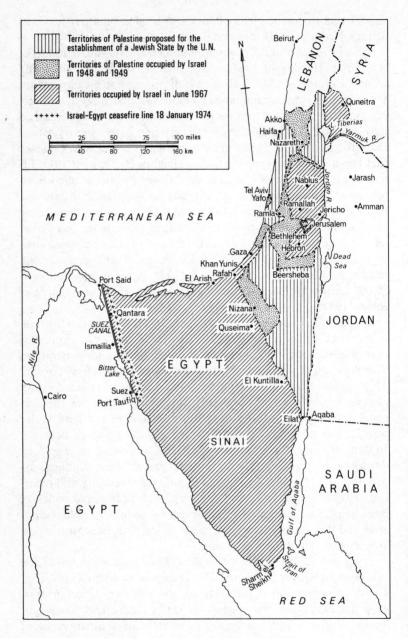

10.1   Israel's conquests 1948–67

about sixty per cent of Egypt's oil production. However, the area was of prime strategic significance, because of the buffer it provided along the east bank of the Suez Canal. The loss of the peninsula resulted in the closing of the Canal, and this was a serious economic blow to Egypt, partially offset by subventions from oil-producing states. As in Golan and parts of the West Bank, it seems beyond doubt that Israel will insist on retaining the Gaza strip. Plans to build a new port, called Yamit, south of Gaza, and smaller Jewish settlements between Rafah and Khan, confirm that this Arab salient is to be eliminated. However, it is equally clear that Israel has no desire to hold all the Sinai peninsula, and in January 1974 it agreed to withdraw from a strip of territory forty-two kilometres (twenty-six miles) wide along the east bank of the Suez Canal. In trying to guess which part of Sinai Israel will wish to retain, a valuable clue is given by the importance attached to Sharm el Sheikh, a fort guarding the strait of Tiran, which leads to the gulf of Aqaba and the Israeli port of Eilat. Egyptian threats to close this strait in 1967 contributed to the outbreak of war, and since then Israel has built a new road from Eilat to the fort, and constructed a new airport there. It therefore seems likely that, if Israel insists on holding the fort, it will strive for a boundary linking this point with the Mediterranean coast north of El Arish. Such a line would lie close to longitude 34° E. There is no evidence that any of the Arab states concerned will settle for less than the total return of all occupied lands.

Lebanon alone of Israel's neighbours has not lost territory, and this situation is probably due to two factors. First, Israel's boundary with Lebanon is the only approved international boundary possessed by Israel, although the boundary was constructed before the creation of Israel. Second, the Lebanese governments showed an obvious desire to avoid involvement in the various wars if possible. More recently Lebanon has been unable to avoid retaliatory raids by Israeli forces following attacks by Arab guerrillas.

The Middle East countries east of Jordan and Syria have contributed funds and sometimes forces to the struggle against Israel, but they have been much less directly involved than Israel's neighbours, and their most pressing problems are of a different nature. These nine states fall into four clear groups.

As table XI shows, Saudi Arabia dominates this part of the Middle East alike in area and wealth derived from petroleum, and this country alone shares a common boundary with all the other states.

The major problem for the authorities in Saudi Arabia is to use its enormous wealth wisely in developing an arid country, where per-

TABLE XI

SELECTED STATISTICS FOR STATES IN THE ARABIAN PENINSULA

State	Area (sq km)	Population (thousands)	Petroleum output (million long tons)
Bahrain	368	216	3.4
Iraq	438,331	9750	69.0
Kuwait	16,913	914	162.0
Oman	212,380	750	13.6
Qatar	10,360	170	22.8
Saudi Arabia	2,149,700	8199	296.6
United Arab Emirates	82,880	230	57.7
Yemen (Sanaa)	194,949	6062	—
Yemen (Aden)	285,094	1475	—

NB. The discrepancies in population figures between those given here and those listed in other tables are due to the lack of reliable data.

SOURCE: *Middle East and North Africa 1973–4*, Europa Publications, London.

haps half the population is nomadic, without creating strains because of the traditional and religious nature of the country's society. The Government also faces the problem of conducting close political relations with revolutionary, socialist governments in neighbouring Arab states. In many ways Saudi Arabia has given a lead to its five small neighbours along its northeast and southeast borders, which form the second group. Kuwait, Bahrain, Qatar, the United Arab Emirates and Oman all have populations less than one million, occupying comparatively small areas, which contain valuable petroleum fields. These states are aware that their military weakness calls for the careful cultivation of friendly relations with their larger neighbours. They are also aware that their dependence on finite oilfields is an economic fact that calls for careful planning if it is not to prove dangerous. The plan, produced by the Organisation of Petroleum Exporting Countries in 1973, of curtailing production and increasing the price, makes sound economic sense providing that alternative sources of fuel do not become available. The increased profits are being used by these small states for overseas investment and to encourage developed countries to establish industries in the Gulf states which will provide future employment and reduce the need for imports.

The two states of Yemen, with their capitals at Sanaa and Aden respectively, form the third group. They are distinguished from the Persian Gulf states by their republican constitutions, their larger populations, and their lack of petroleum reserves. Their pressing problem is to generate enough capital to allow the initiation of development projects, without which they will remain economic backwaters. Both countries have depended heavily on foreign aid since their creation. Iraq, like Saudi Arabia, stands apart in the Middle East. It has the largest population, the second largest area, a socialist, republican government, and significant petroleum reserves. Iraq also possesses a larger area available for cultivation than the other eight states. Despite these favourable characteristics Iraq faces many unique and serious problems. First, there is the threat to the integrity of the state posed by the Kurdish secessionist movement which has continued intermittently since 1932. The efforts to crush various rebellions have led to some conflict with Iran, which also possesses a Kurdish minority in its borderlands with Iraq. Relations between the two countries have also been made difficult by the boundary arrangements in the lower Shatt el Arab, which belongs entirely to Iraq, and by disputes over the division of the continental shelf at the head of the Persian Gulf. Iraq is one of the world's shelf-locked countries, a condition which also brings it into conflict with Kuwait. Iraq also regards Iran's control of the Strait of Hormuz as a security risk, and this risk becomes greater during the periodic interruptions to the flow of Iraq's oil through Syrian pipelines. Finally, Iraqi authorities have also experienced difficulties in converting the conservative peasant population to the processes of collective farming.

The major powers outside the Middle East take different attitudes towards the important international questions raised there, and accordingly fashion different policies. The Soviet Union apparently has decided its best interests will be served by giving strong support to the Arab cause. We can only guess at these interests, but they appear to include the following. The Middle East Arab states, together with those of north Africa, constitute an important voting bloc in the United Nations, and their populations represent a very large market. The re-opening of the Suez Canal will improve the mobility of Soviet naval forces in the Mediterranean and Indian Oceans. There is no disadvantage, and there may be advantages for the Soviet Union if it has some degree of influence with the oil-producing states on which Japan and the states of western Europe rely so heavily. The United States seems to have placed itself at a dis-advantage by giving support to Israel, and it must be presumed that these policies are dictated partly by electoral considerations in the United States itself. More recently the United States authorities, through their efforts to promote peace and the withdrawal of Israel from occupied lands, have established more cordial relations with Egypt. These fresh policies are probably designed to reduce the Soviet Union's advantage in this area. China, the third major power, seems to find in the Middle East an opportunity to criticise Russia and the United States, as it seeks to identify itself closely with the developing countries.

The mercantile, developed countries of western Europe and Japan wish to guarantee their supplies of petroleum from the Persian Gulf, and desire peace so that trade can flourish, and the convenient route through the Suez Canal can be used. Increasingly, individual coun-tries are reaching accommodations with the oil-producing states, often through bilateral, commercial agreements, which in some cases involve the provision of weapons. Predictably the leverage which the Arab states can exert through restrictions on petroleum production and increases in prices will be reduced, as alternative sources of fuel are made available, and if, as seems probable, increasing oil prices cause a reduction in world trade, which will adversely affect the deve-loping countries.

5 Contemporary Problems of the Post-Colonial Period

At present the international situation is most favourable to the developing countries and the peoples of the world. More and more, the old order based on colonialism, imperialism and hege-monism is being undermined and shaken to its foundations. Inter-national relations are changing drastically. The whole world is in turbulence and unrest. The situation is one of 'great disorder under Heaven', as we Chinese put it. (Vice Premier Teng Hsiao-ping, at a special session of the United Nations General Assembly, 10 April 1974).

Given the apparent desire of Chinese leaders to translate the ideology of class struggle to the international arena, this optimistic,
revolutionary view is understandable. However, it is certainly debat-
able whether the present level of turbulence and unrest is exceptionally high, and it is plainly untrue to lay all the blame for such
disturbances on the developed states of the world. There are four important problems besetting the post-colonial world, in addition to
those concerned with relations between great powers which have
already been noted. First, there is pressure from a number of countries to destroy those governments dominated by Whites in Africa.
Second, a number of states which have become independent since the
Second World War exhibit a high level of political and economic
instability. Third, serious conflicts have occurred between countries
which have recently achieved independence. Fourth, there is dissatisfaction on the part of most developing countries with the continuing discrepancy between their levels of economic achievement
and those of developed countries. Each of these problems deserves
further consideration.

With the exception of Spanish Sahara and Portugal's Cabinda, the
areas controlled by white governments are concentrated in southern
Africa. Although the world's main attention is focused on southern
Africa's minority governments, it is possible that the future development of Spanish Sahara will cause critical disputes between the
neighbouring states of Morocco, Mauritania and Algeria. This arid
colony, which was acquired by Spain to secure title to the rich fishing
grounds off the coast, is a richer prize than might be expected. At
Bou-Craa there are phosphate deposits, totalling about 1000 million
tons, which are believed to possess the highest ore content in the
world, and can be economically mined by opencast methods.
Morocco and Mauritania have both expressed the desire to incorporate this territory within their own borders. Morocco claims the
territory on the grounds of historical control, and the sacrifices it has
made for Magrebian, African and Islamic solidarity in recognising
Mauritania and settling its border dispute with Algeria. Mauritania
also bases its claim on another set of historical interpretations, and
on the ethnic ground that the R'Guibates tribe straddles its boundary with Spanish Sahara.

Until April 1974 the cohesion of white governments in southern
Africa was not in doubt. The Portuguese authorities in Angola and
Mozambique, the Rhodesian Government, and the South African

administration in South Africa and South West Africa, called Namibia by the United Nations, shared a common purpose to maintain the rates of political, economic and social change at levels which would avoid risks to the peace of the area. That cohesion did not seem threatened in any way by the existence of Botswana, Lesotho and Swaziland, three enclaves governed by Blacks. However, the cohesion was called into question by the 1974 military coup d'état in Portugal, and suggestions emanating from this country that its African colonies would be given early independence. It is likely to be a considerable time before the true significance of events in Lisbon to the situation in southern Africa can be assessed. Mozambique and Angola are both territories with rich natural resources of minerals and agriculture: if racial harmony could be maintained they are both capable of becoming prosperous members of the world community, and as such would hardly become bases for the overthrow of governments in neighbouring Rhodesia and South Africa. It must also be noted that if Portugal loses its links with these two territories, it will be reduced to perhaps the least significant country in Europe; this would be a bitter blow for a people proud of their culture and imperial history. However, if Mozambique and Angola become the scene of bitter racial conflict, perhaps following the attempt of Portuguese settlers to follow the Rhodesian policy of a unilateral declaration of independence, then the outlook for Rhodesia, and to a lesser extent South Africa, will become increasingly critical. At the moment the Rhodesian authorities are concerned to protect their border with Zambia and part of their border with Mozambique in the Zambezi valley from infiltration. The burden would become much heavier if the entire Mozambique boundary had to be guarded, especially if, at the same time, communication with the outside world, through the ports of Beira and Lourenço Marques, was dislocated. Finally it must be noted that in any violent transition to independence, it may not prove possible for the territories of Angola and Mozambique to remain united. Apart from the risk that large tribes might secede with the territory they control, there can be little doubt that Zaïre would welcome the opportunity of increasing its coastline, and Malawi would be glad of any opportunity to secure an outlet to the Indian Ocean.

Whatever the future brings to Rhodesia, its history since 1965 demonstrates very clearly that the importance of 'world opinion' is generally overrated. This country, unrecognised by any other government, its trade officially boycotted by most independent states, has an enviable record of peace and economic progress in Africa. This success has been achieved through a vigilant security system, by an electoral system which enables Whites to elect the majority of representatives, by significant economic changes in the country's industrial structure, and through the assistance of friendly governments in South Africa and Mozambique. The electoral system ensures that the number of African representatives in the House of Assembly is increased as the proportion of income tax paid by Africans grows. Income tax paid by companies is excluded from the calculations. In the Senate Blacks and Whites are represented by the same number of members. The indirect election of Africans for some positions by chiefs, headmen and elected councillors gives additional weight to conservative opinion. In order to conserve foreign exchange the Rhodesian Government has encouraged the establishment of new consumer industries, which have had the added advantage of increasing employment opportunities. Further, there has been a switch from the production of high grade tobacco, which can be more easily identified, to grades which are more commonly available, and which can be sold on world markets. The development of extensive irrigation schemes in the lowveld of the Sabi valley has allowed the cultivation of a wider range of tropical crops.

The political philosophy of the Nationalist Party of South Africa is based on the view that the country contains many nations, such as Xhosa, Zulu, Tswana and persons of European descent. The policy of separate development is designed to allow each of these nations to determine their own future according to a time-table which they set. The South African Government, therefore, looks forward to the day when there are eight or nine independent Black states, and one independent White state occupying the present area of South Africa. The severest critics of this policy discount the difference between the nations of South Africa and press for the establishment of a unitary state with a government elected by the total population with equal voting rights. The South African authorities have continued with their policies and nine homelands have been created, each of which has advanced some way down the road towards independence. The South African authorities have repeatedly stated that independence cannot be qualified, and that each of the homelands will become independent states. There are several hurdles which must be crossed before this situation will obtain. Three, which have already been mentioned (chapter 6), are fragmentation of the homelands, doubts about their capacity to support their populations and provide the opportunity of improving living standards, and the absence of good ports for those homelands with a coastline. It is also plain that the co-operation of African leaders is essential, and while this has been forthcoming during the initial and middle stages of constitutional advance, it is possible that they may become more insistent on various territorial and economic demands being met during the final stages, which can be expected in the next decade. At a conference of six homeland leaders in November 1973, there was agreement in principle that their territories should federate after they were independent, and some commentators were surprised at the ease with which they stressed Black unity at the expense of personal interests and tribal loyalties.

The political instability of many developing countries in recent years can be attributed mainly to a number of different causes, although it must be recognised that in any particular situation there may be a complex interaction among a number of important factors.

Secessionist movements and civil wars have been most common in countries with a heterogeneous population structure. The Kurds of Iraq, the Baganda of Uganda, the Ibo of Nigeria and the Mizos of India have all waged unsuccessful campaigns for separation from the state. Chad and the Sudan, neighbouring states of the Sahel zone, experienced secessionist movements which were mirror images of each other. In Chad the Hamitic population of the north sought to escape from the Bantu domination of the south; in the Sudan it was the Nilotic tribes of the equatorial regions who fought a long campaign to end Arab administration from the north. Civil wars, unrelated to secession, have beset Burundi, Zanzibar and Uganda at different times in recent years, and yielded a harvest of deaths, which in other circumstances would have shocked world opinion. Ideological differences, generally involving Marxist and other groups, have caused political instability, and sometimes very heavy fighting in Indonesia, South Vietnam, Cambodia and Chile. Political dissatisfaction with individual rulers, usually because they were unable to fulfil their economic promises, or because of an intolerable level of oppression, have caused coups d'état in Uganda, Nigeria, Dahomey, Zaïre, Indonesia and Niger. Similar events have also occurred in Greece and Portugal. The unrest that developed in Ethiopia in 1973–4 was related to the dictatorial constitution, the unequal distribution of wealth, especially land, throughout the community, food shortages consequent upon drought, and the activities of a secessionist movement in Eritrea. While the political geographer cannot assess the role of personal ambition in causing political unrest, he can point to the economic problems which exacerbate political difficulties. In modern times it is very easy for people in the developing, non-communist states to learn about the living standards in the developed countries. When this knowledge is set alongside the sometimes extravagant promises made by political leaders in the pre-independence and post-colonial periods, it is understandable that dissatisfaction may develop. This dissatisfaction is likely to be greater when there is manifest economic mismanagement, as there was in President Nkrumah's Ghana, President Amin's Uganda and President Sukarno's Indonesia. It is also unfortunately true that some independent states simply do not have the resource base to support the superstructure of government, and at the same time give hope of a rising standard of living. Chad, Mali, Gambia, Bangladesh, Yemen (Sanaa) and Honduras are almost certain to remain poor countries, no matter which political party forms the government, and there are others where the prospects of significant development are slight.

There have been conflicts at brigade strength or greater between several developing countries, such as Somalia and Ethiopia, India and Pakistan, Iran and Iraq, Algeria and Morocco, China and India and North and South Korea. In addition there have been boundary disputes and the threat of force used in other cases such as Guatemala and British Honduras (now Belize), and Malaysia with Indonesia and the Philippines.

The foregoing comments have not been written to try to apportion blame for unrest and conflict between the developed and developing countries, but simply to indicate that it is fallacious to speak of the Third World as though it were a coherent group of states with uniform aspirations. All the states of the world act in accord with selfish, national interests, and these are just as likely to lead developing countries into disputes with each other, as they are to cause friction between the developed and developing states.

The new policies of the oil-producing states in 1973 have been interpreted by some commentators to herald a new era, when co-operation by developing countries will secure a fairer distribution of the world's wealth. This view was strengthened by the speeches made by representatives of some developing countries at the special session of the United Nations General Assembly on problems of raw materials and development in April 1974. The meeting ended with a declaration calling for a new international economic order. It will be interesting to see what results flow from this special session, but it will be surprising if the developed countries will be persuaded to adopt self-denying policies for the benefit of the developing states. It is, therefore, necessary to discuss the extent to which the developed states can be compelled, by associations of raw material producers, to change their economic policies. For co-operative action of this type to be successful, the commodity and its pattern of production should have the following characteristics. First, it must be an item of major importance to the economies of a number of developed countries, in order to provide a satisfactory lever. Second, production should be concentrated in a few countries with similar economic and political aims, because this will make it easier to secure a unified front. Third, the developed states should not possess large stockpiles of the particular commodity, and it should not be capable of increased production in other states not associated with the co-operative action. Fourth, the commodity should not be capable of replacement by substitutes. And finally, the developing states concerned should be capable of surviving without export revenue for a reasonable period. It is apparent that all of these conditions were initially present when the oil-producing countries launched their programme of restricting production and increasing prices, and that explains the success they enjoyed, although it must be added that the need to offset damage to the economies of developing countries that import oil requires further study. Within a few months of the new oil policy being implemented, the circumstances were changing, and it is predictable that the developed countries are taking steps to ensure that this situation does not recur. These steps will include the more economical use of petroleum, the substitution of coal where possible, research into new forms of nuclear and solar power, and the exploration for oil in new areas. A survey of the commodities, listed in the United Nations *Statistical Yearbook 1972*, does not reveal any item which satisfies all the conditions mentioned above. It must be further realised that the 'closed political system', which Mackinder identified in 1904, has subsequently become a closed economic system, and any violent action to change that economic system in one area will produce unpredictable consequences in other parts. The fallacy that there are coherent blocs of developed and developing countries is only matched by the foolish proposition that one or the other group can impose its economic will on the world system.

Conclusion

The politically divided, yet interdependent world of the mid-1970s makes its way precariously towards peace and stability under the shadow of the military might of the two superpowers, whose orbiting satellites carry out relentless espionage and whose weapons of war, for use on land, in the air and from the sea, by their deterrent effect, sustain peace, if not everywhere at least for most of the world. On a global view the world is clearly fragmented politically, even though the degree of division ranges from that of the Caribbean islands to the relatively integrated North America and Euro-Asia, where the Soviet Union, by its own distinctive methods, holds together many races and nations in working unity. It is clear that sovereign states, which are in varying degrees largely nation states, have many short-comings as they vary sharply in the resources which they control, in the health, skills, living standards, aspirations and attitudes of their populations. The sovereign state still concentrates great power and, acting in pursuit of its own interests, can deny freedom to its citizens and defy other states, as did France in 1973 over its nuclear tests in the Pacific. Indeed, as Arnold Toynbee noted (see p. 1), it acts like a god of ancient Greece, although it is only a public utility which exists to serve as a framework for the life of individual citizens, whose lives are lived in numerous social groups, starting with the family. There is increasing recognition today of the state's excessive power which has conditioned some movement, albeit haltingly, towards the creation of supranational authorities and supranational communities.

We have noted, too, how colonialism has been bowed out, thus providing opportunities for peoples to learn by the hard way of trial and error how to manage their own affairs. However, states remain that rule their populations by coercion rather than by consensus, thus applying at home the colonialism that has been largely aban-doned abroad. We have noted also that, in practice, powerful states cannot always control small ones, despite their evident weakness.

The divided world of states, we recall, faces divisions of universal concern and danger, notably those related to poverty, underdevelop-ment and race. There has been too much simple optimism that the application to underdeveloped countries of capital for investment and of modern technology would result in major improvement and too much optimism that major social and economic problems could be quickly solved since, although man can change rapidly the face of the earth, he is slow to change acquired habits and attitudes of mind. While, it is true, the rich countries are no longer only those that are highly industrialised and now include the major oil producers, the rich industrial nations appear to get richer, although at heavy social costs, as, for example, by the pollution of the atmosphere, rivers and coastal waters and by overdevelopment, which has produced the crowded and polluted conditions for living in Tokyo and the motorised urban sprawl of Los Angeles. Perhaps the coup d'état in Portugal in the spring of 1974 may prepare the way for the end of colonialism in Portuguese Africa and the easement of racial tensions in southern Africa as a whole.

We may end with two evident points. 'Man was born to trouble': it is in the nature of human life that problems abound, are dealt with, if not solved, as it were to prepare the ground for more. Also, the panaceas suggested by such phrases as 'universal peace and goodwill' and 'political integration' are not so seductive on reflection as they may at first appear. While national feeling and national cultures remain strong and matters for emotional appraisal, at least they eschew and reduce standardisation and monotony. Certainly the short cuts to the integration of human societies by coercion make no appeal. Man and the world of states will inevitably change, and not always for the best, but it is better to travel hopefully than to arrive.

References

1 The World Political Map

ACHESON, DEAN [1970]: *Present at the Creation*, Hamish Hamilton, New York and London, p. 40

ACTON, LORD [1862]: Essay on 'Nationality', reproduced in *The History of Freedom and Other Essays* (1909), Macmillan, London, p. 290

BROOKFIELD, H. C. [1972]: *Colonialism, Development and Independence: The Case of the Melanesian Islands in the South Pacific*, University Press, Cambridge

EAST, W. G., SPATE, O. H. K. and FISHER, C. A., eds [1971]: *The Changing Map of Asia*, 5th edn, Methuen, London, pp. 16–23

FEBVRE, LUCIEN [1925]: *A Geographical Introduction to History*, Kegan Paul, London, pt 4, ch. 1

FRASER, ANTONIA [1970]: *Mary Queen of Scots*, Panther, London. Chapter 8, 'The State of the Realm', examines the political, social and economic background to sixteenth-century Scotland.

HARRISON CHURCH, R. J. [1951]: *Modern Colonisation*, Hutchinson, London

HERTSLET, Sir E. [1875–91]: *The Map of Europe by Treaty*, vol. IV, H.M.S.O., London

HOBBES, THOMAS [1651]: *Leviathan*, edition cited is Routledge, London, 1885

OPPENHEIM, H. [1955]: *International Law*, vol. I, edited by H. Lauterpacht, 8th edn, Longmans, London, pp. 120–3

POUNDS, N. J. G. [1964]: 'History and geography: A perspective on partition', *J. International Affairs*, XVIII, 161–72 (This issue consists of essays on the politics of partition.)

PRESCOTT, J. R. V. [1970]: 'Geography and secessionist movements', *Proceedings of the Geographical Society of Rhodesia*, III, 50–6

TOZER, H. J. [1920]: *Rousseau's Social Contract*, George Allen & Unwin, London

WAINHOUSE, DAVID W. [1964]: *Remnants of Empire: The United Nations and the End of Colonialism*, Harper & Row, New York

WALKER, ERIC A. [1944]: *Colonies*, University Press, Cambridge

WOOLF, LEONARD [1969]: *The Journey not the Arrival Matters*, The Hogarth Press, London, p. 18

2 The Inhabitants of States

BEAUJEU-GARNIER, J. [1966]: *Geography of Population*, Longmans, London, pp. 143–4

BONJOUR, E. and OFFLER, H. S. [1952]: *A Short History of Switzerland*, Clarendon Press, Oxford

BORROW, GEORGE [1846]: *The Zincale; Or an Account of the Gypsies in Spain*, John Murray, London, pp. 101–2

BROGAN, D. W. [1940]: *The Development of Modern France, 1870–1939*, Hamish Hamilton, London, p. 621

Canadian News Facts [1973]: Vol. VII, 1093–4

COBBAN, ALFRED [1969]: *The Nation State and National Self-Determination*, 2nd edn, Collins, London

FIFER, VALERIE J. [1972]: *Bolivia: Land, Location and Politics since 1825*, University Press, Cambridge, pp. 27–8; 260–2

FREEMAN, E. A. [1881]: *The Historical Geography of Europe*, Longmans, London, vol. I, p. 299

GENTILCORE, R. L. [1971]: *Geographical Approaches to Canadian Problems*, Prentice-Hall, Hamilton, Ontario

GOTTMANN, JEAN [1952]: *La politique des états et leur géographie*, Armand Colin, Paris

GRAHAM, G. S. [1950]: *Canada: A Short History*, Hutchinson University Library, London, p. 132

KRISTOF, LADIS K. D. [1968]: 'The Russian image of Russia: An applied study in geopolitical methodology', in C. A. Fisher, ed., *Essays in Political Geography*, Methuen, London

MACKINDER, J. H. [1905]: 'Manpower as a measure of national and imperial strength', *National and English Review*, XLV, 136–43

ROSE, J. HOLLAND [1916]: *Nationality as a Factor in Modern History*, Rivingtons, London, p. 153

SAYWELL, JOHN, ed. [1968]: 'Nationalism and federalism', *Canadian Annual Review for 1967*, University Press, Toronto

SCHWARZENBERGER, GEORG [1964]: *Power Politics*, 2nd edn, Stevens, London, p. 64

STEPHENSON, GLENN V. [1972]: 'Cultural regionalism and the unitary state idea in Belgium' *The Geographical Review* (New York), LXII, 501–23

WILLIAMS, RT HON ERIC [1973]: 'Proportional representation in Trinidad and Tobago', *Round Table*, CCL, 233–45

3 The Territories of States

COUPER, A. D. [1972]: *The Geography of Sea Transport*, Hutchinson University Library, London, pp. 62–3

GOTTMANN, JEAN [1973]: *The Significance of Territory*, University Press of Virginia, Charlottesville

HOFFMAN, G. W. [1967]: 'The political-geographic bases of the Austrian nationality problem', *Austrian History Yearbook* (Rice University, Houston, Texas), III, pt 1, 121–46

MAUDE, H. E. and DORAN, E. [1966]: 'The precedence of Tarawa Atoll', *Annals*, Association of American Geographers, LVI, 269–89

POUNDS, N. J. G. [1972]: *Political Geography*, 2nd edn, McGraw-Hill, New York, p. 62

ROBINSON, G. W. S. [1953]: 'West Berlin: the geography of an exclave', *Geographical Review*, XLIII, 540–57

ROBINSON, G. W. S. [1959]: 'Exclaves', *Annals*, Association of American Geographers, XLIX, 283–95

TAYYEB, A. [1972]: *Pakistan: A Political Geography*, 2nd edn, Oxford University Press, London

WEIGERT, H. W. *et al.* [1957]: *Principles of Political Geography*, Appleton Century-Crofts, New York, p. 174

4 Frontiers and International Boundaries

ANCEL, J. [1936]: 'Les frontières: étude de géographie politique', *Receuil des Cours*, LV, 207–97

ANCEL, J. [1938]: *Les frontières,* Gallimard, Paris, p. 196

BILLINGTON, R. A. [1960]: *Westward Expansion*, 2nd edn, Macmillan, New York

BLAKEMORE, H. and SMITH, C. I., eds [1971]: *Latin America: Geographical Perspectives*, Methuen, London, pp. 537–8

BOGGS, S. W. [1940]: *International Boundaries: A Study of Boundary Functions and Problems*, Columbia University Press, New York

British and Foreign State Papers: Volumes 63 (1872–3), 75 (1883–4), 76 (1884–5), 77 (1885–6), 78 (1886–7), 79 (1887–8) and 87 (1894–5), H.M.S.O., London

DAVIES, C. C. [1932]: *The Problem of the Northwest Frontier, 1890–1908*, University Press, Cambridge, p. 179

EAST, W. G. [1937]: 'The nature of political geography', *Politica,* XI, 259–86

EAST, W. G. [1960]: 'The geography of landlocked states', *Transactions and Papers*, Institute of British Geographers, no. 28, 1–20

EAST, W. G. [1962]: *An Historical Geography of Europe*, 4th edn, Methuen, London

FAWCETT, C. B. [1918]: *Frontiers: A Study in Political Geography*, Clarendon Press, Oxford

FIFER, J. V. [1966]: 'Bolivia's boundary with Brazil: A century of evolution', *Geographical Journal*, CXXXI, 360–71

GENICOT, L. [1970]: 'Ligne et zone: la frontière des principautés mediévales', Academie Royale de Belgique, *Bulletin de la Classe des Sciences Morales et Politiques*, 5th series, LVI, 29–42

HARRISON, J. A. [1953]: *Japan's Northern Frontier*, University of Florida Press, Gainesville, Florida

HERTSLET, SIR E. [1909]: *Map of Africa by Treaty*, H.M.S.O., London

HILL, J. E. [1965]: 'El Chamizal: A century-old boundary dispute', *Geographical Review*, LV, 510–22

HILL, N. L. [1945]: *Claims to Territory in International Law and Relations*, Oxford University Press, London

HINKS, A. R. [1921]: 'Notes on the techniques of boundary delimitation', *Geographical Journal*, LVIII, 417–43

HUNTINGFORD, C. W. B. [1955]: *The Galla of Ethiopia: The Kingdom of Kafa and Janjero*, International African Institute, London

JONES, S. B. [1945]: *Boundary-making: A Handbook for Statesmen*, Carnegie Endowment for International Peace, Washington

KRISTOF, L. A. D. [1959]: 'The nature of frontiers and boundaries', *Annals*, Association of American Geographers, XLIX, 269–82

LAPRADELLE, P. de [1928]: *La Frontière: Étude de Droit International*, Les Editions Internationales, Paris

LAWS, J. B. [1932]: 'A minor adjustment in the boundary between Tanganyika Territory and Ruanda', *Geographical Journal*, LXXX, 244–7

MITCHELL, R. D. [1972]: 'The Shenandoah Valley Frontier', *Annals*, Association of American Geographers, LXII, 461–86

PALLIS, A. A. [1925]: 'Racial migrations in the Balkans during the years 1912–24', *Geographical Journal*, LXVI, 315–51

PAULLIN, C. O. [1932]: *Atlas of the Historical Geography of the United States*, Hoen, New York

PEAKE, E. R. L. [1934]: 'Northern Rhodesia–Belgian Congo boundary', *Geographical Journal*, LXXXIII, 263–80

POUNDS, N. J. G. [1951]: 'The origin of the idea of natural frontiers in France', *Annals*, Association of American Geographers, XLI, 146–57

POUNDS, N. J. G. [1954]: 'France and "Les limites naturelles" from the seventeenth to the twentieth centuries', *Annals*, Association of American Geographers, XLIV, 51–62

PRESCOTT, J. R. V. [1967]: *The Geography of Frontiers and Boundaries*, Hutchinson, London

RATZEL, F. [1897]: *Politische Geographie*, Oldenbourg, Munich

SMITH, G. E. [1907]: 'From the Victoria Nyanza to Kilimanjaro', *Geographical Journal*, XXIX, 249–73

TURNER, F. J. [1953]: *The Frontier in American History*, 3rd impression, Rinehart & Winston, New York

WILKINSON, H. R. [1955]: 'Jugoslav Kosmet', *Transactions and Papers*, No. 21, Institute of British Geographers, 171–93

WILKINSON, J. C. [1971]: 'The Oman question: The background to the political geography of South-east Arabia', *Geographical Journal*, CXXXVII, 361–71

WISKEMANN, E. [1956]: *Germany's Eastern Neighbours*, University Press, London, p. 213

WYMAN, W. D. and KROEBER, C. B. [1957]: *Frontier in Perspective*, University of Wisconsin Press, Madison

5 The Categories of States

AUTY, PHYLLIS [1970]: *Tito: A Biography*, Longmans, London

BENEDICT, B., ed. [1967]: *Problems of Smaller Territories*, Athlone Press, London

BERRY, B. J. L. [1969]: 'Review of Russett's *International Regions and the Industrial System'*, *Geographical Review* (New York), LIX, 450–1

BLIJ, H. J. de [1967]: *Systematic Political Geography*, Wiley, New York, p. 104

BONJOUR, E. and OFFLER, H. S. [1952]: *A Short History of Switzerland*, University Press, Cambridge, pp. 270–3

BOWMAN, ISAIAH [1922]: *The New World: Problems in Political Geography*, Harrap, London

CVIIC, K. F. [1972]: 'Yugoslavia: The missing dimension', *International Affairs*, XLVIII, 414–23

DALE, E. H. [1962]: 'The state-idea: Missing prop of the West Indies

Federation', *Scottish Geographical Magazine*, LXXVIII, 166–76

EAST, W. G. and MOODIE, A. E., eds [1956]: *The Changing World: Studies in Political Geography*, Harrap, London and World Book Co., Yonkers-on-Hudson

EAST, W. G., SPATE, O. H. K. and FISHER, C. A., eds [1971]: *The Changing Map of Asia*, Methuen, London, paperback 1973

FAIRGRIEVE, J. [1941]: *Geography and World Power*, 8th edn, University of London Press, London, chapter 1

FORD, RICHARD [1846]: *Gatherings from Spain*, Everyman edn, 1970, Dent, London, p. 9

FOX, A. B. [1959]: *The Power of Small States*, University of Chicago Press, p. 186

FRANK, T. M., ed. [1968]: *Why Federations Fail*, University Press, New York

FUCKS, W. [1965]: *Formeln zur Macht* (Formula for Power), Stuttgart

GERMAN, F. C. [1960]: 'A tentative evaluation of world power', *Journal of Conflict Resolution*, IV, 138–44

GOBLET, Y. M. [1955]: *Political Geography and the World Map*, Philip, London, pp. 187–200

HARTSHORNE, R. [1954]: 'Political geography', in Preston E. James and Clarence F. Jones, eds, *American Geography: Inventory and Prospect*, Syracuse University Press, Ithaca, p. 185

HARTSHORNE, R. [1968]: 'Morphology of the state area: Significance for the state', in C. A. Fisher, ed., *Essays in Political Geography*, Methuen, London, pp. 27–30

MENDELSON, W. H. [1972]: 'The two Germanies', *The Times*, 14 November

PRESCOTT, J. R. V. [1972]: *Political Geography*, Methuen, London, pp. 40–5

RUSSETT, B. M. [1967]: *International Regions and the International System*, Rand McNally, Chicago

TEMPERLEY, H. W. V. [1919]: *History of Serbia*, Bell, London, p. 230

VALKENBURG, S. van [1939]: *Elements of Political Geography*, Pitman, London, chapter 1

WEIGERT, H. W. *et al.* [1957]: *Principles of Political Geography*, Appleton Century Crofts, New York, chapter 1

WHITTLESEY, DERWENT [1956]: 'The United States: The origin of a federal state', in W. G. East and A. E. Moodie, eds, *The Changing World: Studies in Political Geography*, Harrap, London, p. 239

6 The Economic Structure of States

Africa Research Bulletin [1973]: Africa Research Limited, Exeter

AHMED, I. and TIMMONS, J. F. [1971]: 'Current land reforms in East Pakistan', *Land Economics*, XLVII, 55–64

BLACK, L. D. [1963]: 'U.S. economic aid to Africa' (abstract), *Annals*, Association of American Geographers, LIII, 579–80

BLANKSTEIN, C. S. and ZUVEKAS, C. [1973]: 'Agrarian reform in Ecuador: An evaluation of past efforts and the development of a new approach', *Economic Development and Cultural Change*, XXII, 73–94

BLIJ, H. J. de [1967]: *Systematic Political Geography*, Wiley, New York, pp. 77–80; 90–9

BOWDEN, P. J. [1965]: 'Regional problems and policies in the northeast of England', *J. of Industrial Economics*, supplement, 20–39

BRUNN, S. I. and WHEELER, J. O. [1971]: 'Spatial dimensions of poverty in the U.S.', *Geografiska Annaler*, LIII B, 6–15

BURKE, M. [1970]: 'Land reform and its effects upon production and productivity in the Lake Titicaca Region', *Economic Development and Cultural Change*, XVIII, 410–50

COURTENAY, P. P. [1961]: 'International tin restriction and its effects on the Malayan tin mining industry', *Geography*, XLVI, 223–31

CULBERTSON, W. S. [1924]: 'Raw materials and foodstuffs in the commercial policies of nations', *Annals*, American Academy of Political and Social Science, CXII, 1–133

FERNEA, R. A. [1969]: 'Land reform and ecology in post-revolutionary Iraq', *Economic Development and Cultural Change*, XVII, 356–81

GWYER, G. D. [1972]: 'Three international commodity agreements: The experience of East Africa', *Economic Development and Cultural Change*, XXI, 465–76

HAMILTON, F. E. I. [1968]: *Yugoslavia: Patterns of Economic Activity*, Bell, London

HUDSON, S. C. [1961]: 'Role of commodity agreements in international trade', *J. of Agricultural Economics*, XIV, 507–30

JACKSON, W. A. D. and SAMUELS, M. S. [1971]: *Politics and Geographic Relationships*, Prentice Hall, Englewood Cliffs, New Jersey

JONES, S. B. [1954]: 'The power inventory and national strategy', *World Politics*, VI, 421–52

KASPERSON, R. E. and MINGHI, J. V. [1969]: *The Structure of Political Geography*, Aldine, Chicago

KOROPECKYJ, I. S. [1972]: 'Equalisation of regional development in socialist countries: An empirical study', *Economic Development and Cultural Change*, XXI, 68–86

MAINA, C. [1974]: 'What future for the Community?', *African Development*, VIII, EA7–EA9

MALEFAKIS, E. E. [1970]: *Agrarian Reform and Peasant Revolution in Spain: Origins of the Civil War*, Yale University Press, New Haven, Conn., p. 6

MORRILL, R. L. and WOHLENBERG, E. H. [1972]: *The Geography of Poverty in the United States*, McGraw-Hill, New York

MORRIS, A. S. [1972]: 'The regional problem in Argentina's economic development', *Geography*, LVII, 289–306

ODELL, P. R. [1973]: 'The future of oil: A rejoinder', *Geographical Journal*, CXXXIX, 436–54

OJALA, E. M. [1967]: 'Some current aspects of international commodity policy', *J. of Agricultural Economics*, XVIII, 27–46

POUNDS, N. J. G. [1972]: *Political Geography*, 2nd edn, McGraw-Hill, New York

PRESCOTT, J. R. V. [1968]: *The Geography of State Policies*, Hutchinson, London

RENAUD, B. M. [1972]: 'Conflicts between national growth and regional income equality in a rapidly growing economy: The case of Korea', *Economic Development and Cultural Change*, XXI, 429–45

SCHEEL, W. [1963]: 'Die Politische und Wirtschaftliche Bedeutung der Entwicklungshiffe für die Länder Afrikas', *Die Erde*, XCIV, 182–90

SYMONS, L. [1967]: 'Russia and the Third World', paper presented to The Thirty-Ninth Congress, at Melbourne, of the Australian and New Zealand Association for the Advancement of Science, Section P

TOWLE, L. W. [1956]: *International Trade and Commercial Policy*, Harper, New York, pp. 439–45

WARMAN, H. R. [1972]: 'The future of oil', *Geographical Journal*, LXXXVIII, 287–97

WARRINER, D. [1969]: *Land Reform in Principle and Practice*, Clarendon Press, Oxford

WEIGERT, H. W., *et. al.* [1957]: *Principles of Political Geography*, Appleton Century Crofts, New York, pp. 451–2

WILLIAMSON, J. G. [1965]: 'Regional inequality and the process of national development', *Economic Development and Cultural Change*, XIII, pt 2, 44

7 The Territorial Structure of the State's Administration

ALDERFER, H. F. [1964]: *Local Government in Developing Countries*, McGraw-Hill, New York

BILLINGTON, M. [1959]: 'The Red River boundary controversy', *Southwestern Historical Quarterly*, LXII, 356–63

BOWMAN, I. [1923]: 'An American boundary dispute: Decision of the Supreme Court with respect to the Texas–Oklahoma boundary', *Geographical Review*, XII, 161–81

CARPENTER, W. C. [1925]: 'The Red River boundary dispute', *American Journal of International Law*, XIX, 517–29

DAY, W. M. [1949]: 'The relative permanence of former boundaries in India', *Scottish Geographical Magazine*, LXV, 113–22

DESPICHT, N. [1971]: 'From regional planning to regional government' in E. Kalk, ed., 65–74 (see below under Kalk)

DOUGLAS, J. N. H. [1964]: 'A method of analysing the effectiveness of local government areas in Great Britain', paper delivered to the International Geographical Union's symposium on political geography, at Sheffield

FAWCETT, C. B. [1961]: *Provinces of England: A Study of Some Geographical Aspects of Devolution*, revised by W. G. East and S. W. Wooldridge, Hutchinson, London

FENELON, P. [1956]: 'Structure géographique et frontières des départements français', *Abstract of Papers*, Eighteenth International Geographical Congress, Rio de Janeiro, 186

FESLER, J. W. [1949]: *Area and Administration*, University of Alabama Press, Birmingham, Alabama

FIELDING, G. J. [1964]: 'The Los Angeles Milkshed: a study of the political factor in agriculture', *Geographical Review*, LIV, 1–12

GILBERT, E. W. [1948]: 'The boundaries of local government areas', *Geographical Journal*, CXI, 172–206

HELIN, R. A. [1967]: 'The volatile administrative map of Rumania', *Annals*, Association of American Geographers, LVII, 481–502

KALK, E., ed. [1971]: *Regional Planning and Regional Government in Europe*, International Union of Local Authorities, The Hague

LIPMAN, V. D. [1949]: *Local Government Areas 1834–1945*, Blackwell, Oxford

LOGAN, W. S. [1963]: '*The Evolution and Significance of Selected Intra-national Boundaries in Southwest Victoria*', unpublished dissertation for the degree of B.A. at the University of Melbourne

LOGAN, W. S. [1968]: 'The changing landscape significance of the Victoria-South Australia boundary', *Annals*, Association of American Geographers, LVIII, 128–54

MCCOLL, R. W. [1963]: 'Development of supra-provincial administrative regions in Communist China 1949–60', *Pacific Viewpoint*, IV, 53–64

MAES, R. [1971]: 'Emergent forms of regional administration in Belgium', in E. Kalk, ed., 199–206 (see above under Kalk)

NELSON, H. J. [1952]: 'The Vernon area of California: A study of the political factor in urban geography', *Annals*, Association of American Geographers, XLII, 177–91

NICHOLSON, N. L. [1954]: *The Boundaries of Canada, Its Provinces and Territories*, Department of Mines and Technical Survey, Geography Branch, Memoir 2, Ottawa, p. 119

NICHOLSON, N. L. [1968]: 'The further partition of the Northwest Territories of Canada', in C. A. Fisher, ed., *Essays in Political Geography*, Methuen, London, 311–24

O'CONNELL, D. P. [1968]: 'Problems of Australian coastal jurisdiction', *Australian Law Journal*, XLII, 39–51

O'CONNELL, D. P. [1970]: 'The Australian maritime domain', *Australian Law Journal*, XLIV, 192–208

POUNDS, N. J. G. [1972]: *Political Geography*, McGraw-Hill, New York

PRESCOTT, J. R. V. [1959]: 'Nigeria's regional boundary problems', *Geographical Review*, XLIX, 485–505

PRESCOTT, J. R. V. [1968]: *The Geography of State Policies*, Hutchinson, London

PRESCOTT, J. R. V. [1972]: 'Overpopulation and overstocking in the native areas of Matabeleland', in R. M. Prothero, ed., *People and Land in Africa South of the Sahara*, Oxford University Press, London and New York

ROSE, A. J. [1955]: 'The border zone between Queensland and New South Wales', *Australian Geographer*, VI, 3–18

SCHWEINFURTH, U. [1968]: 'The problems of Nagaland', in C. A. Fisher, ed., *Essays in Political Geography*, Methuen, London, 161–76

SHABAD, T. [1956]: 'The administrative territorial patterns of the Soviet Union', in W. G. East and E. A. Moodie, eds., *The Chang-*

ing World, Harrap, London and World Book Co., Yonkers-on-Hudson, 365–84

SHARPE, L. J. [1971]: 'Regionalism and local government in Great Britain', in E. Kalk, ed. (see above under Kalk)

SPATE, O. H. K. [1957]: *India and Pakistan*, 2nd edn, Methuen, London

STEINER, K. [1965]: *Local Government in Japan*, University Press, Stanford, California

TAYLOR, E. G. R. [1942]: 'Discussion on the geographical aspects of regional planning', *Geographical Journal*, XCIX, 61–80

ULLMAN, E. L. [1939]: 'The eastern Rhode Island-Massachusetts boundary zone', *Annals*, Association of American Geographers, XXIX, 291–302

YONEKURA, J. [1956]: 'Historical development of the political–administrative divisions of Japan', *Abstract of Papers*, Eighteenth International Geographical Congress, Rio de Janeiro

8 The Political Geography of the Sea

ALEXANDER, LEWIS M. [1963]: *Offshore Geography of Northwestern Europe*, McNally, Chicago

BERBER, F. J. [1959]: *Rivers in International Law*, Stevens, London

BROWN, E. D. [1971]: *The Legal Regime of Hydrospace*, Stevens, London, p. 9

BUTLER, WILLIAM E. [1971]: *The Soviet Union and the Law of the Sea*, Johns Hopkins Press, Baltimore and London

COUPER, A. D. [1972]: *The Geography of Sea Transport*, Hutchinson University Library, London, pp. 62–3

DALE, E. H. [1968]: 'Some geographical aspects of African land-locked states', *Annals*, Association of American Geographers, LVIII, 485–505

DEPARTMENT OF EXTERNAL AFFAIRS [1958]: *Current Notes on International Affairs*, XXIX, Canberra, p. 355

EAST, W. G. [1960]: 'The geography of land-locked states', *Transactions and Papers*, Institute of British Geographers, No. 28, 1–20

EAST, W. G. and MOODIE, A. E., eds [1956]: *The Changing World: Studies in Political Geography*, Harrap, London and World Book Co., Yonkers-on-Hudson

EAST, W. G., SPATE, O. H. K. and FISHER, C. A. [1971]: *The Changing Map of Asia*, 5th edn, Methuen, London, p. 208

FAWCETT, J. E. S. [1973]: 'How free are the seas?', *International Affairs*, XLIX, 14–22

The Geographer [1973]: 'Claims to national jurisdiction', *Limits in the Sea*, No. 36, Washington

GLASSNER, MARTIN IRA [1970]: *Access to the Sea for Developing Landlocked States*, Martinus Nijhoff, The Hague

HILLS, T. L. [1959]: *The St Lawrence Seaway*, Methuen, London

LEIFER, MICHAEL and NELSON, DOLLIVER [1973]: 'Conflict of interest in the Straits of Malacca', *International Affairs*, XLIX, 190–203

LEVINE, I. O. [1937]: 'Les projets de percement de l'isthme de Kra et leur histoire', *Affaires Etrangères*, II, 83–97

LUARD, EVAN [1968]: 'Legal tangles over sea-bed wealth', *The Times*, 3 June 1968

LUARD, EVAN [1974]: 'The Law of the Sea Conference', *International Affairs*, L, 268–78

MAHAN, CAPTAIN A. T. [1890]: *The Influence of Sea Power upon History*, Sampson Low, Marston, London

OPPENHEIM, H. [1955]: *International Law*, vol. I, 8th edn, Longmans, London, p. 508

OSBORNE, H. [1954]: *Bolivia: A Land Divided*, 3rd edn, Oxford University Press London, p. 38

TROEBST, CORD CHRISTIAN [1963]: *Conquest of the Sea*, Hodder & Stoughton, London

9 The Grouping of States

ALBRECHT-CARRIÉ, RENÉ [1965]: *The Unity of Europe: An Historical Survey*, Martin Secker & Warburg, London

ALEXANDER, LEWIS M. [1957]: *World Political Patterns*, Rand McNally, Chicago

BARRACLOUGH, G. [1963]: *European Unity in Thought and Action*, Blackwell, Oxford

BROOKFIELD, H. C. [1972]: *Colonialism, Development and Independence: The Case of the Melanesian Islands in the South Pacific*, University Press, Cambridge

CARRINGTON, C. E. [1961]: *The Liquidation of the British Empire*, Harrap, London

CARRINGTON, C. E. [1962]: 'Decolonization: The last stages', *International Affairs* (London), XXXVIII, 219–40

EAST, W. G. [1951]: 'The new frontiers of the Soviet Union', *Foreign Affairs* (New York), XXIX, 591–607

EAST, W. G. [1953]: 'The Mediterranean: Pivot of peace and war', *Foreign Affairs* (New York), XXXI, 619–33

EAST, W. G. [1968]: 'Political organizations at higher ranks', in C. A. Fisher, ed., *Essays in Political Geography*, Methuen, London, pp. 39–60

Focus [1973]: 'International co-operation for development: The Andean Common Market', *Focus*, XXIV, 1–8

FOX, A. B. [1959]: *The Power of Small States*, University Press, Chicago

FRANKEL, JOSEPH [1969]: *International Politics. Conflict and Harmony*, Penguin, London

GASTEYGER, CURT [1974]: *The Times: European Defence Supplement*, 19 February, VIII

HARTSHORNE, RICHARD [1954]: 'Political geography', in Preston E. James and Clarence F. Jones, eds, *American Geography: Inventory and Prospect*, University of Syracuse Press, Ithaca, pp. 211–14

JACKSON, W. A. DOUGLAS [1964]: *Politics and Geographic Relationships: Readings on the Nature of Political Geography*, Prentice-Hall, Englewood Cliffs, New Jersey

JENNINGS, SIR IVOR [1949]: *The Commonwealth in Asia*, Clarendon Press, Oxford

JENNINGS, SIR IVOR [1954]: *The British Commonwealth of Nations*, 2nd edn, Hutchinson, London, pp. 108–14

KISH, GEORGE [1968]: 'Eastern Europe's power grid', *Geographical Review*, LVII, 137–40

MACKINDER, SIR H. J. [1919]: *Democratic Ideals and Reality*, Constable, London 1919; republished 1962, Norton, New York (see entry under Mackinder in reference to Chapter 10)

NKRUMAH, KWAME [1965]: *Neocolonialism. the Last Stage of Imperialism*, Nelson, London

NYSTROM, J. WARREN and MALOF, PETER [1962]: *The Common Market: European Community in Action*, Van Nostrand, Princeton, New Jersey, p. 75

RUSSETT, BRUCE M. [1967]: *International Regions and the International System*, Rand McNally, Chicago

RUSTOW, D. A. [1967]: *A World of Nations: Problems of Political Modernization*, The Brookings Institution, Washington, D.C.

SETON-WATSON, HUGH [1964]: *Nationalism and Communism: Essays 1946–63*, Methuen, London

SHONFIELD, ANDREW [1968]: 'Changing commercial policies in the Soviet bloc', *International Affairs*, XLIV, 1–13

SNOW, C. P. [1967]: *Variety of Men*, Macmillan, London and New York, p. 86

SPROUT, HAROLD and SPROUT, MARGARET [1962]: *Foundations of International Politics*, Van Nostrand, Princeton, N. J.

WAINHOUSE, DAVID W. [1964]: *Remnants of Empire: The United Nations and the End of Colonialism*, Harper & Row, New York and Evanston, p. 133

10 Compass of the World

ACHESON, DEAN [1970]: *Present at the Creation*, Hamish Hamilton, New York and London, p. 220

ANCEL, JACQUES [1936]: *Géopolitique*, Delagrave, Paris

Arab Report and Record [1973]: Mendip Press, London, p. 358

BOWMAN, ISAIAH [1922]: *The New World: Problems of Political Geography*, Harrap, London

BOWMAN, ISAIAH [1944]: 'Geography vs geopolitics', in Hans W. Weigert and Vilhjalmur Stefansson, eds, *Compass of the World*, Harrap, London

DEMANGEON, A. [1932]: 'Géographie politique', *Annales de Géographie*, XLI, 22–31

EAST, W. G. [1937]: 'The nature of political geography', *Politica*, XI, 259–86

EAST, W. G. and MOODIE, A. E., eds [1956]: *The Changing World: Studies in Political Geography*, Harrap, London and the World Book Co., Yonkers-on-Hudson

MACKINDER, SIR H. J. [1919]: *Democratic Ideals and Reality*, Constable, London 1919; republished 1962, Norton, New York. This American edition, in the Norton Library, includes also 'The Pivot of History' [1904] and other earlier and later articles by Mackinder

PARKER, W. H. [1972]: *The Superpowers: The United States and U.S.S.R. Compared*, Macmillan, London

SNOW, C. P. [1967]: *Variety of Men*, Macmillan, London and New York, p. 80

Index

Page numbers in italics refer to maps